INTERNATIONAL AUTHORITY
AND THE RESPONSIBILITY
TO PROTECT

The idea that states and the international community have a responsibility to protect populations at risk has framed internationalist debates about conflict prevention, humanitarian aid, peacekeeping and territorial administration since 2001. This book situates the responsibility to protect concept in a broad historical and jurisprudential context, demonstrating that the appeal to protection as the basis for de facto authority has emerged at times of civil war or revolution – the protestant revolutions of early modern Europe, the bourgeois and communist revolutions of the following centuries and the revolution that is decolonisation. This analysis, from Hobbes to the UN, of the resulting attempts to ground authority on the capacity to guarantee security and protection is essential reading for all those seeking to understand, engage with, limit or critique the expansive practices of international executive action authorised by the responsibility to protect concept.

ANNE ORFORD is the Michael D. Kirby Professor of International Law, an Australian Research Council Professorial Fellow and Director of the Institute for International Law and the Humanities at the University of Melbourne.

Executive rule

INTERNATIONAL AUTHORITY AND THE RESPONSIBILITY TO PROTECT

ANNE ORFORD

CAMBRIDGE UNIVERSITY PRESS
Cambridge, New York, Melbourne, Madrid, Cape Town, Singapore,
São Paulo, Delhi, Dubai, Tokyo, Mexico City

Cambridge University Press
The Edinburgh Building, Cambridge CB2 8RU, UK

Published in the United States of America by Cambridge University Press, New York

www.cambridge.org
Information on this title: www.cambridge.org/9780521199995

First published 2011

Printed in the United Kingdom at the University Press, Cambridge

A catalogue record for this publication is available from the British Library

Library of Congress Cataloguing in Publication data
Orford, Anne.
International authority and the responsibility to protect / Anne Orford.
p.   cm.
Includes bibliographical references and index.
ISBN 978-0-521-19999-5 – ISBN 978-0-521-18638-4 (pbk)
1. International police.   2. Peacekeeping forces.   3. Intervention
(International law)   I. Title.
KZ6374.O74   2011
341.3–dc22
2010039189

ISBN 978-0-521-19999-5 Hardback
ISBN 978-0-521-18638-4 Paperback

CONTENTS

Acknowledgements   *page vii*

1 **Protection in the Shadow of Empire**   1

   The role of the UN in the decolonised world   3

   From deeds into words: systematising peace and protection   6

   The powers of the international executive under the UN Charter   10

   The responsibility to protect and the question of authority   13

   From endorsement to implementation   17

   The normative significance of the responsibility to protect concept   22

   Humanitarian intervention, police action and the responsibility to protect   27

   Recognition, protection and authority: chapter overview   34

2 **Practices of Protection: From the Parliament of Man to International Executive Rule**   42

   From conference diplomacy to executive action   44

   Neutrality, impartiality and the international civil servant   47

   The space of empire: the UN experiment at Suez   57

   Protecting life and maintaining order: the United Nations in the Congo   69

   The master texts of executive action   87

   The expansion of executive rule and the challenge to international authority   90

   The responsibility to protect and the legacy of Hammarskjöld   103

3   How to Recognise Lawful Authority: Hobbes, Schmitt and the Responsibility to Protect   109

Civil war and the turn to protection   109

Thomas Hobbes, natural law and the preservation of life   112

Carl Schmitt, the European order and protection as war   125

International executive rule and the politics of protection   133

4   Who Decides? Who Interprets?: Jurisdiction, Recognition and the Institutionalisation of Protection   139

Jurisdiction, control and the modern state   143

Completing the Reformation: Hobbes, Bellarmine and the struggle of institutions   150

Recognition, revolution and the family of nations   161

International jurisdiction and decolonisation: from form to function   164

Jurisdiction, recognition and the responsibility to protect   178

Law, politics and the conflict of competences   186

5   The Question of Status and the Subject of Protection   189

The crisis of parliamentary democracy in international relations   189

The impossibility of neutrality   192

Rethinking functionalism   196

The form of international rule   199

The question of status   205

Revolution, counter-revolution and the future of international law   207

Institutionalising protection: the work of law and politics   210

Bibliography   213
Index   231

ACKNOWLEDGEMENTS

I gratefully acknowledge the financial support of the Australian Research Council, which awarded me a fellowship to undertake research on a project entitled 'Cosmopolitanism and the Future of International Law' from 2007 to 2011. This book is part of that broader project.

My thanks go to colleagues and doctoral students at Melbourne Law School, particularly those associated with the Institute for International Law and the Humanities, for the conversations that have enriched my thinking on this project and for the camaraderie that has enriched my working life. Early work on the book was undertaken as an Edward Clarence Dyason Fellow at the Faculty of Law, Lund University and I am very grateful to Gregor Noll, Dean Per Ole Träskman and the faculty at Lund for their hospitality. The book was largely completed while I was in residence at Queen's College, University of Melbourne, and I am grateful to the Master of Queen's College, David Runia, and to my colleague Margaret Young for making that stay possible. The final stages of editing and proofing of the manuscript were undertaken in the wonderful peace of the Radcliffe Camera and I would like to thank Dean Timothy Endicott for enabling my visit to Oxford in June 2010.

I am particularly grateful to Martti Koskenniemi for his generous and energetic engagement with this argument in its many and varied forms, to Andrew Robertson for insightful comments on (many) earlier versions of these chapters and to Finola O'Sullivan at Cambridge University Press for her ongoing support for the project and her patience in the face of shifting deadlines for the submission of the manuscript. My warm thanks also to Aidan Hehir for the opportunity to present this work at the University of Westminster and to the audience at that seminar, particularly David Chandler, for critical engagement with the project; to Brett O'Bannon for inviting me to be part of the rich conversation at his symposium on 'Imperfect Duties? Humanitarian Intervention in Africa and the Responsibility to Protect in a Post-Iraq Era' held at the Prindle

Institute for Ethics, DePauw University; to Philip Lorenz and the participants at his Theo-Political Renaissance workshop held at Cornell University Department of English for responses to material from Chapter 3 on Hobbes, Schmitt and the early modern state; to Susan Zimmerman and Karin Fischer for the opportunity to present this work in its early stages as part of a joint lecture series programme at the Institute for International Development, University of Vienna and at the Department of History, Central European University, Budapest; to Richard Falk, Vesselin Popovski and Ramesh Thakur for the invitation to write a paper on the responsibility to protect which was the initial impetus for this book; and to Hilary Charlesworth and Ann Genovese for many forms of intellectual and practical advice and support. I have also presented talks drawn from work on this project over the past four years at the Australian National University, Brown University, the joint meeting of the Indian Society of International Law and the Australian and New Zealand Society of International Law, Jindal Global Law School, the London School of Economics and Political Science, Lund University, the University of Hong Kong, the University of Melbourne, the University of Michigan, the University of Oxford, the University of Stockholm, the University of Toronto and Uppsala University. My argument has benefited enormously from formal and informal discussions at and around those presentations.

My thanks to the staff at Melbourne Law School Library, Kungliga Biblioteker in Stockholm and the National Archives in Kew for their help in accessing resources and archival material related to this project. I also benefited from a chance virtual encounter with Steve Askin through Amazon and feel privileged to have been able to use parts of the library on Congo put together by his late wife Carole Collins. I am very grateful to Sara Dehm and Mary Quinn for their excellent editorial and proofing assistance, and in addition to Sara Dehm for creating the bibliography. My thanks also to Vesna Stefanovski for the efficient and cheerful way in which she has kept the Institute for International Law and the Humanities running smoothly during my lengthening periods of absent-mindedness (and, by the end, absence) while I finalised this manuscript.

Chapter 4 includes revised material originally published in Anne Orford, 'Jurisdiction without Territory: From the Holy Roman Empire to the Responsibility to Protect' (2009) 30 *Michigan Journal of International Law* 981, and Chapter 5 includes material originally published in Anne Orford, 'International Territorial Administration and the Management of Decolonization' (2010) 59 *International and Comparative Law Quarterly*

227. An early version of the argument developed in Chapter 3 is forthcoming as Anne Orford, 'Lawful Authority and the Responsibility to Protect' in Richard Falk, Ramesh Thakur and Vesselin Popovski (eds.), *Legality and Legitimacy in International Order* (Oxford: Oxford University Press, forthcoming).

Finally, my love and thanks to Andrew, Hamish and Felix – your wonderful company, good humour and encouragement helped me to write this book, and the thought of having more time to spend with you helped me to finish it.

1

Protection in the Shadow of Empire

Since the late 1950s, the United Nations (UN) and other international actors have developed and systematised a body of practices aimed at 'the maintenance of order' and 'the protection of life' in the decolonised world.[1] These practices range from fact-finding and the provision of humanitarian assistance to peacekeeping, the management of refugee camps and territorial administration. As the UN and humanitarian organisations expanded and consolidated those practices, a new form of authority began to emerge. This book is an exploration of the ways in which those practices of governing and that form of authority have been represented. It focuses in particular upon a new basis for justifying and rationalising international rule that emerged at the beginning of the twenty-first century. The international authority to undertake executive action for protective ends was given a detailed normative articulation in the form of a 2001 report by the International Commission on Intervention and State Sovereignty (ICISS) entitled 'The Responsibility to Protect'.[2] ICISS was an initiative, sponsored by the Canadian government, undertaken in response to serious concerns about the legality and legitimacy of the 1999 North Atlantic Treaty Organization (NATO) action in Kosovo. The responsibility to protect concept is premised upon the notion, to quote former UN Secretary-General Kofi Annan, that 'the primary raison d'être and duty' of every state is to protect its population.[3] If a state 'manifestly' fails to protect its population, the responsibility to do so shifts to the international community.

The idea that states and the international community have a fundamental responsibility to protect populations has rapidly colonised

---

[1] UN SCOR, 15th Sess., 873rd Mtg., UN Doc. S/PV.873, 13–14 July 1960, para. 19.
[2] International Commission on Intervention and State Sovereignty, 'The Responsibility to Protect' (Ottawa: International Development Research Centre, 2001).
[3] UN Secretary-General, 'In Larger Freedom: Towards Development, Security and Human Rights for All', UN GAOR, 59th Sess., Agenda Items 45 and 55, UN Doc. A/59/2005, 21 March 2005, para. 135.

internationalist debates about conflict prevention, humanitarian action, peacekeeping and territorial administration, and has garnered the support of a strikingly diverse range of states, international and regional organisations and civil society groups since 2001. The responsibility to protect concept came of age with its unanimous adoption by the General Assembly in the World Summit Outcome of 2005.[4] The General Assembly there endorsed the notion that both the state and the international community have a responsibility to protect populations from genocide, war crimes, ethnic cleansing and crimes against humanity. Although the General Assembly confined the situations in which the international community might intervene militarily to those in which a state was 'manifestly failing' to protect its population, it endorsed a broad range of preventive, early warning and capacity-building actions to assist states 'before crises and conflicts break out'.[5] The UN is now committed to the project of 'implementing the responsibility to protect'.[6] The description of that project by UN officials makes clear that the aim is not to develop new actions or operations in order to implement the abstract ideal of protection. Instead, the implementation of the responsibility to protect concept can be seen as an attempt to integrate pre-existing but dispersed practices of protection into a coherent account of international authority.

According to UN Secretary-General Ban Ki-moon, the challenge now facing those who support the responsibility to protect concept is to transform the concept from 'promise to practice' or from 'words into deeds'.[7] In contrast, this book will argue that the significance of the responsibility to protect concept lies not in its capacity to transform promise into practice, but rather in its capacity to transform practice into promise, or deeds into words. The project of developing and seeking to implement the responsibility to protect concept engages with the way in

---

[4] 2005 World Summit Outcome, GA Res. 60/1, UN GAOR, 60th Sess., Provisional Agenda Items 46 and 120, Supp. No. 49, UN Doc. A/RES/60/1, 24 October 2005, paras. 138–9.

[5] *Ibid.*

[6] UN Secretary-General, 'Implementing the Responsibility to Protect: Report of the Secretary-General', UN GAOR, 63rd Sess., Agenda Items 44 and 107, UN Doc. A/63/677, 12 January 2009, p. 7.

[7] On the need to move from 'promise to practice', see UN Secretary-General, 'Implementing the Responsibility to Protect'. On the need to move from 'words to deeds', see UN Secretary-General, 'Remarks at a Stanley Foundation Conference on "Implementing the Responsibility to Protect"', Tarrytown, 15 January 2010, www.stanleyfoundation.org/publications/policy_memo/SGresptoprotect15jan2010.pdf.

which the UN thinks.[8] The implementation of the responsibility to protect concept is designed to produce an 'international reflex' action directed to protecting populations at risk whenever decisions about those populations are made.[9] Yet unlike earlier periods in which the scope of international executive action has been justified, redefined or expanded, the articulation of the responsibility to protect concept does not simply offer a reflection upon past practice or an attempt to produce modest lessons learned from previous experience. Instead, it develops an ambitious conceptual framework aimed at systematising and giving formal expression to the protective authority exercised by international actors in the decolonised world since 1960.

The role of the UN in the decolonised world

The idea that the UN has a responsibility to maintain order and protect life in the decolonised world began to take shape with the creation of the United Nations Emergency Force (UNEF) in response to the Suez crisis of 1956 and the UN offer of military assistance to the Government of the Republic of the Congo in 1960. When the UN was requested to intervene in Egypt and the Congo, both the requesting governments and the Secretary-General believed that the UN could operate as a neutral force to protect the interests of newly independent states and prevent the expansion of Cold War conflicts. That Secretary-General was Dag Hammarskjöld. Hammarskjöld is considered by many to have been the most important Secretary-General of the UN to date. His significance lies in the fact that he successfully transformed the office of the UN Secretary-General and championed the expansion of 'dynamic executive action' to fill the power vacuums created by the 'liquidation of the colonial system'.[10]

---

[8] See generally Mary Douglas, *How Institutions Think* (Syracuse: Syracuse University Press, 1996), p. 126 (arguing that if we want to change human action in the modern world '[o]nly changing institutions can help', and that the only way to change institutions is to understand how they think).

[9] Gareth Evans, *The Responsibility to Protect: Ending Mass Atrocity Crimes Once and For All* (Washington DC: Brookings Institution Press, 2008), pp. 54, 235 (suggesting that the aim is for the responsibility to protect concept 'to become the accepted international reflex in principle' and that achieving that aim requires 'institutional processes capable of translating knowledge, concern, and confident belief in the utility of action into actual action').

[10] UN Secretary-General, 'Introduction to the Annual Report of the Secretary-General on the Work of the Organization', UN GAOR, 16th Sess., Supp. No. 1A, UN Doc. A/4800/Add.1, 1961, p. 7.

When Hammarskjöld took office, the Secretary-General was still largely regarded in the terms set out in Article 97 of the UN Charter as 'the chief administrative officer of the Organization'. In the words of his colleague Brian Urquhart: 'It was Hammarskjöld's development – perhaps creation is not too strong a word – of the political role of the Secretary-General that is his most lasting practical legacy.'[11] In a sense, Hammarskjöld did not so much create the political role of the Secretary-General as re-imagine the role of 'chief administrative officer' in political terms. He was thus a man for his time. Administration was to become the principal means of governing, both in terms of the administrative rule that has come to dominate the governance of industrialised states and in the form of managerial rule by international actors over the people and territories of the decolonised world.

On 8 September 1961, five days before he left for the Congo and ten days before he was killed in a plane crash there, Hammarskjöld addressed his staff for the last time, and said:

> If the Secretariat is regarded as truly international, and its individual members as owing no allegiance to any national government, then the Secretariat may develop as an instrument for the preservation of peace and security of increasing significance and responsibilities.[12]

As Hammarskjöld foresaw, the UN has since developed as an instrument for the preservation of peace and security, and its significance and responsibilities have increased dramatically as a result. International intervention in the decolonised world from Congo onwards has been represented as necessary to preserve international peace and security, to prevent a political vacuum being filled by imperialist states and to protect order and maintain life. The UN understands itself as neutral and impartial – a mediator between factions (an expansive term that can encompass elected governments, insurgents, revolutionaries and *génocidaires*) unable to reach consensus. The effect has been to create a long-term policing and managerial role for the UN in the decolonised world.

---

[11]   Sir Brian Urquhart, 'The Secretary-General – Why Dag Hammarskjöld?' in Sten Ask and Anna Mark-Jungkvist (eds.), *The Adventure of Peace: Dag Hammarskjöld and the Future of the UN* (New York: Palgrave Macmillan, 2005), p. 14 at pp. 19–20.

[12]   Dag Hammarskjöld, 'Last Word to the Staff' in Wilder Foote (ed.), *The Servant of Peace: A Selection of the Speeches and Statements of Dag Hammarskjöld* (London: The Bodley Head, 1962), p. 329.

That form of executive rule gradually expanded, until by the 1990s much of the decolonised world was subject to some form of international administration. Despite the scope and complexity of the forms of executive action undertaken by international actors in the decolonised world, the nature of the authority to undertake such action received very little attention for much of the twentieth century. The expansion of executive rule has not been the subject matter of Charter amendments, new treaties or doctrinal elaboration. Instead, the practices of executive rule have been transmitted through operationally oriented documents such as Security Council mandates, rules of engagement, instruction manuals, reports and studies outlining lessons learned from previous experiences. In the words of Hammarskjöld, these documents have functioned as digests of experience, blueprints for action and 'master texts' of the kind needed to guide future operations.[13] To the extent that such master texts have sought to justify the authority to undertake executive rule in the decolonised world, they have done so from the beginning on functional grounds.

According to Hammarskjöld, the development of executive rule was necessary for the performance of the UN's duty to maintain peace and security. Decolonisation had given rise to new conflicts, made more threatening by the possibility that Africa in particular might become a new theatre for the Cold War. Decolonisation had expanded the membership of the UN and made conferencing too slow and cumbersome. The UN could not perform its key functions of guaranteeing peace and protecting independent states if it were understood only as conference machinery. The challenges to peace and security posed by decolonisation made it necessary to abandon the static 'conference approach' to international relations and focus instead upon dynamic 'executive action'.[14] In order to do so, the UN had to ensure that peace operations conformed to certain principles distilled from previous actions. The UN must act independently of the ideologies and interests of specific governments, remain impartial as between warring parties, ensure that

---

[13] See Dag Hammarskjöld, 'The Uses of Private Diplomacy' in Wilder Foote (ed.), *The Servant of Peace: A Selection of the Speeches and Statements of Dag Hammarskjöld* (London: The Bodley Head, 1962), p. 170 at p. 173 (discussing the study of the UN operation in the Suez that he had initiated in the Secretariat as an attempt to 'digest our experiences, work out some kind of blueprint, master texts of the kind needed for this kind of operation').

[14] UN Secretary-General, 'Introduction to the Annual Report of the Secretary-General', p. 1.

the parties involved consented to the UN's operations and only take actions necessary to achieve the mandate.

From deeds into words: systematising peace and protection

Executive rule thus developed through the systematisation of practice rather than through the development of detailed doctrines or norms. Perhaps it would be more precise to say that UN culture 'transcended the conventional split between norms and actions by elevating the actions themselves to norms'.[15] To the generations of international civil servants who came after him, Hammarskjöld did not bequeath norms or 'lifeless ideas ... whose believers might or might not ever translate them into deeds'.[16] Instead, Hammarskjöld and his colleagues bequeathed deeds – deeds that were then systematically rationalised and translated into programmes for further dynamic executive action. The result has been the gradual consolidation of an impressive apparatus of international rule accompanied by a minimalist articulation of the nature and form of international authority.

The terms in which the practices of international rule were rationalised remained remarkably stable for almost forty years. The UN and other humanitarian internationalists understood themselves to be impartial and neutral actors, intervening to maintain peace and protect life with the consent of those they governed. For Hammarskjöld, the commitment to impartiality meant that 'UN personnel cannot be permitted in any sense to be a party to internal conflicts'.[17] The commitment to neutrality meant more broadly 'that the international civil servant, also in executive tasks with political implications, must remain wholly uninfluenced by national or group interests or ideologies'.[18] The Secretary-General in particular has a duty 'to carry out his tasks in controversial political situations with full regard to his exclusively

---

[15] Isabel V. Hull, *Absolute Destruction: Military Culture and the Practices of War in Imperial Germany* (Cornell: Cornell University Press, 2005), p. 333. Hull explores the way in which imperial German military culture worked to elevate actions to norms by transmitting 'habits of action' or practices, rather than 'lifeless ideas'.

[16] *Ibid.*

[17] UN Secretary-General, 'Summary Study of the Experience Derived from the Establishment and Operation of the Force: Report of the Secretary-General', UN GAOR, 13th Sess., Agenda Item 65, UN Doc. A/3943, 9 October 1958, annex, para. 166.

[18] Dag Hammarskjöld, 'The International Civil Servant in Law and in Fact' in Wilder Foote (ed.), *The Servant of Peace: A Selection of the Speeches and Statements of Dag Hammarskjöld* (London: The Bodley Head, 1962), p. 329 at p. 338.

international obligation under the Charter and without subservience to a particular national or ideological character'.[19] Even as early as the Congo operation, the capacity of the UN to act as an impartial and independent guarantor of international peace and security was questioned, but the Secretary-General was able successfully to dismiss such criticisms as mistaken or made in bad faith. The idea that the UN in particular, and international humanitarians more generally, could intervene as neutral actors to alleviate suffering without becoming party to internal conflicts persisted throughout the Cold War.

With the ending of the Cold War, international executive action expanded. During the 1990s, humanitarian missions, peace operations and territorial administration became more frequent and more ambitious. As a result, the stakes of the conceptualisation of international authority became apparent and the inadequacy of existing accounts of international rule could no longer be ignored. With the expansion in the scope and complexity of international operations, it became clear that existing political and legal concepts could not adequately grasp the nature of this form of rule or address the problems and contests to which it gave rise. Both the achievements and the failures of UN operations placed the legitimacy of international executive action on the table. In Kosovo and East Timor, for example, local actors challenged the legitimacy of the authority exercised by international administrators. In Rwanda and Srebrenica, critics argued that the commitment of the UN to protecting its own personnel and to complying with principles of impartiality and neutrality meant that UN peacekeepers failed to protect civilian populations from genocide. As the ambition and complexity of peacekeeping, humanitarian and administration operations grew, so too did the difficulties faced by international actors in determining the proper limits of their responsibility and authority. These difficulties found expression in the many auditing and other reports produced by the UN and humanitarian actors seeking to rationalise their processes or reflect upon lessons learned from past practice, as well as in external critiques of the failures of intervention. While the practices of international rule introduced under Hammarskjöld were characterised in terms of technical expertise and political impartiality, by the end of the 1990s that framework for understanding international practice was increasingly unable to address pressing questions about the legitimacy, authority and credibility of international action.

[19] Ibid.

Many of the issues raised by humanitarian practice were most clearly exemplified by the disastrous effect of attempts to create 'safe havens' or humanitarian spaces in which the UN and humanitarian non-governmental organisations could alleviate the suffering and protect the lives of civilians in situations of civil war or genocide. Critics of the UN argued that its reliance upon principles of impartiality and the use of force only in self-defence had led to its complicity in allowing genocide to unfold in Rwanda in 1994 and again in the UN-protected safe haven of Srebrenica in 1995. The humanitarian principles of impartiality and neutrality came under sustained challenge, with Western journalists and activists arguing that 'impartial peacekeeping between two unequal sides was its own form of side-taking'.[20] Within the UN, official reports questioned the viability of the long-standing commitment to impartiality and neutrality on the part of UN peace-keepers and humanitarian agencies when confronted with situations of war or genocide.[21] In the words of a major UN report on the future of UN peace operations, although impartiality should remain one of the 'bedrock principles' of peacekeeping, there are cases where 'local par-ties consist not of moral equals but of obvious aggressors and victims'.[22] In such situations, 'continued equal treatment of all parties by the United Nations can in the best case result in ineffectiveness and in the worst may amount to complicity with evil'.[23] The report called on world leaders 'to strengthen the capacity of the United Nations to fully accomplish the mission which is, indeed, its very *raison d'être*: to help communities engaged in strife and to maintain or restore peace'.[24] The massacre of civilians who had relied on the UN for protection in Srebrenica and Rwanda had shown 'how easy it was to declare land "safe", yet how difficult it was to persuade the major powers in fact to secure civilians'.[25]

---

[20] Samantha Power, *Chasing the Flame: Sergio Vieira de Mello and the Fight to Save the World* (New York: Penguin Books, 2008), p. 179.

[21] UN Secretary-General, 'Report of the Secretary-General pursuant to General Assembly Resolution 53/35: The Fall of Srebrenica', UN GAOR, 54th Sess., Agenda Item 42, UN Doc. A/54/549, 15 November 1999; 'Report of the Independent Inquiry into the Actions of the United Nations during the 1994 Genocide in Rwanda', UN SCOR, 54th Sess., UN Doc. S/1999/1257, 16 December 1999, annex.

[22] Panel on UN Peace Operations, 'Report to the Secretary-General', UN GAOR, 55th Sess., Provisional Agenda Item 87, UN Doc. A/55/305-S/2000/809, 21 August 2000, pp. ix, 9.

[23] Panel on UN Peace Operations, 'Report to the Secretary General', p. ix.

[24] Parel on UN Peace Operations, 'Report to the Secretary General', p. xv.

[25] Power, *Chasing the Flame*, p. 206.

During the 1990s, international humanitarians who had been involved in development, refugee, famine assistance and emergency relief work began to publish subtle analyses of the problems that their increased operations had faced, particularly in Africa. These analyses were also framed in terms of responsibility and protection. They explored the difficult issues raised by the involvement of the development enterprise in contributing to conditions leading to genocide,[26] the responsibility of protection agencies in situations where humanitarian spaces and refugee camps were providing safe havens for belligerents,[27] and the effects of the over-inflated claims that humanitarians made in representing their capacity to offer protection to people at risk.[28] This literature began to ask questions about the lawfulness or ethics of humanitarian internationalists, both in terms of how they represented their presence and how they understood their responsibility for the effects of their actions and decisions. It also addressed issues of effectiveness, asking whether humanitarian protection was in fact assisting populations at risk, and whether humanitarian actors were fulfilling their responsibilities to those people they claimed to be assisting. Academic commentators in turn suggested that representatives of the international humanitarian community were involved in governing, and that the responsibility of these actors may be better addressed if international presence were recognised as an ongoing factor shaping the dynamics of conflict in the decolonised world rather than characterised as a series of temporary interventions.[29]

The increased scope and ambition of international executive rule in the post-Cold War period thus gave rise to two sets of questions about authority. The first set of questions related to the legitimacy and the effectiveness of international authority. Why should the international executive, and particularly executive organs of the UN, have the power to govern in the decolonised world, rather than domestic authorities, other international institutions claiming functional authority or even

[26] Peter Uvin, *Aiding Violence: The Development Enterprise in Rwanda* (Connecticut: Kumarian Press, 1998).
[27] Fiona Terry, *Condemned to Repeat?: The Paradox of Humanitarian Action* (New York: Cornell University Press, 2002).
[28] Alex de Waal, *Famine Crimes: Politics and the Disaster Relief Industry in Africa* (International African Institute, Bloomington: Oxford and Indiana University Press, 1997).
[29] Anne Orford, *Reading Humanitarian Intervention: Human Rights and the Use of Force in International Law* (Cambridge: Cambridge University Press, 2003); David Kennedy, *The Dark Sides of Virtue: Reassessing International Humanitarianism* (Princeton: Princeton University Press, 2004).

coalitions of willing states? Is the international executive in fact able to govern effectively? Should the UN or other international actors have the right to judge the legitimacy of rulers or governments? The second set of questions referred to the relation between international rulers and local claimants to authority. Why do international administrators recognise and liaise with particular local claimants to authority? Upon what grounds is the choice made to recognise one actor rather than another as the legitimate authority or the appropriate collaborator in a territory? Can international humanitarians really act impartially in making such choices? What effects does the choice to collaborate with one group or leader rather than another have in situations of civil war or protracted conflict? Because international actors were operating in the decolonised world without an adequate characterisation of their political and legal role, they had no coherent answer to questions about the political choices they were inevitably making by treating *génocidaires* in the same way as insurgents, or by liaising with warlords as well as parliamentarians. While this problem was already apparent as early as the Congo action, it became unavoidable in the aftermath of situations such as Rwanda and Srebrenica. During the 1990s, it appeared increasingly necessary for representatives of international authority to find a more coherent account of the power they exercised and the political choices they made. The responsibility to protect concept is a response to that need.

The powers of the international executive under the UN Charter

The responsibility to protect concept can best be understood as offering a normative grounding to the practices of international executive action that were initiated in the era of decolonisation and that have been gradually expanding ever since. To the extent that there existed an explicit legal basis for that form of executive rule, it can be found in the provisions of the UN Charter that define the authority of the Secretariat and the Secretary-General. Article 97 of the Charter describing the Secretary-General as the 'chief administrative officer of the Organization', together with Article 100 providing that the Secretary-General and the staff of the Secretariat 'shall not seek or receive instructions from any government or from any other authority external to the Organization' and Article 101 providing that Secretariat staff are to be appointed by the Secretary-General rather than by Members, established the character of the executive. According to Hammarskjöld, those provisions were of 'fundamental importance' for the status of the

Secretariat, as together they created for the Secretariat an administrative position of 'full political independence'.[30] Article 98 provides that the Secretary-General shall perform the functions entrusted to him by the Security Council and the General Assembly, and it is that provision that 'entitles the General Assembly and the Security Council to entrust the Secretary-General with tasks involving the execution of political decisions, even when this would bring him – and with him the Secretariat and its members – into the arena of possible political conflict'.[31]

Perhaps the most important article for the subsequent development of executive action is Article 99. Article 99 is the article that 'more than any other was considered by the drafters of the Charter to have transformed the Secretary-General of the United Nations from a purely administrative official to one with an explicit political responsibility'.[32] It provides that: 'The Secretary General may bring to the attention of the Security Council any matter which in his opinion may threaten the maintenance of international peace and security.' The express provision in the UN Charter of a political role for the head of the organisation represented a significant departure from earlier international organisations, including the League of Nations.[33] Article 99 gave the Secretary-General considerable discretion to invoke the article by bringing to the attention of the Security Council any matter that in his opinion may threaten the maintenance of international peace and security. According to Hammarskjöld, that article did not only confer upon the Secretary-General the right to bring matters before the Security Council, but also necessarily carried with it 'a broad discretion to conduct inquiries and to engage in informal diplomatic activity in regard to matters which "may threaten the maintenance of international peace and security"'.[34] In order to decide whether a matter should be brought before the Security Council, the Secretary-General must have access to 'full and impartial data concerning the matter in point. From this assumption it follows that the Secretary-General has the right to make such inquiries and investigations as he may think necessary in order to determine whether or not to invoke his powers.'[35] The Article has thus been 'interpreted as providing a specific legal authorization for

[30] Hammarskjöld, 'The International Civil Servant', p. 334.   [31] Ibid., p. 335.
[32] Ibid.
[33] S. M. Schwebel, 'The Origins and Development of Article 99 of the Charter' British Year Book of International Law 28 (1951), 371 at 372.
[34] Hammarskjöld, 'The International Civil Servant', p. 335.
[35] Schwebel, 'Origins and Development of Article 99', 379.

that extensive, informal, behind-the-scenes political activity of the Secretary-General for which the propensities of his position, and the precedent of the League, provide a non-textual basis'.[36]

More generally, to the extent that Article 99 affirms the political authority of the Secretary-General, it has been said to have 'set the tone of the office of the Secretary-General'.[37] Thus even if Article 99 is 'not formally invoked, its presence provides the likeliest legal source for the continuing political initiative of the Secretary-General, which takes forms other than the implementation of Article 99 in terms'.[38] The functions and powers conferred by Articles 98 and 99, together with the Secretary-General's position as the chief administrative officer of the organisation and the figure who represents the organisation as a whole, constitutes 'the legal basis for the Secretary-General's political author- ity'.[39] In light of the potential that these Charter provisions offered for the expansion of that political authority, Stephen Schwebel, writing in 1951, presciently commented:

> Perhaps it is not too much to suggest that, as the development of the great
> national civil services profoundly affected the national histories of the
> nineteenth and twentieth centuries, so the growth of the powers of the
> international executive may in time influence the future course of world
> affairs.[40]

The growth of the powers of the international executive have since developed through the expansion of practices aimed at maintaining peace and protecting life in the decolonised world. In his Introduction to the 1961 Annual Report of the Secretary-General to the General Assembly, Hammarskjöld noted that although 'great attention is given' in the UN Charter 'to the principles and pur- poses, and considerable space is devoted to an elaboration of what may be called the parliamentary aspects of the Organization, little is said about executive arrangements'.[41] He concluded that as a result, 'the executive functions and their form have been left largely to practice'.[42] For Oscar Schachter, reflecting a decade later upon the developments that had occurred during Hammarskjöld's tenure as Secretary-General, the expansion of 'executive action' was 'widely regarded as constituting a major feature' of Hammarskjöld's

---

[36] *Ibid.*, 375.   [37] *Ibid.*, 381–2.   [38] *Ibid.*, 381.   [39] *Ibid.*, 379.   [40] *Ibid.*, 382.
[41] UN Secretary-General, 'Introduction to the Annual Report of the Secretary-General',
UN Doc. A/4800/Add.1, p. 5.
[42] *Ibid.*

'political legacy'.[43] The forms of executive action developed by Hammarskjöld had been directed to filling 'power vacuums' in the 'peripheral' or 'underdeveloped areas'.[44] Although such '"operational" measures' might 'not at first seem to be related to international law', Schachter argued that in fact they 'have an impact on the evolution of the standards of international behaviour, and the effective implementation of such standards'.[45] Collective intervention 'involves more than "action"'.[46] It necessarily creates 'new conceptions of permissible and impermissible interference' as well as new conceptions 'of the Charter obligations for mutual assistance and co-operation'.[47] Such actions can therefore be 'regarded in a broader and more subtle sense' as giving 'a new dimension to the efforts to give rigor and efficacy to a normative structure based on the common interest of all peoples'.[48] Over time, the practices of executive action initiated by Hammarskjöld have led to the creation of a new form of administrative rule. As that form of rule began to be consolidated and centralised, it began to seem necessary to develop a full conceptualisation of the normative basis for executive authority.

The responsibility to protect and the question of authority

The ICISS report returned the question of authority to its proper place at the centre of debates about international law and order. The report is premised upon the idea that states and the international community have a 'responsibility to protect' populations at risk. The inspiration for the responsibility to protect concept came from the work done by Francis Deng during the 1990s on conflict management in Africa.[49] In *Sovereignty as Responsibility*, Deng and his co-authors had argued that responsibility, rather than control, should be seen as the essence of sovereignty.[50] They developed a theory of authority to justify the exercise of governmental functions by international actors in Africa. *Sovereignty as Responsibility* argues that the state has an obligation 'to preserve life-

---

[43] Oscar Schachter, 'Dag Hammarskjöld and the Relation of Law to Politics', *American Journal of International Law* 56 (1962), 1 at 8.
[44] *Ibid.*, 7.   [45] *Ibid.*, 8.   [46] *Ibid.*   [47] *Ibid.*   [48] *Ibid.*
[49] Gareth Evans, 'From Humanitarian Intervention to the Responsibility to Protect', *Wisconsin International Law Journal* 24 (2006), 703 at 708.
[50] Francis M. Deng *et al.*, *Sovereignty as Responsibility: Conflict Management in Africa* (Washington: The Brookings Institution, 1996), pp. 1–2.

sustaining standards for its citizens'.[51] That obligation is a 'necessary condition of sovereignty'.[52] In early modern Europe, it was thought that situations of civil war, instability and disorder 'could only be overcome by viable governments capable of establishing firm and effective control over territory and populations'.[53] The state could only continue to claim legitimacy as long as it was 'capable or willing' of establishing order and providing protection.[54] Deng and his co-authors refer to the famous debate between H. L. A. Hart and Lon Fuller, siding with Fuller's claim that the sovereign does not exist above the law but that the legitimacy of the sovereign is instead judged according to law.[55] According to Fuller, 'a dictatorship which clothes itself with a tinsel of legal form can so far depart from the morality of order, from the inner morality of law itself, that it ceases to be a legal system'.[56] Fuller resisted the idea that the demands of security and justice, or 'order' and 'good order', were contradictions. Indeed, Fuller chose the language of 'order' and 'good order' so as to avoid the sense of 'opposing demands that have no living contact with one another, that simply shout their contradictions across a vacuum'.[57] According to Fuller:

> As we seek order, we can meaningfully remind ourselves that order will do us no good unless it is good for something. As we seek to make our order good, we can remind ourselves that justice is impossible without order, and that we must not lose order itself in the attempt to make it good.[58]

For Deng and his co-authors, a government will only be recognisable as the lawful authority over a territory if it can guarantee both security and justice. *Sovereignty as Responsibility* suggested that 'to qualify for the name of government, a government has now to meet certain standards, all of which involve restraints on the use of power'.[59] The 'international community' has a 'responsibility' to ensure that the state meets these standards and is in fact able and willing to guarantee protection to its citizens.[60] Sovereignty understood in that sense of an obligation to

---

[51] *Ibid.*, p. xviii.   [52] *Ibid.*   [53] *Ibid.*, p. 2.   [54] *Ibid.*, p. 1.   [55] *Ibid.*, p. 3.

[56] Lon L. Fuller, 'Positivism and Fidelity to Law – A Reply to Professor Hart', *Harvard Law Review* 71 (1958), 630 at 660.

[57] *Ibid.*, 657.   [58] *Ibid.*

[59] Deng *et al.*, *Sovereignty as Responsibility*, p. 4, citing W. Michael Reisman, 'Through or Despite Governments: Differentiated Responsibilities in Human Rights Programs', *Iowa Law Review* 72 (1987), 391 at 392.

[60] Deng *et al.*, *Sovereignty as Responsibility*, p. 6.

preserve life has become 'a pooled function'.[61] If local claimants to
authority in Africa – whether they be 'governments, rebel leaders, militia
leaders, civil society, or the general population' – fail to exercise the
responsibility to protect citizens, 'they cannot legitimately complain
against international humanitarian intervention'.[62] Indeed, a government that cannot protect its citizens may no longer even be recognisable
as the lawful authority in a territory:

> After all, internal conflicts in Africa as elsewhere often entail a contest of
> the national arena of power and therefore sovereignty. Every political
> intervention from outside has its internal recipients, hosts, and benefi-
> ciaries. Under those circumstances, there can hardly be said to be an
> indivisible quantum of national sovereignty behind which the nation
> stands united.[63]

Following Deng's lead, the ICISS report argued that 'the changing international environment' required a rethinking of the fundamental notion
of authority. ICISS proposed a 'necessary re-characterization' of sovereignty from '*sovereignty as control* to *sovereignty as responsibility*'.[64]
According to ICISS, thinking of sovereignty in those terms enabled a
clearer focus upon the 'functions' of 'state authorities'.[65] Sovereignty as
responsibility 'implies that the state authorities are responsible for the
functions of protecting the safety and lives of citizens and promotion of
their welfare'.[66] That responsibility to perform the functions of protecting citizens and promoting their welfare 'resides first and foremost with
the state whose people are directly affected'.[67] However, those functions
are often not performed by the state, as evidenced by the fact that:
'Millions of human beings remain at the mercy of civil wars, insurgencies, state repression and state collapse.'[68] In such circumstances, where
the state does not have the power, the capacity or the will to meet its
responsibility to protect, the need for international action arises. In that
situation, a 'residual' or 'fallback' responsibility to protect on the part of
the 'broader community of states' is activated.[69] The situations in which
this international responsibility may arise were spelt out in broad terms
in the ICISS report:

> Where a population is suffering serious harm, as a result of internal war,
> insurgency, repression or state failure, and the state in question is

---

[61] *Ibid.*   [62] *Ibid.*, p. xvi.   [63] *Ibid.*, p. 16.
[64] ICISS, 'Responsibility to Protect', p. 13 (emphasis in original).   [65] *Ibid.*   [66] *Ibid.*
[67] *Ibid.*, p. 17.   [68] *Ibid.*, p. 11.   [69] *Ibid.*, p. 17.

unwilling or unable to halt or avert it, the principle of non-intervention yields to the international responsibility to protect.[70]

The responsibility to protect concept places a renewed emphasis on de facto rather than de jure grounds for authority. In doing so, it represents a significant departure from the conception of lawful authority that has formed the normative basis of the modern international legal system since 1945. International law has long treated effective control over territory as an important criterion of statehood.[71] In that sense, statehood has in part been premised upon de facto authority. Yet the creation of the UN in 1945 saw the emergence of an international regime in which the principles of self-determination, sovereign equality and the prohibition against acquisition of territory through the use of force were also treated as central to determining the lawfulness of particular claimants to authority.[72] These principles shaped the process of formal decolonisation and delegitimised alien rule. Under the UN Charter, the lawfulness of authority over a given territory thus became a matter both of fact and of right. Where occupation by foreign states or administration by international organisations was permitted, it was conceived of as temporary, authorised for limited periods and for restricted ends. Humanitarian intervention in turn was understood (and championed) as an exceptional measure that properly did little 'to threaten the traditional rights of sovereigns'.[73] The responsibility to protect concept is a significant departure from that vision. It is premised on the notion that authority, to be legitimate, must be effective at guaranteeing protection, and that the failure to protect a population is a factual matter that can be determined by the international community. The responsibility to protect concept thus grounds authority – both of states and of the international community – on the capacity to provide effective protection to populations at risk. This de facto grounding of authority marginalises the more familiar claims to authority grounded on right, whether that right be understood in historical, universal or democratic terms.

---

[70] Ibid., p. xi.
[71] James Crawford, *The Creation of States in International Law*, 2nd edn Oxford: (Oxford University Press, 2006), pp. 37–89.
[72] Ibid., pp. 96–173.
[73] José Alvarez, 'The Schizophrenias of R2P', *American Society of International Law Newsletter* 23(3) (2007), 1, www.asil.org/newsletter/president/pres070927.html.

From endorsement to implementation

The inclusion of the responsibility to protect concept in the World Summit Outcome 'transformed the principle, from a commission proposal actively supported by a relatively small number of like-minded states' to a concept 'endorsed by the entire UN membership'.[74] Yet despite the inclusion of the concept in the World Summit Outcome, it was not clear whether states and international organisations would take up the concept institutionally. The most enthusiastic early adopter of the responsibility to protect concept was the UN, particularly under the leadership of Secretary-General Ban Ki-moon. Throughout his campaign for UN Secretary-General, Ban Ki-moon made clear that he was a strong supporter of the responsibility to protect. Since his appointment as Secretary-General, Ban has said he will 'spare no effort to operationalize the responsibility to protect',[75] and has spoken of the need to translate the concept 'from promise into practice, words into deeds'.[76] The Secretary-General signalled the emphasis to be placed on the responsibility to protect with the creation of two senior positions to oversee its implementation. Francis Deng was appointed to the newly styled position of UN Special Adviser on the Prevention of Genocide in 2007 and Edward Luck was appointed to the new position of Special Adviser to the Secretary-General on the Responsibility to Protect in 2008. The two advisers 'share an office on genocide prevention and RtoP, helping the United Nations to speak and act as one'.[77]

In the wake of the World Summit, Western states began to refer to the responsibility to protect in policy statements, stressing the concept's relevance to questions of international order, development and security. For example, members of the US administration stated that the US has a responsibility to protect in cases involving genocide, war crimes, ethnic cleansing and crimes against humanity, and that it had acted upon this

---

[74] Alex J. Bellamy, *Responsibility to Protect: The Global Effort to End Mass Atrocities* (Cambridge: Polity Press, 2009), p. 95.

[75] UN Secretary-General, 'Address to the Summit of the Africa Union', Addis Ababa, Ethiopia, 31 January 2008, www.un.org/apps/news/infocus/sgspeeches/search_full.asp?statID=180#.

[76] UN, 'Secretary-General Defends, Clarifies "Responsibility to Protect" at Berlin Event on "Responsibility to Protect: International Cooperation for a Changed World"', UN Press Release SG/SM/11701, 15 July 2008, www.un.org/News/Press/docs/2008/sgsm11701.doc.htm.

[77] *Ibid.*

responsibility as a member of the Security Council.[78] In a series of speeches concerned with the conflict in Sudan, the Swedish Minister for International Development Cooperation stated that Sweden must 'put our responsibility to protect into practice' and 'contribute to an improved situation for the suffering civilians' in Darfur.[79] The provision of humanitarian aid, diplomatic efforts to support implementation of the North–South peace agreement and Sweden's contribution to reconstruction have been characterised as part of Sweden's 'responsibility to protect civilians' in Darfur.[80] In November 2007, then UK Prime Minister Gordon Brown declared that: 'We now rightly recognise our responsibility to protect behind borders where there are crimes against humanity.'[81] If that responsibility is to be honoured, Brown argued, it would require a 'new framework for reconstruction', involving the systematic combination of 'traditional emergency aid and peacekeeping with stabilisation, reconstruction and development', so that the 'international community' is 'able to offer a practical route map from failure to stability'.[82] In August 2008, Australia's Foreign Minister Stephen Smith also publicly stated that 'Australia supports the R2P principle' and is 'committed to making the principle central to conflict prevention and resolution'.[83] He announced the establishment of a $2 million 'Responsibility to Protect Fund', to be administered by Australia's aid agency. In its 2009 'Defence White Paper', the Australian government endorsed the responsibility to protect concept, stating that if a 'rules-based global security order' is to work, 'occasionally it is necessary to act to restore order'.[84] In that context, the

---

[78]   John R. Crook (ed.), 'US Officials Endorse "Responsibility to Protect" through Security Council Action', *American Journal of International Law* 100 (2006), 463 at 463–4.

[79]   Gunilla Carlsson, Swedish Minister for International Development Cooperation, 'The Challenge of Protecting Civilians in Darfur: Sweden's Response', speech given to the ICRC Seminar on the humanitarian challenges in Darfur, 2 July 2007, www.sweden.gov. se/sb/d/8812/a/85206.

[80]   *Ibid.* For the announcement of specific measures to be taken to 'increase Sweden's efforts for humanitarian protection' in Darfur, see Swedish Ministry for Foreign Affairs, 'New Strategy for Swedish Support to Sudan', Press Release, 15 June 2007, www.sweden.gov. se/sb/d/9227/a/84264.

[81]   Prime Minister Gordon Brown, 'Lord Mayor's Banquet Speech', 12 November 2007, www.pm.gov.uk/output/Page13736.asp.

[82]   *Ibid.*

[83]   Stephen Smith, Australian Minister for Foreign Affairs, 'A New Era of Engagement with the World', speech given to the Sydney Institute, 9 August 2008, www.foreignminister. gov.au/speeches/2008/080819_si.html.

[84]   Australian Government Department of Defence, 'Defending Australia in the Asia Pacific Century: Force 2030: Defence White Paper', (Canberra: Australian Government

government declared its support for the "'responsibility to protect" principle' and recognised 'that, on occasion, it may be necessary for other states to intervene, under the auspices of a UN Security Council resolution, if a state cannot or will not protect its population'.[85] In addition, ongoing support for the responsibility to protect concept was evidenced by its inclusion in a series of thematic and operational resolutions of the Security Council during that period.[86]

Regional support for the responsibility to protect concept was also apparent in Africa. In the lead-up to the World Summit, the African Union developed a common position on the proposed reform of the UN that formally endorsed the responsibility to protect concept.[87] A 2007 resolution of the African Commission on Human and Peoples' Rights called for the strengthening of the responsibility to protect concept, and endorsed the 2007 Security Council decision to deploy an AU/UN Hybrid Operation in Darfur as an exercise of the responsibility to protect.[88] Individual states including Botswana, Ghana, Lesotho, Nigeria, Rwanda and Tanzania continued to make strong statements endorsing the responsibility to protect concept and the need for collective action to protect populations under threat of genocide, war crimes, ethnic cleansing and crimes against humanity.

Department of Defence, 2009), para. 5.19, www.defence.gov.au/whitepaper/docs/defence_white_paper_2009.pdf.

[85] *Ibid.*

[86] See, for example, SC Res. 1674, UN SCOR, 61st Sess., 5430th Mtg., UN Doc. S/RES/1674, 28 April 2006; SC Res. 1706, UN SCOR, 61st Sess., 5519th Mtg., UN Doc. S/RES/1706, 31 August 2006 ('*Recalling* also its previous resolutions . . . and 1674 (2006) on the protection of civilians in armed conflict, which reaffirms inter alia the provisions of paragraphs 138 and 139 of the 2005 United Nations World Summit outcome document'); SC Res. 1755, UN SCOR, 62nd Sess., 5670th Mtg., UN Doc. S/RES/1755, 30 April 2007; SC Res. 1769, UN SCOR, 62nd Sess., 5727th Mtg., UN Doc. S/RES/1769, 31 July 2007 (recalling the Security Council's previous resolutions and presidential statements on Darfur and on the protection of children, civilians and humanitarian workers in armed conflict, determining that the situation in Sudan continues to constitute a threat to international peace and security and deciding to authorise and mandate the establishment of an AU/UN Hybrid Operation in Darfur).

[87] Executive Council, African Union, 'The Common African Position on the Proposed Reform of the United Nations: "The Ezulwini Consensus"', 7th Extraordinary Sess., Ext/EX.CL/2 (VII), 7–8 March 2005 (adopting the principle of the responsibility to protect).

[88] African Commission on Human and Peoples' Rights, 'Resolution on Strengthening the Responsibility to Protect in Africa', 42nd Ordinary Sess., ACHPR/Res. 117 (XXXXII), 28 November 2007 (endorsing the 2007 Security Council decision to deploy an AU/UN Hybrid Operation in Darfur as an exercise of the responsibility to protect). www.responsibilitytoprotect.org/files/Govt%20Statements%202005–2007–Africa%20pdf.pdf.

Yet reports also began to circulate of a growing unease about the concept, particularly among members of the Non-Aligned Movement. A lack of consensus about the desirability of acting upon the responsibility to protect concept not only threatened to sideline the concept as a relevant factor in state decision-making about international relations, but also threatened the viability of the concept at the UN. Without a General Assembly resolution formally endorsing the responsibility to protect concept, the Secretary-General could not gain access to the institutional resources that would be needed to implement the concept within the UN system. In January 2009, the Secretary-General produced a report for debate in the General Assembly setting out strategies for implementing the responsibility to protect concept.[89] The Secretary-General's Special Adviser Ed Luck, backed up by an informal governmental grouping of Friends of the Responsibility to Protect and a broad coalition of civil society groups, engaged in a concerted programme of negotiation and discussion with states in the lead-up to the General Assembly meeting to discuss the responsibility to protect.

At the subsequent General Assembly meeting, held in July 2009, ninety-four representatives spoke, revealing wide support for the Secretary-General's focus upon prevention, capacity-building and assistance to states as the basis for implementing the responsibility to protect concept. States and the representatives of groups such as the Non-Aligned Movement displayed little opposition to proposals for the further development and implementation of the concept.[90] On 14 September 2009, the General Assembly passed its first resolution on the responsibility to protect concept, noting the Secretary-General's report on implementing the responsibility to protect concept and deciding to continue discussions of the responsibility to protect concept within the General Assembly.[91] The resolution, co-sponsored by sixty-seven Member States, provides the authority for the Secretary-General to seek further financial and institutional resources for implementing and

---

[89] UN Secretary-General, 'Implementing the Responsibility to Protect'.

[90] Of the ninety-four speakers at the debate, only a handful (representing Venezuela, Cuba, Sudan, Nicaragua, Sri Lanka and the Democratic People's Republic of Korea) expressed strong scepticism or hostility towards the responsibility to protect concept. Those that did treated the responsibility to protect concept primarily as a justification for military intervention. See further the statements at www.un.org/ga/president/63/interactive/responsibilitytoprotect.shtml.

[91] 'The Responsibility to Protect', GA Res. 63/308, UN GAOR, 63rd Sess., Agenda Items 44 and 107, Supp. No. 49, UN Doc. A/RES/63/308, 7 October 2009.

mainstreaming the responsibility to protect concept within the UN system.[92] According to the Secretary-General, implementing the responsibility to protect concept now 'demands a system-wide UN effort' and 'should also inform our development and peacebuilding work not just our efforts in the areas of human rights, humanitarian affairs, peacekeeping and political affairs'.[93]

With that endorsement by the General Assembly, the responsibility to protect concept has moved into a new phase. The discussion has moved from whether the responsibility to protect concept should be endorsed, to how it should be implemented. In addressing the General Assembly, the European Union (EU) has declared that the focus should now be on 'operationalisation and implementation' of the concept,[94] and in a statement to the Security Council at its eighth meeting on the protection of civilians in armed conflict, the EU called for the concept of the responsibility to protect 'to be integrated in our overall normative framework'.[95] In its statement to the Security Council, Rwanda noted that the 'General Assembly debate and resolution 63/308 on the responsibility to protect make it necessary for this concept to be operationalized as an additional element in the protection of populations from genocide, war crimes, ethnic cleansing and crimes against humanity'.[96] The likelihood that the responsibility to protect concept will be implemented has been increased by the decision of the US to throw its weight behind the concept. The US National Security Strategy released in May 2010 includes an explicit commitment to the responsibility to protect concept in the section dealing with 'international order':

> The United States and all member states of the U.N. have endorsed the concept of the 'Responsibility to Protect.' In so doing, we have recognized

[92] UN Secretary-General, 'Remarks at a Stanley Foundation Conference on "Implementing the Responsibility to Protect"'.

[93] *Ibid.*

[94] Anders Lidén, Ambassador and Permanent Representative of Sweden to the UN, 'Statement on behalf of the European Union to the General Assembly Debate on the Responsibility to Protect', UN GAOR, 63rd Sess., 97th Plen. Mtg., UN Doc. A/63/PV.97, 23 July 2009, pp. 3–5.

[95] Anders Lidén, Ambassador and Permanent Representative of Sweden to the UN, 'Statement on behalf of the European Union at the Security Council Debate on Protection of Civilians in Armed Conflict', UN SCOR, 64th Sess., 6216th Mtg., UN Doc. S/PV.6216, 11 November 2009, pp. 29–30.

[96] Bugingo Rugema, Representative of Rwanda, 'Statement by Rwanda at the Security Council Debate on Protection of Civilians in Armed Conflict', UN SCOR, 64th Sess., 6216th Mtg., UN Doc. S/PV.6216 (Resumption 1), 11 November 2009, pp. 52–3.

that the primary responsibility for preventing genocide and mass atrocity rests with sovereign governments, but that this responsibility passes to the broader international community when sovereign governments themselves commit genocide or mass atrocities, or when they prove unable or unwilling to take necessary action to prevent or respond to such crimes inside their borders. The United States is committed to working with our allies, and to strengthening our own internal capabilities, in order to ensure that the United States and the international community are proactively engaged in a strategic effort to prevent mass atrocities and genocide. In the event that prevention fails, the United States will work both multilaterally and bilaterally to mobilize diplomatic, humanitarian, financial, and – in certain instances – military means to prevent and respond to genocide and mass atrocities.[97]

The normative significance of the responsibility to protect concept

In making the argument that this embrace of the responsibility to protect concept is an important normative development, I depart from the consensus position that is developing in academic literature about the *insignificance* of the responsibility to protect concept. For some critics, the indeterminate content and uncertain status of the responsibility to protect concept seem to have been left deliberately vague, suggesting that states have no intention of taking on new obligations to protect suffering peoples in foreign lands.[98] From this perspective, the invocation of the responsibility to protect concept is at best an empty rhetorical gesture cynically made by the leaders of Western states to assuage the growing popular pressure for action in situations of humanitarian crisis. At worst, the ambiguity and contingency of the responsibility to protect concept will mean that it can serve as a front for business-as-usual on the part of powerful states – any unilateral military action can potentially be justified as necessary to 'protect populations at risk'.[99] The apparent commitment of states to the concept may simply operate to reinforce the

---

[97] 'National Security Strategy of the United States' (Washington, May 2010), p. 48, www.whitehouse.gov/sites/default/files/rss_viewer/national_security_ strategy.pdf.

[98] David Chandler, 'Unravelling the Paradox of "The Responsibility to Protect"', *Irish Studies in International Affairs* 20 (2009), 27 ('the R2P is conceptually and institutionally a reflection of the evasion of Western responsibility for others'); Nicholas J. Wheeler and Frazer Egerton, 'The Responsibility to Protect: "Precious Commitment" or a Promise Unfulfilled?', *Global Responsibility to Protect* 1 (2009), 114.

[99] Noam Chomsky, 'Statement to the United Nations General Assembly Thematic Dialogue on the Responsibility to Protect', United Nations, New York, 23 July 2009,

Western world's 'moral ownership' of civil war, famine and other crises in the decolonised world,[100] without providing any mechanism for requiring organisations to take responsibility for protecting populations. In that sense, the responsibility to protect concept can be added to the proliferating list of unrealised tasks, deadlines and projects that the international community has set itself during the post-Cold War period.

At the heart of such critiques is the assumption that if the responsibility to protect concept imposes no new binding duties or obligations upon states or international organisations, then it has no normative effect. Indeed, for many international lawyers, the only legally relevant question to ask about the responsibility to protect concept is whether it gives rise to a new norm that binds states.[101] Most agree that the World Summit Outcome cannot be understood to impose new legal obligations that are binding upon states acting either unilaterally or collectively.[102] There is nothing added to (although there may be something subtracted from) existing international law by the Secretary-General's claim referred to earlier that 'the primary raison d'être and duty' of every state is to protect those within its territory.[103] The obligation of the state to protect those within its territory or jurisdiction from genocide and other mass atrocities was already reflected in the Genocide Convention,[104] international and regional human rights treaties and

---

www.un.org/ga/president/63/interactive/protect/noam.pdf; Alvarez, 'The Schizophrenias of R2P'.

[100] On that 'moral ownership', see de Waal, *Famine Crimes*, p. xvi.

[101] Carlo Focarelli, 'The Responsibility to Protect Doctrine and Humanitarian Intervention: Too Many Ambiguities for a Working Doctrine', *Journal of Conflict and Security Law* 13 (2008), 191 at 193 ('without support from states as a whole, an "emerging" norm can hardly "emerge" and credibly be binding upon them'); Amrita Kapur, '"Humanity as the A and Ω of Sovereignty": Four Replies to Anne Peters', *European Journal of International Law* 20 (2009), 560 at 562 (arguing that the responsibility to protect is not a legal norm because 'there are no identified consequences for the failure to fulfil the R2P by either the subject state or the P5'); Gelijen Molier, 'Humanitarian Intervention and the Responsibility to Protect after 9/11', *Netherlands International Law Review* 53 (2006), 37.

[102] See, however, Anne Peters, 'Humanity as the A and Ω of Sovereignty', *European Journal of International Law* 20 (2009), 513 at 540, 544 (arguing that the emergence of the responsibility to protect concept has promoted 'a significant evolution of international law in the direction of a legal obligation of the Security Council to take humanitarian action').

[103] UN Secretary-General, 'In Larger Freedom', para. 135.

[104] Convention on the Prevention and Punishment of the Crime of Genocide, opened for signature 9 December 1948, 78 UNTS 277 (entered into force 12 January 1951).

the laws of war.[105] Nor does it appear that the declaration of an *international* responsibility to protect has imposed a legal obligation upon states to engage in unilateral or collective intervention in situations of humanitarian crisis.

It seems clear that the responsibility to protect concept has been carefully couched so as not to impose legal duties upon states or international organisations to take particular actions in specific circumstances. The idea that the responsibility to protect concept might impose obligations of that nature upon states has been resisted both by states that might be subjected to intervention and by states that might be obliged to intervene. In the negotiations leading up to the World Summit, 'states with major force projection capabilities' made clear that they were 'decidedly unenthusiastic – as were many other Member States as well – about allowing multilateral organizations to decide how, where, and when their forces would be deployed'.[106] In particular, John Bolton, the US Representative to the UN, spelt out in a letter to Members that 'the Charter has never been interpreted as creating a legal obligation for Security Council members to support enforcement action in various cases involving serious breaches of international peace' and accordingly 'a determination as to what particular measures to adopt in specific cases cannot be predetermined in the abstract but should remain a decision within the purview of the Security Council'.[107] According to the US, 'the responsibility of the other countries in the international community is not of the same character as the responsibility of the host, and we thus want to avoid formulations that suggest that the other countries are inheriting the same responsibility that the host state has'.[108] States that had experienced or that could be likely targets of Western intervention, including the members of the Non-Aligned Movement, were also strongly opposed to any endorsement of the notion that inclusion of the responsibility to protect concept in the World Summit Outcome might create a right of

---

[105] Louise Arbour, 'The Responsibility to Protect as a Duty of Care of International Law and Practice', *Review of International Studies* 34 (2008), 445 at 449–50; Carsten Stahn, *The Law and Practice of International Territorial Administration: Versailles to Iraq and Beyond* (Cambridge: Cambridge University Press, 2008), p. 118.

[106] Edward C. Luck, 'Sovereignty, Choice, and the Responsibility to Protect', *Global Responsibility to Protect* 1 (2009), 10 at 19.

[107] John R. Bolton, Ambassador and Representative of the US to the UN, 'Letter to UN Member States', 30 August 2005, www.reformtheun.org/index.php/government_statements/c74?theme=alt2.

[108] *Ibid.*

humanitarian intervention.[109] During the formal plenary debate of the Secretary-General's report on 'Implementing the Responsibility to Protect' at the General Assembly in July 2009, many states continued to express their strong opposition to any linkage of the responsibility to protect concept with unilateral intervention.[110] Similarly, the responsibility to protect concept appears to authorise but not mandate particular forms of executive action by the UN in situations of mass atrocity. Legal scholars have therefore concluded that because the responsibility to protect concept appears not to impose new obligations upon states or international organisations to take action in particular situations, it has no normative effect, introduces no conceptual innovation and merely amounts to 'political rhetoric'.[111]

This book argues in contrast that even if the responsibility to protect concept does not impose any new obligations upon states or the UN to take action in situations of humanitarian crisis, it nonetheless raises fundamentally important legal questions. The responsibility to protect concept is not a form of law that imposes duties on subjects. Rather, it can best be understood as a form of law that confers powers 'of a public or official nature' and that allocates jurisdiction.[112] In *The Concept of Law*, H. L. A. Hart distinguished between 'laws that confer powers' and 'those that impose duties'.[113] Commentators have tended to treat the inclusion of the responsibility to protect concept in the World Summit Outcome as an attempt to do the latter and criticised the imperfection of the duties thus imposed.[114] Instead, the responsibility to protect concept should be understood as normative in the former sense of providing legal authorisation for certain kinds of activities. Officials are not bound to 'obey' the responsibility to protect concept, and nor does the World Summit Outcome dictate the precise means by which the international

---

[109] Luck, 'Sovereignty, Choice and the Responsibility to Protect', 17–18.

[110] For an assessment of the positions taken by states during the debate, see Global Centre for the Responsibility to Protect, 'Implementing the Responsibility to Protect – The 2009 General Assembly Debate: An Assessment', GCR2P Report, August 2009.

[111] Carsten Stahn, 'Responsibility to Protect: Political Rhetoric or Emerging Legal Norm?', *American Journal of International Law* 101 (2007), 99; Focarelli, 'Responsibility to Protect Doctrine'; Kapur, '"Humanity as the A and Ω of Sovereignty": Four Replies'; Molier, 'Humanitarian Intervention'.

[112] H. L. A. Hart, *The Concept of Law* (Oxford: Clarendon Press, 1961), p. 28.

[113] *Ibid.*, p. 32.

[114] Kledja Mulaj, 'Humanitarian Protection: Prevention, Reaction, and Reconstruction', *Journal of Intervention and Statebuilding* 3(1) (2009), 122 at 125–7.

community should implement the responsibility to protect.[115] The vocabulary of 'responsibility' works here as a language for conferring authority and allocating powers rather than as a language for imposing binding obligations and commanding obedience.[116] In that sense, the responsibility to protect concept has a similar character to the articles providing the legal basis for the political authority of the Secretary-General and Secretariat under the UN Charter. In particular, it has long been accepted that Article 99 of the Charter does not impose a duty or obligation upon the Secretary-General to exercise his political authority in a particular way, but rather provides a discretionary mandate to undertake executive action.

To think about the responsibility to protect concept in this way, as a means of conferring or expanding authority, represents a departure from dominant accounts of international law. Much international legal doctrine is premised upon understanding international law as a system of law akin to private law.[117] International law, like private law, is understood as a system for governing relations between equals. In the case of international law, the equality of subjects plays an even more fundamental role than in domestic legal systems, where the idea that agreements must be honoured finds a guarantor in the state.[118] Because international law is a system in which there is no sovereign guarantor of the law, international legal jurisprudence is strongly shaped by the notion of consent and by the idea that law exists to bind states to their commitments. Yet international law is not only a form of law that binds sovereign states, but also a form of law that orders relations between those who claim to represent particular political communities and those who claim to represent the universal in some sense. International law has

---

[115] In distinguishing between the two broad types of laws, Hart comments that conformity with a law that confers powers is not well captured by the idea that an official has obeyed the law. For example, if a certain number of votes are necessary before a measure can be passed by a legislative body, 'the voters in favour of the measure have not "obeyed" the law requiring a majority decision nor have those who voted against it either obeyed or disobeyed it': Hart, *The Concept of Law*, p. 31.

[116] For the related argument that the work of the International Law Commission on the responsibility of international organisations has to date largely concerned 'the allocation of powers, rather than providing reparation for injury', see André Nollkaemper, 'Constitutionalization and the Unity of the Law of International Responsibility', *Indiana Journal of Global Legal Studies* 16 (2009), 535 at 537.

[117] *Ibid.*, at 542–3 (discussing inter alia the claim made by Hersch Lauterpacht that public international law 'belongs to the genus private law').

[118] Alain Supiot, *Homo Juridicus: On the Anthropological Function of the Law*, Saskia Brown trans., (London: Verso, 2007), pp. 86–100.

historically been concerned with mediating relations between representatives of sovereign states and representatives of the universal (such as the Pope, the Holy Roman Emperor or the Secretary-General of the UN).[119] Sovereignty is a concept that has been deployed to limit universal jurisdiction as well as to limit the jurisdiction of other sovereign states. The responsibility to protect concept can best be understood as part of that international legal tradition. The concept is not primarily concerned with the distribution of jurisdiction and authority between sovereign states, but rather with the distribution of jurisdiction and authority between states and international actors. Just as medieval jurists argued that princes or kings could have jurisdiction over particular places or things (like England or France) while the Holy Roman Emperor retained jurisdiction over the world 'considered as a single whole',[120] so the responsibility to protect concept develops the idea that while states are responsible for their own citizens or populations the UN is responsible for the international community as a whole.

Humanitarian intervention, police action and the responsibility to protect

Many critical responses to the development of the responsibility to protect concept have focused upon its potential to authorise unilateral police action or humanitarian intervention. For example, in an interactive dialogue that took place before the General Assembly debate on the responsibility to protect in July 2009, Noam Chomsky focused upon the danger that the doctrine of the responsibility to protect could be misused by powerful states seeking to engage in military intervention.[121] Many states also expressed concern that the responsibility to protect concept might be misused by powerful states to justify unilateral humanitarian intervention. Yet most states were willing to endorse the use of the responsibility to protect concept to justify the expansion of gentler forms of international action, such as humanitarian assistance, capacity-building, development aid and reform. Academic critics of the concept have also focused upon the possibility that it might be misused to justify

---

[119] Anne Orford, 'Jurisdiction without Territory: From the Holy Roman Empire to the Responsibility to Protect', *Michigan Journal of International Law* 30 (2009), 981.

[120] Constantin Fasolt, *The Limits of History* (Chicago: University of Chicago Press, 2004), p. 192.

[121] Chomsky, 'Statement to the United Nations General Assembly Thematic Dialogue on the Responsibility to Protect'.

unilateral interventions by powerful states claiming the role of human-itarian protector.[122] There has been much less critical attention paid to the possibility that the responsibility to protect concept might be used precisely as its proponents suggest it should be used – that is, to expand international executive rule in the name of protecting life.

International executive rule, and now the responsibility to protect concept as an expression of that form of rule, has a complex relationship to practices of unilateral police action and humanitarian intervention. On the one hand, from Hammarskjöld onwards advocates of interna-tional executive action have been opponents of imperial intervention and champions of sovereign equality. The new mechanisms of executive rule that have grown up over the past sixty years have developed in opposi-tion to the idea that powerful states have authority to intervene in the name of protecting human rights and maintaining order in the decolon-ised world. On the other hand, those advocating international executive action have assumed, as did Hammarskjöld, that it would be possible for the international civil servant to occupy the space claimed by intervening states, and in so doing take the sting out of the tail of intervention. International civil servants have wagered that by occupying the space of the humanitarian intervener or global police officer and performing that role in good faith, the UN could both render humanitarianism implausible as an excuse for neoimperial adventures and at the same time in fact become 'the main protector' of those newly independent states 'who feel themselves strong as members of the international family but who are weak in isolation'.[123]

For example, during the Suez crisis the UN took action in order to replace powerful Western interveners with UN forces. In an address to the General Assembly, the British Ambassador to the UN, Sir Pierson Dixon, had characterised the Franco-British invasion of Egypt in the aftermath of the 1956 nationalisation of the Suez Canal as a 'temporary police action necessitated by the turn of events in the Middle East and occasioned by the imperative need not only to protect the vital interests of my own and many other countries, but also to take immediate

---

[122]   Alvarez, 'The Schizophrenias of R2P'; Alex de Waal, 'No Such Thing as Humanitarian Intervention: Why We Need to Rethink How to Realize the "Responsibility to Protect" in Wartime', *Harvard International Review* (21 March 2007), 1, http://hir.harvard.edu/index.php?page=article&id=1482&p=1.

[123]   UN Secretary-General, 'Introduction to the Annual Report of the Secretary-General on the Work of the Organization', UN GAOR, 15th Sess., Supp. No. 1A, UN Doc. A/4390/Add.1, 1960, p. 7.

measures for the restoration of order'.[124] According to Dixon, British action was not intended to threaten the 'sovereignty' or the 'territorial integrity' of Egypt, but instead 'to protect a vital water-way'.[125] Dixon, however, suggested that: 'If the United Nations were willing to take over the physical task of maintaining peace in the area, no-one would be better pleased than we. But police action there must be, to separate the belligerents and to stop the hostil-ities.'[126] The introduction of UNEF was designed to take the British at their word and to remove the justification for the Franco-British attack on Egypt.

Similarly, the United Nations Operation in the Congo (*Organisation des Nations Unies au Congo*, or ONUC) was undertaken to remove the stated justifications for Belgian intervention. The crisis in the Congo had erupted days after the Congo's accession to independ-ence on 30 June 1960, when soldiers of the *Armée Nationale Congolaise* (ANC, formerly the infamous *Force Publique*) revolted against their Belgian officers.[127] The revolt was accompanied by rioting, attacks against European residents and looting. On 10 July, Belgium intervened, justifying its military action as a 'human-itarian intervention in the Congo' undertaken 'with the sole purpose of ensuring the safety of European and other members of the population and of protecting human lives in general'.[128] The Belgian intervention started in the resource-rich province of Katanga, which declared its independence on 11 July, and extended to the occupation of the Port of Matadi, which was also of

---

[124] UN GAOR, 1st Emergency Special Sess., 561st Plen. Mtg., Agenda Item 5, UN Doc. A/PV.562, 1 November 1956, para. 101.

[125] *Ibid.*, para. 102.   [126] *Ibid.*, para. 111.

[127] For the history of the *Force Publique*, see Adam Hochschild, *King Leopold's Ghost* (Boston: Mariner Books, 1999), pp. 123–31. The *Force Publique* was created by King Leopold II of Belgium in 1888 as 'counterguerrilla troops, an army of occupation, and a corporate labor police force' for his new Congo Free State. The *Force Publique* was a central part of the system of terror that enabled the production of raw materials for export from the Congo Free State and later the Belgian Congo. From its inception, the soldiers of the *Force Publique* were African, and the commissioned officers were European, usually Belgian. Soldiers regularly mutinied as a result of the ill-treatment meted out by European officers. Hochschild argues that those early rebellions should be understood as 'more than mutinies of disgruntled soldiers; they were precursors of the anticolonial guerrilla wars': p. 129.

[128] UN SCOR, 15th Sess., 873rd Mtg., UN Doc. S/PV.873, 13–14 July 1960, paras. 183, 197.

commercial significance to the Belgians.[129] On 12 July, Lumumba and the President of the Republic of the Congo, Joseph Kasavubu, jointly wrote to the UN Secretary-General condemning 'the dispatch to the Congo of metropolitan Belgian troops' and requesting UN military assistance 'to protect the national territory of the Congo from the present external aggression which is a threat to international peace'.[130] In his report to the Security Council placing the Congo on the agenda and successfully requesting UN intervention, the Secretary-General recharacterised UN involvement as necessary to achieve 'the maintenance of order in the country and the protection of life'.[131] Hammarskjöld made clear his understanding that 'were the United Nations to act as proposed' and as a result 'the national security forces are able to fully meet their tasks', the Belgian Government would then 'see its way to a withdrawal'.[132]

Hammarskjöld considered that operations such as UNEF and ONUC were necessary as a means of allowing independent states to make their own political choices while preventing the decolonised world from becoming a site of proxy wars between the Cold War blocs.

> The Organization must further and support policies aiming at independence, not only in the constitutional sense but in every sense of the word, protecting the possibilities of the African peoples to choose their own way without undue influences being exercised and without attempts to abuse the situation. This must be true in all fields – the political, the economic, as well as the ideological – if independence is to have a real meaning.[133]

[129] The cable from Kasavubu and Lumumba claimed that the Belgian Government had 'carefully prepared the secession of the Katanga with a view to maintaining a hold on our country' and declared that the Congolese Government, 'supported by the Congolese people, refuses to accept a "fait accompli" resulting from a conspiracy between Belgian imperialists and a small group of Katanga leaders'. For a discussion of the relation between the Congolese secessionists and Belgian military forces, see Carole J. L. Collins, 'The Cold War Comes to Africa: Cordier and the 1960 Congo Crisis', *Journal of International Affairs* 47 (1993), 243 at 250; and Georges Abi-Saab, *The United Nations Operation in the Congo 1960–1964* (Oxford: Oxford University Press, 1978), pp. 21–53.
[130] 'Cable dated 12 July 1960 from the President of the Republic of the Congo and Supreme Commander of the National Army and the Prime Minister and Minister of National Defence Addressed to the Secretary-General of the United Nations', UN SCOR, 15th Sess., UN Doc. S/4382, 13 July 1960.
[131] UN SCOR, 15th Sess., 873rd Mtg., UN Doc. S/PV.873, 13–14 July 1960, para. 19.
[132] *Ibid.*, para. 26.
[133] UN Secretary-General, 'Introduction to the Annual Report of the Secretary-General on the Work of the Organization', p. 2.

The UN had a particular role to play, working with 'the best and most responsible elements of all the countries of the continent'.[134] The UN could play this role because of its unique characteristics of universality and neutrality.

> As a universal organization neutral in the big Power struggles over ideology and influence in the world, subordinated to the common will of the Member Governments and free from any aspirations of its own to power and influence over any group or nation, the United Nations can render service which can be received without suspicion and which can be absorbed without influencing the free choice of peoples.[135]

Yet for Hammarskjöld there were also definite limits to the capacity of the new nations to determine their own political personality. These limits became clear when Lumumba and members of his government disagreed with Hammarskjöld's interpretation of the meaning of protection and the ends to which UN assistance should be put in the Congo. In response, Hammarskjöld declared:

> In this situation spokesmen of the central government speak about the assistance rendered by the international community through the United Nations as if it were an imposition and treat the Organization as if they had all rights and no obligations. They seem to believe that the independence of the Republic of the Congo, in the sense of the international sovereignty of the state which everybody respects, means independence also in a substantive sense of the word which, in our interdependent world of today, is unreal even for a country living by its own means and able to provide for its own security and administration.
>
> A government without financial means is dependent on those who help it to meet its needs. It may depend financially on another state, or group of states, and thereby tie its fate to that of the donors. Or it may depend on the international community in its entirety, represented by the United Nations, and so remain free. There is no third alternative this side of a complete breakdown of the state through inflation or a speedy disintegration of all social and economic services.[136]

Hammarskjöld was clear that when the UN took the place of Britain and France at Suez or the Belgians in the Congo, it was acting as a protector of the interests of decolonised states. When the UN sent forces into Suez, it

not quite

---

[134] *Ibid.* [135] *Ibid.*

[136] Dag Hammarskjöld, 'Opening Statement in the Security Council: New York, September 9, 1960' in Andrew W. Cordier and Wilder Foote (eds.), *Public Papers of the Secretaries-General of the United Nations, Volume V: Dag Hammarskjöld 1960–1961* (New York: Columbia University Press, 1975), p. 163.

prevented the British and French from claiming that their presence was necessary in order to maintain peace in the area. When the UN sent forces into the Congo, it prevented the Belgians from claiming that their presence was necessary to maintaining order and protecting life. Hammarskjöld and many UN supporters since have been confident that the resulting form of UN rule was not imperialist, because unlike the British, French or Belgian forces, the UN did not seek to acquire territory or gain discriminatory advantages over other European or American powers. The bona fides of the UN in that respect was guaranteed by its independence, its impartiality as between the parties to each conflict and its neutrality as between competing ideologies and interests. The UN could properly play this role because it was a universal organisation committed to the principle of peace. In claiming the political authority to take executive action independent of the interests of Great Powers, the Secretary-General successfully challenged other twentieth-century visions of world order, such as those projected by the British and the French at Suez or the Belgians in the Congo. Yet the effect of Hammarskjöld's innovations in the practice of governance was to replace those imperial visions of order with a new form of international executive rule.

It is in that sense that the responsibility to protect concept can be seen to relate to the practices of protection that emerged in the early years of decolonisation. As was the case in 1960, the immediate context for the articulation of the idea that the international community has a responsibility to protect populations at risk was a controversial humanitarian intervention conducted by Western states. The 1999 NATO action in Kosovo had exposed the fault-lines that divided world opinion on issues of international authority and intervention. While some states and commentators saw the NATO intervention as illegal and ineffective, others asserted that there was strong 'moral or humanitarian justification for the action' and welcomed the intervention as 'a long overdue internationalization of the human conscience'.[137] Key to the division of opinion on the legitimacy of humanitarian intervention in general, and NATO's action in particular, was its link to imperialism. Was it really possibly to divorce the interests of powerful states from their role as humanitarian interveners? Did the UN and other humanitarian organisations lose their authority and their claim to impartiality if they aligned themselves with powerful states to defend human rights or end human

---

[137]   ICISS, 'The Responsibility to Protect', p. vii.

suffering?[138] Yet if humanitarian actors or international organisations did not create alliances with powerful states, how would they ensure a supply of the resources (whether financial, administrative or military) necessary to bring about the social change or the end to suffering that they sought? This issue had particular importance for the UN. For UN officials, the failure to respond in situations that 'shock the conscience of mankind' would mean abandoning what many had come to see as the mission of the organisation.[139] Kosovo (and later Iraq) represented a possible dystopian future in which powerful states or coalitions of the willing sidelined the UN and took its place as the representatives of humanity. In the aftermath of the Kosovo intervention, then UN Secretary-General Kofi Annan issued a challenge to the Members of the General Assembly: 'if humanitarian intervention is, indeed, an unacceptable assault on sovereignty, how should we respond to a Rwanda, to a Srebrenica – to gross and systematic violations of human rights that affect every precept of our common humanity?'[140] He warned that: 'If the collective conscience of humanity ... cannot find in the United Nations its greatest tribune, there is a grave danger that it will look elsewhere for peace and for justice.'[141]

The ICISS report was designed to respond to that challenge. In the name of preventing the misuse of humanitarian motives to justify intervention by powerful states, it called for the international community to take collective action to prevent conflict, to respond to conflict and to react after conflict. The result is a detailed argument for the political authority of the international community and for the consolidation and integration of executive rule by international actors. That message was reinforced by the Secretary-General in his report on 'Implementing the Responsibility to Protect'. Ban Ki-moon urged the 'UN community' to articulate and implement a strategy for responding to situations in which a state is manifestly failing to protect its population.[142] According to the

---

[138] David Rieff, *A Bed for the Night: Humanitarianism in Crisis* (New York: Simon and Schuster, 2003); Fabrice Weissman (ed.), *In the Shadow of 'Just Wars': Violence, Politics and Humanitarian Action* (Ithaca: Cornell University Press, 2004).

[139] ICISS, 'Responsibility to Protect', p. 31.

[140] UN Secretary-General, 'We the Peoples: The Role of the United Nations in the 21st Century', UN GAOR, 54th Sess., Agenda Item 49(b), UN Doc. A/54/2000, 27 March 2000, p. 48.

[141] UN, 'Secretary-General Presents His Annual Report to General Assembly', UN Press Release SG/SM/7136 GA/9596, 20 September 1999, www.un.org/News/Press/docs/1999/19990920.sgsm7136.html.

[142] UN Secretary-General, 'Implementing the Responsibility to Protect', p. 28.

Secretary-General, the development of a 'credible multilateral alternative' would 'make it more difficult for States or groups of States to claim that they need to act unilaterally or outside of United Nations channels, rules and procedures to respond to emergencies relating to the responsibility to protect'.[143] That report stresses that 'the best way to discourage States or groups of States from misusing the responsibility to protect for inappropriate purposes would be to develop fully the United Nations strategy, standards, processes, tools and practices for the responsibility to protect'.[144]

The significant feature of the responsibility to protect concept thus lies not only in its relation to humanitarian intervention, but also in its relation to the practices of international executive action that have been developed to displace humanitarian intervention. The responsibility to protect concept makes those practices intelligible in new ways and seeks to strengthen and consolidate them to ends defined by the international community. It is the resulting form of international executive rule that should be the focus of critical engagement with the responsibility to protect concept.

Recognition, protection and authority: chapter overview

Rather than marking the moment at which the international community has initiated a new set of practices or states have accepted new obligations of conduct, the emergence of the responsibility to protect concept instead marks a shift in the way in which existing practices of international rule will be made intelligible. In order to understand why the responsibility to protect concept is a significant normative development, it is therefore necessary to understand the practices that it seeks to rationalise and make coherent.[145] Chapter 2 focuses upon these practices

---

[143] *Ibid.*   [144] *Ibid.*, p. 1.

[145] For a related approach to the emergence of concepts such as 'state and society, sovereign and subjects', see Michel Foucault, *The Birth of Biopolitics: Lectures at the Collège de France 1978–1979*, Graham Burchell trans. (New York: Palgrave Macmillan, 2008), pp. 2–3. Foucault argues that what we now recognise as the state emerged first as a set of governmental practices. Once those practices were established, concepts like sovereignty or statehood begin to be used in order to make sense or meaning of those practices of rule. For the argument that the emergence of administrative techniques was key to the consolidation of the power and authority of the modern state, see John Brewer, *War, Money and the English State 1688–1783* (Cambridge: Harvard University Press, 1988); Michel Foucault, *Society Must Be Defended: Lectures at the Collège de France, 1975–76*, David Macey trans. (London: Penguin Books, 2004); Philip S. Gorski,

of protection and the ways in which they have been rationalised and given meaning within international institutions and internationalist scholarship. The Suez and Congo operations initiated the development of practices aimed at maintaining order and protecting life that rapidly expanded during the era of decolonisation. Executive action was seen as a means for the UN to fill 'the "power vacuums" that arose in under-developed areas'.[146] In retrospect, it is clear that even in the earliest days of UN intervention for protection purposes in the Congo, the idea that the UN could act as a neutral or impartial force was not plausible.[147] Yet the idea that the UN in particular, and international humanitarians more generally, could intervene as neutral actors to alleviate suffering without becoming party to internal conflicts persisted throughout the Cold War. The adequacy of this account of international authority became a major question during the 1990s, as the enormous expansion of international humanitarian action necessitated and enabled by the ending of the Cold War produced new practical and theoretical challenges. This chapter concludes that the responsibility to protect concept can best be under-stood as an attempt to respond to those challenges, and to reassert the authority of the state and the UN in the face of proliferating rival claim-ants to authority in the decolonised world.

Chapter 3 explores the implications of arguing that the lawfulness of authority is determinable by reference to the fact of protection. While I have suggested that the turn to protection represents something novel in modern discussions about international authority and its proper role, the linking of state authority with the office of protection is not a new idea – indeed it is as old as the European state itself. The appeal to protection has often emerged at times of civil war or revolution, and has been used to explain how to distinguish between competing claimants to authority. Chapter 3 focuses upon the work of two political and legal theorists who sought to argue that the factual capacity to guarantee protection grounds lawful authority: Thomas Hobbes and Carl Schmitt. To invoke protec-tion as the 'raison d'être' of the state is to be in a complicated relation to a long tradition of absolutist theories of statehood. Thomas Hobbes is often treated as the originator of this tradition. The treatment of protec-tion as central to the relation between state and subject is given detailed

---

The Disciplinary Revolution: Calvinism and the Rise of the State in Early Modern Europe (Chicago and London: University of Chicago Press, 2003).

[146] Schachter, 'Dag Hammarskjöld', 7.

[147] See further the detailed discussion of the UN action in the Congo in Chapter 2.

elaboration in Hobbes' *Leviathan*, published in London in 1651.[148] This was just three years after the Peace of Westphalia brought the devastation of the Thirty Years' War in Europe to an end, two years after the execution of Charles I 'in the name of the people of England' had shaken the established political order of Europe and led many countries to cut off diplomatic relations with the English republic,[149] and not long before the final defeat of the Royalists in the English civil wars would see the first Commonwealth of England replaced with a Protectorate led by the Puritan Oliver Cromwell. Hobbes was thus writing in the context of the challenge posed to traditional authority and universal values by religious warfare in Europe. Appeals to the truth of competing religious beliefs were everywhere shaking the foundations of established political orders. At the time Hobbes was writing *Leviathan*, it was still uncertain how the fundamental divisions between political and religious groups within European states, and particularly within England, would ever be mended, or which if any values and political forms would emerge triumphant. In writing *Leviathan*, Hobbes was thus addressing an audience who were repeatedly confronted with the open question of how to distinguish the representative of a lawful sovereign from an enemy or a usurper. How to recognise lawful authority remains an open question for those asked to choose between competing national and international claimants to authority in places such as Iraq, Kosovo and Darfur today.

It was under such conditions that Hobbes sought to argue that the creation of a political order depended upon the establishment of a common power with the capacity to protect its subjects. According to Hobbes, the lawful authority is recognisable as the one who achieves protection in the broad sense of bringing into being a condition in which the safety of the people can be achieved.[150] This was the 'office', or in other words the responsibility, of the sovereign.[151] For Hobbes, the question of public authority did not turn on issues of authenticity, or

---

[148] Thomas Hobbes, *Leviathan* J. C. A. Gaskin (ed.), (Oxford: Oxford University Press, 2006) (first published 1651).

[149] Christopher Hill, *Puritanism and Revolution: Studies in Interpretation of the English Revolution of the 17th Century* (New York: St Martin's Press, 1997), p. 112.

[150] *Ibid.*, p. 222.

[151] The history of linking sovereignty and protection in order to justify state authority has been invoked by Edward Luck, the UN Special Adviser on the Responsibility to Protect. See Edward C. Luck, UN Special Adviser, 'Statement to the UNSC Working Group on Conflict Resolution and Prevention in Africa', 1 December 2008, www.responsibility toprotect.org/index.php/eupdate/1965 ('From the dawn of the nation-state era, it has been the intrinsic and inherent responsibility of the sovereign to offer protection to its

on who was the true representative of God or the people. The authority of such a common power was instead grounded on its capacity in fact to ensure protection in accordance with the terms of the covenant. Indeed, Hobbes argued that the 'obligation of subjects' to obey the sovereign would 'last as long, and no longer, than the power lasteth, by which he is able to protect them'.[152] The linkage of sovereignty and protection thus emerged alongside the modern state, as a way of distinguishing the state's de facto capacity to protect from de jure claims to authority, whether those claims were made by the peasantry (such as the revolutionary claimants to authority in seventeenth-century England), the Pope, the Holy Roman Emperor or rival claimants to territory in the new world.

Hobbes' attempt to ground the legitimacy of authority upon the responsibility to protect was explicitly revived in the twentieth century by Carl Schmitt.[153] Schmitt was writing at a time when Germany, and indeed Europe more generally, was struggling to come to terms with the devastation of the First World War and with 'the swell of revolutions and class-based civil wars that ran all across the continent from 1918 to 1923' in the aftermath of the Russian revolutions.[154] Schmitt agreed with Hobbes that 'the factual, current accomplishment of genuine protection is what the state is all about'.[155] However, the end of protection for Schmitt was neither the fulfilment of the needs of individuals (self-preservation) nor the procurement of the material well-being of the population (the safety of the people). Rather, for Schmitt, the authority of the state as protector was premised upon its capacity to represent the will of an 'indivisibly similar, entire, unified people'.[156] In developing his justification for de facto authority as the solution to civil war, Hobbes legitimised the political structure of the absolutist state. This potential was realised in the fascist states of twentieth-century Europe. Yet as

people. In return, they offer their loyalty. What higher purpose could sovereignty serve?').
[152] Hobbes, *Leviathan*, p. 147.
[153] See particularly Carl Schmitt, *The Concept of the Political*, George Schwab trans. (Chicago and London: University of Chicago Press, 1996) (first published 1932), pp. 52–3; Carl Schmitt, *The Leviathan in the State Theory of Thomas Hobbes: Meaning and Failure of a Political Symbol*, George Schwab and Erna Hilfstein trans., (Westport: Greenwood Press, 1996) (first published 1938).
[154] Eric D. Weitz, 'Foreword to the English Edition' in Pierre Broué, *The German Revolution 1917–1923*, John Archer trans. (Chicago: Haymarket Books, 2006) (first published 1971), p. i at p. xi.
[155] Carl Schmitt, *The Leviathan in the State Theory of Thomas Hobbes*, p. 34.
[156] Carl Schmitt, *Legality and Legitimacy*, Jeffrey Seitzer trans. (Durham and London: Duke University Press, 2004) (first published 1932), p. 28.

Chapter 3 concludes, the philosophy of Hobbes also sowed the seeds of liberal and revolutionary state forms. The turn to protection does not have a predetermined political effect and can give rise to a range of projects directed towards quite different ends. How the responsibility to protect concept is implemented will depend in large part upon who gets to decide what protection will mean and how it will be administered.

The key problem for an account of authority based on protection is thus the question of who decides. That question is taken up in Chapter 4. Early modern state theorists such as Hobbes proposed that the representative of lawful authority is recognisable as the one capable of guaranteeing protection. Yet as both Hobbes and Schmitt were aware, this left open the question of who has the worldly responsibility to recognise the legitimacy of rulers. Who is responsible for bestowing recognition upon a government? Who decides whether an authority is functioning effectively? Who decides what protection means in a particular time and place, and whether achieving it is always more important than anything else? Chapter 4 shows that as the authority of the modern state was consolidated, the authority of the Pope to determine such questions about the legitimacy of temporal rulers was effectively challenged. However, these questions did not disappear – instead they changed form. In particular, the questions of 'who decides' and 'who interprets' have persisted in legal debates about recognition and jurisdiction.

One form in which the question of 'who decides' has been addressed is through international legal doctrines concerning the effect of the recognition of a government or of a new state. According to the declaratory theory of recognition, which was dominant until the late eighteenth century, the 'legal status' of a ruler was understood to be 'derived and perfected from within'.[157] As a result, 'internal legality' determined 'external legality'.[158] The question of whether a duly appointed or elected ruler properly had authority over territory was *not* treated as a question for external actors or the law of nations, because to give foreign rulers or powers 'the *right to recognition*' would be to give them the right to intervene in the internal affairs of states, and would threaten sovereign equality.[159] Yet beginning in the early nineteenth century, in response to revolutions in Europe and the New World, this began to change. International lawyers were confronted with 'frequent changes in membership of the Family of Nations' as a result of those revolutions,

---

[157] C. H. Alexandrowicz, 'The Theory of Recognition *in Fieri*', *British Year Book of International Law* 34 (1958), 176 at 179.
[158] *Ibid.*   [159] *Ibid.*

and questions about the normative criteria of statehood therefore began to appear in urgent need of resolution.[160] The law of nations began to treat legitimacy as a question that had to be determined both internally and externally.

A second form in which the question of the authority to recognise the legitimacy of rulers persists is in conflicts over jurisdiction. Jurisdiction is often understood as raising fairly flat or technical questions concerned with the administration of law. Yet recent theoretical work has enlivened the study of jurisdiction, pointing out that the administration of law through jurisdiction 'is not only a reflective cultural phenomenon, but also a productive one'.[161] Jurisdiction addresses the question of who has 'the power and authority to speak in the name of the law' in a particular territory in a given situation.[162] With the creation of the UN, the role of external actors in determining the legitimacy of governments became linked to international jurisdiction. In that context, the question of who decides took the form of debates about whether governmental legitimacy was properly a matter for the international community. From the 1960s onwards, the question of whether and when the conduct of a ruler threatens international peace has been claimed as a matter of international jurisdiction. As the practices of international executive rule expanded in the decolonised word, international lawyers developed detailed explanations as to why the expansion of international jurisdiction was necessary in order to maintain peace and security, and why that expansion of executive rule did not affect the status of territories under administration. Today, it is an axiom of international legal scholarship that the expansion of international jurisdiction over the decolonised world has had no effect upon the juridical status of states being administered or governed by international actors. Indeed, even to raise the question of status in discussions of administration is dismissed as anachronistic. The expansion of executive rule is said to have no effect on status because international actors do not seek to acquire title to territory but instead seek only to exercise control over territory for specific purposes and for limited ends. Once that separation of ownership and control is properly understood, the governance of the decolonised world

---

[160] *Ibid.*, at 196.

[161] Bradin Cormack, *A Power to Do Justice: Jurisdiction, English Literature, and the Rise of Common Law, 1509–1625* (Chicago: University of Chicago Press, 2007), p. 3.

[162] Shaunnagh Dorsett and Shaun McVeigh, 'Questions of Jurisdiction' in Shaun McVeigh (ed.), *Jurisprudence of Jurisdiction* (Oxford: Routledge-Cavendish, 2007), p. 3 at p. 5.

can be seen simply to involve the distribution of 'functions'. International authority needs no further justification than the functionalist claim to be managing the world and acting as executive agent of the international community.

That expansion of international jurisdiction over the decolonised world has left open the question of which body representing the universal or the international community has the authority to determine the lawfulness of rulers. The NATO intervention in Kosovo revealed particularly clearly that an increasing number of actors were enthusiastically ready to assume responsibility for guaranteeing peace and protecting community values. Chapter 4 concludes that the question of who has the authority to decide the meaning of peace and protection has been reopened but not resolved by the responsibility to protect concept. At stake in the implementation of the concept is what form of power it will consolidate in the decolonised world.

Contemporary legal accounts of the administration of life in the decolonised world systematically avoid the question of status, that is, the question of who is the subject of protection and of law. Chapter 5 suggests that the turn to protection as the ground for international authority re-enlivens that notion of status (or, in vernacular terms, the state). While the language of 'status' initially referred to the majestic persona of the ruler in medieval jurisprudence,[163] it gradually came to express the abstracted forms of protective authority and corporate life soon to be represented by the institutions of the modern state. In time, the apparatus or institutions of the state began to be separated from the person of the ruler. The emergence of the modern conception of the state was completed when in turn the people could also be thought of as separate from the impersonal state. With this double abstraction of ruler and ruled from the state, something resembling the modern state form was conceivable.[164] Political and legal theories have ever since sought to wrestle with the relations between these component parts of modern political authority – the relation, that is, between the state, the ruler and the people who are ruled. What form should the relation between ruler and ruled take? How is the legitimacy of that relation to

---

[163] Gaines Post, *Studies in Medieval Legal Thought: Public Law and the State, 1100–1322* (Princeton: Princeton University Press, 1964), pp. 338–40.

[164] Quentin Skinner, 'From the State of Princes to the Person of the State' in *Visions of Politics: Renaissance Virtues*, vol. II (Cambridge: Cambridge University Press, 2002), p. 368.

be determined? How are the representatives of lawful authority to be recognised? By whom? It is those core questions about status and authority that have been dismissed as anachronistic by lawyers rationalising the practices of international executive rule in the decolonised world. There is as yet no account of authority in international law that is adequate to the task of understanding those practices and formally integrating them into international legal doctrine.

The emergence of the responsibility to protect concept challenges the theoretical conception of state authority as a given about which questions cannot be raised within the legal discipline. It also challenges the formal commitment to sovereign equality, self-determination and non-intervention as foundational principles of the UN Charter. In grounding the authority of the state and the international community on the capacity to protect, the concept represents a significant shift in thinking about the lawfulness of authority in the modern world. This book concludes that, as a result, the articulation and embrace of the responsibility to protect concept represents one of the most significant normative shifts in international relations since the creation of the UN in 1945.

2

Practices of Protection: From the Parliament of Man to International Executive Rule

The responsibility to protect concept offers a coherent framework for understanding the practices of international executive rule that have shaped the decolonised world since the 1950s. As outlined in Chapter 1, those practices were initiated during the early years of decolonisation by then UN Secretary-General Dag Hammarskjöld. Hammarskjöld argued forcefully that it was necessary to stop thinking of the UN merely as a forum for 'static conference diplomacy' and instead reimagine it as a 'dynamic instrument' for 'executive action, undertaken on behalf of all members'.[1] The techniques of international governance developed during that period – such as preventive diplomacy, peacekeeping and territorial administration – were premised upon the idea that the UN could act as a neutral force and fill the political vacuum caused by a temporary crisis of authority within a territory, thus pre-empting intervention by powerful states with vested interests. In order to understand the implications of the responsibility to protect concept, this chapter explores the development of those practices of executive rule, and the shifting ways in which they have been rationalised and reflected upon over the past fifty years.

Although Hammarskjöld recognised that the UN Charter gave little attention to the development of the executive aspects of the organisation, he did not interpret this as a limitation on executive action. Instead, he argued that the UN's 'executive functions and their form' had 'been left largely to practice'.[2] According to Hammarskjöld, it had become necessary to develop those inchoate executive functions in response to the twinned challenges posed by decolonisation and the Cold War. The UN had a responsibility to protect newly independent states from external

---

[1] UN Secretary-General, 'Introduction to the Annual Report of the Secretary-General on the Work of the Organization', UN GAOR, 16th Sess., Supp. No. 1A, UN Doc. A/4800/ Add.1, 1961, p. 1.

[2] *Ibid.*, p. 5.

interference. That responsibility could best be met by taking action to fill the 'power vacuums' that were arising as the colonial system was being 'liquidated'.[3] By taking such action, the UN could occupy the position of guarantor of order and protector of life otherwise claimed in bad faith by powerful states seeking to control the choices made by the peoples of the decolonised world in general, and Africa in particular. That in turn would prevent the extension of the Cold War to those regions. The maintenance of peace and the protection of independent states were therefore linked.

Hammarskjöld's preference for developing an independent civil service capable of undertaking executive action in the decolonised world was shaped by his early successes at asserting the independence of the Secretariat in administrative matters, and at developing techniques of executive action. His experiments with quiet diplomacy during negotiations with Peking to seek the release of detained American pilots during 1955 and with peacekeeping during the Suez crisis of 1956 confirmed Hammarskjöld's preference for international executive rule as a means of maintaining international peace and security. He was particularly enthusiastic about using executive action as a response to 'the problem of Africa'.[4] That faith in the utility and propriety of executive rule was put to the test in the Congo. Hammarskjöld's vision of the UN as a neutral agent of executive action made it seem as if international civil servants could avoid taking a position on internal political questions or making judgments about the legitimacy of local claimants to authority. The problems with that approach became clear during the Congo operation.

Over the following decades, UN peace and humanitarian operations continued to be based upon the principles of neutrality, impartiality and independence inherited from Hammarskjöld. The insufficiency of the minimalist set of principles grounding international authority became increasingly apparent as international executive rule expanded in the post-Cold War period. Not only did the scope of UN operations expand during the 1990s, but the tasks undertaken by international actors also became increasingly complex and sensitive. The notions of impartiality and neutrality that had supported the emergence of international

---

[3] *Ibid.*, p. 7.
[4] UN Secretary-General, 'Introduction to the Annual Report of the Secretary-General on the Work of the Organization', UN GAOR, 15th Sess., Supp. No. 1A, UN Doc. A/4390/ Add.1, 1960, p. 1.

executive rule were not capable of responding to the problems and challenges to which the rapid expansion of international rule gave rise.

The responsibility to protect concept emerged as a response to those challenges. Hammarskjöld and later UN officials had necessarily developed an implicit account of authority that informed their decisions about which local actors were proper collaborators and that shaped their sense of their own right to rule. The responsibility to protect concept makes that account of authority explicit and coherent. According to the responsibility to protect concept, the lawfulness of both state and international authority is grounded upon the capacity and willingness to protect the population. The responsibility to protect concept is therefore true to the culture of international rule that has developed since the late 1950s because it self-consciously sets out to build upon and rationalise practices of executive rule developed over the past five decades. Yet it is also a departure from that tradition because it seeks to provide a coherent account of international authority and a framework within which to make decisions about future international action.

From conference diplomacy to executive action

Article 1 of the UN Charter includes as the first listed purpose of the UN: 'To maintain international peace and security, and to that end: to take effective collective measures for the prevention and removal of threats to the peace.'[5] According to Hammarskjöld, the goal of preventing and removing threats to the peace in the context of decolonisation required new ways of thinking about the role of the UN. It was no longer sufficient to think of the organisation 'as a static conference machinery for resolving conflicts of interests and ideologies with a view to peaceful co-existence'.[6] Instead, it was necessary to reconceive of the UN 'as a dynamic instrument of Governments' through which 'to develop forms of executive action, undertaken on behalf of all Members, aimed at forestalling conflicts and resolving them, once they have arisen'.[7] The conception of the UN as a 'static conference machinery' referred 'to history and to the traditions . . . of the past'. The conception of the UN as a 'dynamic instrument' of 'executive action' pointed to 'the needs of the present and of the future'.[8] The latter conception was better suited to 'a world of ever-closer international

---

[5] UN Charter, article 1(1).
[6] UN Secretary-General, 'Introduction to the 1961 Annual Report', p. 1.   [7] Ibid.   [8] Ibid.

interdependence where nations have at their disposal armaments of hitherto unknown destructive strength'.[9]

The tension between these two conceptions of the UN had become particularly apparent in the 'practical work of the Organization' relating to 'countries under colonial rule or in other ways under foreign domination'.[10] According to Hammarskjöld, decolonisation had produced the need to reconceptualise the roles, functions and operations of the UN for two reasons. First, it had created new possibilities for conflict as a result of the power vacuums created with the departure of colonial powers. The 'main field of useful activity' of the UN related to the aim of 'keeping newly arising conflicts outside the sphere of bloc differences'.[11] Hammarskjöld developed the technique of 'preventive diplomacy' as a means of responding to situations 'where the original conflict may be said either to be the result of, or to imply risks for, the creation of a power vacuum between the main blocs'.[12] According to Hammarskjöld:

> Preventive action in such cases must in the first place aim at filling the vacuum so that it will not provoke action from any of the major parties, the initiative for which might be taken for preventive purposes but might in turn lead to counter-action from the other side. The ways in which a vacuum can be filled by the United Nations so as to forestall such initiatives differ from case to case, but they have this in common: temporarily, and pending the filling of a vacuum by normal means, the United Nations enters the picture on the basis of its non-commitment to any power bloc, so as to provide to the extent possible a guarantee in relation to all parties against initiatives from others.[13]

The aim of the UN was thus to introduce itself 'into the picture, sometimes with very modest means, sometimes in strength, so as to eliminate a political, economic and social, or military vacuum'.[14]

Hammarskjöld was particularly concerned with 'the problem of Africa and its importance for the international community'.[15] There had been 'mixed' reactions to independence from outside Africa, with some trying 'to maintain what history has already judged' and others trying 'to put in place of the past new and more subtle forms of predominance and influence'.[16] In that situation, the UN had a particular 'responsibility' to put in place a 'framework' within which independent African states could determine their own 'political personality' within 'the setting of

---

[9] *Ibid.*   [10] *Ibid.*, p. 2.
[11] UN Secretary-General, 'Introduction to the 1960 Annual Report', p. 4.   [12] *Ibid.*
[13] *Ibid.*   [14] *Ibid.*   [15] *Ibid.*, p. 1.   [16] *Ibid.*

universality as represented by the United Nations'.[17] The UN was the proper actor to play this role because it was 'a universal organization neutral in the big Power struggles over ideology and influence in the world, subordinated to the common will of the Member Governments and free from any aspirations of its own to power and influence over any group or nation'.[18] The UN could not, however, fulfil its function of protecting self-determination and the independence of all peoples if it were limited to relying upon decisions of the General Assembly or the Security Council taken 'within the framework of a conference pattern'.[19] Current 'African developments' (namely the UN Operation in the Congo (ONUC)) had put the organisational capacity of the UN to the test, raising questions about the 'functions' of the UN's 'parliamentary institutions' and about 'the efficiency and strength of its executive capacity'.[20]

Secondly, decolonisation had also made it necessary to revisit questions about the operations of the UN because of the effect that newly independent states were having upon the capacity of the UN to work 'expeditiously'.[21] The 'irrationality' of a system that allowed a massive shift in voting power to newly independent states put the wisdom of continued parliamentary or conference-based governance of the UN into question.[22]

> The considerable increase in the membership of the United Nations stemming from a region with short independent experience in international politics has led to doubts regarding the possibility of the General Assembly and its committees working expeditiously and in a way which truly reflects considered world opinion.[23]

While the inclusion of new members did 'widen the perspectives' and 'enrich the debate' at the UN, it also posed 'certain practical problems'.[24] For example, the expanded membership led to longer debates and made General Assembly proceedings 'too cumbersome in cases where speed and efficiency are of the essence'.[25] Given the commitment in the UN Charter to equal votes for all Members, there seemed no practical possibility of changing the voting system and diluting the influence of

---

[17] Ibid. [18] Ibid.
[19] UN Secretary-General, 'Introduction to the 1961 Annual Report', p. 7.
[20] UN Secretary-General, 'Introduction to the 1960 Annual Report', p. 2. [21] Ibid.
[22] Ibid., commenting that 'the irrationality of such a system is demonstrated when a new voting balance can be achieved through a sudden expansion of the number of Members by some 20 per cent'.
[23] Ibid. [24] Ibid., pp. 2–3. [25] Ibid., p. 3.

those Members short on independent experience in international politics. The answer for Hammarskjöld was to strengthen the executive organs of the UN. The expansion of the political authority of the Secretary-General had already enabled an increase in the required speed and efficiency of decision-making and action. During the Suez and Hungary crises, the General Assembly had 'found that the most adequate way to meet the challenges which it had to face was to entrust the Secretary-General with wide executive tasks on the basis of mandates of a general nature'.[26] During these crises, the Secretariat proved its 'value and possibilities' as an 'executive organ' of the UN.[27] Although the Security Council had returned to its role as the UN organ with primary responsibility for maintaining peace and security, the shift of emphasis away from the General Assembly had 'not led to a change of working methods' – the Council also treated the Secretariat and Secretary-General 'as its main executive agent'.[28]

Neutrality, impartiality and the international civil servant

Hammarskjöld did not offer a developed account of the reasons why international civil servants should be vested with the authority to exercise core governmental functions in the decolonised world. Indeed, Hammarskjöld generally preferred to avoid dealing with abstract questions of authority or producing doctrines to define – and thus inevitably circumscribe – his actions. Nonetheless, Hammarskjöld was drawn to system-building. He produced detailed memoranda, studies and reports articulating his interpretation of events as they unfolded and setting out principles to be drawn from the experiences of past UN operations. Over the course of his time in office, a set of themes began to emerge from those reflections. In particular, Hammarskjöld returned to the principles of independence, impartiality and neutrality as central to the character of international civil service. His repeated references to the need for an independent, impartial and neutral civil service were the closest Hammarskjöld came to providing an account of the reasons why the UN executive was the proper authority to rule the decolonised world.

According to Hammarskjöld, the League and the UN represented 'an advance beyond traditional "conference diplomacy"' because they introduced 'joint permanent organs, employing a neutral civil service, and the use of such organs for executive purposes on behalf of all the members of

[26] *Ibid.*   [27] *Ibid.*   [28] *Ibid.*

the organizations'.[29] That 'radical innovation in international life' was premised upon the idea that the Secretary-General in particular, and the international civil service more broadly, were capable of acting 'on a truly international basis' and carrying out their tasks 'without subservience to a particular national or ideological attitude'.[30] From his reorganisation of the Secretariat through to the conduct of ONUC, Hammarskjöld treated the commitment to neutrality as a core requirement both of the office of the Secretary-General and of the Secretariat. For Hammarskjöld, the Secretary-General in particular has a duty 'to carry out his tasks in controversial political situations with full regard to his exclusively international obligation under the Charter and without subservience to a particular national or ideological character'.[31] The Secretariat in turn must be made up of 'a dedicated professional service responsible only to the Organization'.[32] Members of the Secretariat could not perform their role properly if they are 'under – or consider themselves to be under – two masters in respect of their official functions'.[33]

Neutrality, independence and the question of loyalty

Hammarskjöld's sense of the need for an independent and active Secretariat and Secretary-General developed early in his time in office. During the tenure of Hammarskjöld's predecessor, the Norwegian Trygve Lie, the US Government had decided to conduct public investigations of the loyalty of American nationals working in the Secretariat and to limit access to UN headquarters in New York by visitors who were considered a threat to US security.[34] Lie had allowed FBI agents to have access to the UN building, and at the request of the US Government had dismissed staff members who had pleaded the Fifth Amendment and refused to answer questions posed by US authorities concerning their involvement in subversive activities. The extent of the FBI's activities in the UN was revealed early in Hammarskjöld's tenure, when a plainclothes agent attempted to take a demonstrator from the public gallery of the Security Council.[35]

---

[29] Dag Hammarskjöld, 'The International Civil Servant in Law and in Fact' in Wilder Foote (ed.), *The Servant of Peace: A Selection of the Speeches and Statements of Dag Hammarskjöld* (London: The Bodley Head, 1962), p. 329.
[30] *Ibid.*, p. 346. [31] *Ibid.* [32] *Ibid.*, p. 342. [33] *Ibid.*
[34] Brian Urquhart, *Hammarskjöld* (New York: W. W. Norton, 1972), pp. 64–5.
[35] *Ibid.*, p. 63.

McCarthy period

One of Hammarskjöld's first tasks after taking office in 1953 was to develop a response to US demands for greater ideological control over the staff of the Secretariat. For Hammarskjöld, such demands 'implicitly challenged the international character of the responsibilities of the Secretary-General and his staff'.[36] Hammarskjöld took the view that it was important to insist upon the need for independent decision-making by the Secretary-General in recruiting and dismissing staff members.[37] To dismiss a staff member because of a conclusion reached by a government based upon evidence not made available to the Secretary-General would be a violation of Article 100 of the UN Charter, which prohibited the Secretary-General from seeking or receiving instructions from any authority external to the organisation. Governments could provide the Secretary-General with information or facts about potential staff members, but it was for the Secretary-General 'to interpret and to judge those facts as far as they affected UN employment'.[38] In the immediate context of the US loyalty investigations, Hammarskjöld therefore announced that he would disregard the taking of the Fifth Amendment by a staff member if he were satisfied with their explanation, but he also made clear that Secretariat members 'must abstain from unsuitable political activities'.[39]

Hammarskjöld saw these and other early successes in resisting interference from governments as significant. Like the theorists of the seventeenth century who explained the necessity of resolving competing loyalties between church and state in favour of the state, Hammarskjöld argued for the necessity of resolving competing loyalties between the national and the international in favour of the international.[40] The Secretary-General had the ultimate authority to judge and interpret whether a matter properly concerned issues of national security or international administration. For Hammarskjöld, the defence of the idea that the UN should have a 'dedicated professional service responsible only to the Organization in the performance of its duties' was an important and necessary step towards strengthening the executive capacity of the UN.[41] In Hammarskjöld's view, Article 97 of the Charter describing the Secretary-General as the 'chief administrative officer of the Organization', together with Articles 100 and 101 (providing that Secretariat staff are to be appointed by the Secretary-General rather than by Member States), were of 'fundamental importance' for the status of

---

[36] Hammarskjöld, 'The International Civil Servant', p. 340.   [37] *Ibid.*
[38] Urquhart, *Hammarskjöld*, p. 62.   [39] *Ibid.*, pp. 67–8.
[40] See further Chapter 4 below.   [41] Hammarskjöld, 'The International Civil Servant', p. 342.

the Secretariat, as together they created for the Secretariat an administrative position 'of full political independence'.[42] However, the administrative role of the Secretary-General did not raise the question of neutrality in a strong form. Hammarskjöld considered that 'the decisions and actions of the Secretary-General as chief administrative officer naturally can be envisaged as limited to administrative problems outside the sphere of political conflicts of interest or ideology'.[43]

Quiet diplomacy and the political role of the Secretary-General

According to Hammarskjöld, it was the granting of political authority to the Secretary-General under Articles 98 and 99 that served to 'open the door to the problem of neutrality'.[44] As discussed in Chapter 1, Article 98 provided that the Secretary-General would carry out the functions entrusted to him by the Security Council and the General Assembly, and Article 99 authorised the Secretary General 'to bring to the attention of the Security Council any matter which in his opinion may threaten the maintenance of international peace and security'. Hammarskjöld considered that the grant of political responsibilities to the Secretary-General in those terms had taken the UN 'beyond the concept of a non-political civil service into an area where the official, in the exercise of his functions, may be forced to take stands of a politically controversial nature'.[45] Nonetheless, provided the Secretary-General undertook his tasks 'on the basis of his exclusively international responsibility and not in the interests of any particular State or group of States',[46] there would be no infringement of the commitment to neutrality.

Hammarskjöld's developing sense of the expansive nature of the Secretary-General's independent political role is well illustrated by his conduct of negotiations with Peking over the release of a group of American pilots shot down during the Korean War. The pilots had been detained by the Chinese Government and subsequently convicted of espionage. The General Assembly passed a resolution condemning 'as contrary to the Korean Armistice Agreement, the trial and conviction of prisoners of war illegally detained after 25 September 1953'.[47] It

---

[42] Ibid., p. 334.   [43] Ibid.   [44] Ibid., p. 335.   [45] Ibid., p. 337.   [46] Ibid., p. 346.
[47] 'Complaint of Detention and Imprisonment of United Nations Military Personnel in Violation of the Korean Armistice Agreement', GA Res. 906 (IX), UN GAOR, 9th Sess., 509th Plen. Mtg., UN Doc. A/RES/906 (IX), 10 December 1954.

requested 'the Secretary-General, in the name of the United Nations, to seek the release, in accordance with the Korean Armistice Agreement, of these eleven United Nations Command personnel, and all other captured personnel of the United Nations still detained' and 'to make, by the means most appropriate in his judgment, continuing and unremitting efforts to this end'.[48]

Hammarskjöld met with the Chinese leader, Chou En-Lai, in Peking from 6 to 10 January 1955. Hammarskjöld decided to conduct those negotiations on the basis of the political authority of his own office rather than on the basis of the General Assembly resolution. That decision was a very pragmatic one. Neither Washington nor the UN had recognised the People's Republic of China, and Hammarskjöld was aware that China, as a non-member of the UN, might well not feel itself bound by a resolution of the General Assembly.[49] Yet Hammarskjöld's conception of the political authority of the Secretary-General to undertake quiet diplomacy also reflected his growing sense of the independent role of the executive under the UN Charter.

Hammarskjöld defined his interpretation of the legal basis of his authority at the first of his meetings with Chou En-Lai. According to Hammarskjöld, the Secretary-General was entitled under the UN Charter 'to take whatever initiative he finds appropriate in order to get under control or reverse developments leading to serious tensions'. The 'rights and obligations' of the Secretary-General in that respect were 'not limited to Member Nations', but were 'of world-wide application'.[50]

> When he acts for the purposes indicated, it is not and can never be permitted to be, on behalf of any nation, group of nations or even majority of Member Nations as registered by a vote in the General Assembly. He acts under his constitutional responsibility for the general purposes set out in the Charter, which must be considered of common and equal significance to Members and Non-Members alike.
>
> The constitutional position of the Secretary-General as I now define it, is the basis on which I have approached you and on which I have come here.

---

[48] *Ibid.*, para. 3.

[49] Manuel Fröhlich, *Political Ethics and the United Nations: Dag Hammarskjöld as Secretary-General* (London and New York: Routledge, 2008), p. 137; Urquhart, *Hammarskjöld*, p. 94.

[50] UN Archives New York, DAG-1/5.1.3–3 'Dag Hammarskjöld. Basic Documents visit to Peking 1954/55. Re: Korean Pow's UN Command Personnel, 6 January 1955', p. 2, cited in Manuel Fröhlich, *Political Ethics and the United Nations*, p. 137.

> Thus, sitting here at this conference table I do so as Secretary-General, not as a representative of an Assembly majority or of any national or individual interests.[51]

It was on the basis of the constitutional responsibility of the office of Secretary-General that Hammarskjöld raised the question of the detention of the US prisoners.

> When the Secretary-General of the United Nations has engaged himself and his office, with all the weight it carries in world opinion, for the fate of the prisoners . . . it does not mean that I *appeal* to you or that I *ask you* for their release. It means that – inspired also by my faith in your wisdom and in your wish to promote peace – I have considered it my duty as forcefully as I can, and with deep conviction, to draw your attention to the vital importance of their fate to the cause of peace. I could have based my approach to you on the fact that the General Assembly has asked me to seek their release. I have not done so. I could have acted as spokesman of the Organization for which, and under the orders of which, the prisoners served. That – although justified – would have made me a representative of a party to a conflict. My position is stronger than that.[52]

In the long run, the negotiations were successful and the Chinese Government decided to release the pilots, announcing that its decision to do so was 'in order to maintain friendship with Hammarskjöld and has no connection with the UN resolution'.[53] The development and success of the 'Peking formula' represented a further step towards the conception of a new form of executive authority that transcended the interests of states.[54]

Economic thinking and the role of the state

Hammarskjöld's sense of the need for administrative neutrality was also a product of his background as an economist. In his various roles as a senior Swedish civil servant, Hammarskjöld had demonstrated his allegiance to an approach that treated the state not as a potential agent of transformation or planning, but merely as an arbiter between competing interests. Hammarskjöld thus understood the challenges facing decolonised states and the UN in terms of the conservative policy prescriptions then gaining currency in post-war European and American economic thinking.

Hammarskjöld had majored in economics as an undergraduate at Uppsala University, and continued his studies in economics at Cambridge with John

---

[51] *Ibid.*   [52] *Ibid.*, pp. 7–8, cited in Fröhlich, *Political Ethics and the United Nations*, p. 138.
[53] *Ibid.*, p. 144.   [54] *Ibid.*, p. 137.

Maynard Keynes.[55] In 1930 he began work for the *Arbetslöshetsutredningen*, the Swedish governmental commission on unemployment,[56] and received his doctorate in economics from the University of Stockholm in 1933. Hammarskjöld continued at the unemployment commission until 1936, when he took up a position at the Department of Finance and began working in close relationship with the Social Democratic Minister of Finance, Ernst Wigforss.[57] In 1941 Hammarskjöld was appointed as state secretary (the most senior official position) in the Department of Finance,[58] and served as chair of the board of governors of the *Riksbank*, the Swedish National Bank, from 1941 to 1948.[59]

During this period, Hammarskjöld played a major role in shaping the economic policy of the Social Democratic government. In his varied roles as an economic adviser and Swedish civil servant, Hammarskjöld influenced the subtle shift that took place between the formulation and the implementation of Swedish economic policy.[60] While advisers to the Social Democratic government were developing government policy that prioritised the goals of full employment and public works in response to the economic crises of the 1930s, Hammarskjöld was responsible for translating that policy into practical measures at the Finance Ministry and the *Riksbank*.[61] In that process of translation, Hammarskjöld systematically prioritised the conservative goals of price stability over full employment and state 'neutrality' over state intervention.

> Dominating Hammarskjöld's perception was the general view of the Civil Service aristocracy of the state as an arbiter between conflicting interests and as the highest expression of the general interest in society. This could be seen in his insistence on 'neutrality' as the leitmotif in the moments of decision in the after-war years in Sweden. Neutrality between debtors and creditors, between the Swedish Treasury and the government bond holders, were invoked as a central argument underlying the goal of the

---

[55] Urquhart, *Hammarskjöld*, p. 368. According to Urquhart, Keynes thought Hammarskjöld 'highly intelligent but not original or creative as an economist' and told the Swedish economist Bertil Ohlin 'I don't think we can expect much from *him*'.

[56] *Ibid.*, p. 368.

[57] Örjan Appelqvist, 'A hidden duel: Gunnar Myrdal and Dag Hammarskjöld in Economics and International Politics 1935–1955', *Stockholm Papers in Economic History No 2* (Department of Economic History, Stockholm University, 2008), pp. 3–4.

[58] *Ibid.*, p. 7.

[59] Örjan Appelqvist, 'Civil servant or politician? Dag Hammarskjöld's role in Swedish government policy in the Forties', *Economic Review* 3 (2005), 33.

[60] Appelqvist, 'A hidden duel', p. 6.

[61] Urquhart, *Hammarskjöld*, p. 369; Appelqvist, 'Civil servant or politician?', 35.

post-war monetary policy: to reflate the price levels to the 1940 level. Neutrality was also invoked by Hammarskjöld as the main argument against a growth oriented financial policy: it was by no means certain that the advantages of such a policy would accrue to those who would bear its costs in terms of higher taxation levels.[62]

Hammarskjöld also played a significant role in determining Sweden's post-war international economic policy. In 1945 he was appointed as an adviser to the Swedish Cabinet on economic and financial issues, and in 1947 took up a position at the Foreign Office as Under-Secretary with responsibility for economic questions. In these roles he shaped Sweden's post-war economic and financial planning, led trade and financial nego-tiations with countries including the US and the UK, and was the Swedish delegate to the Paris Conference at which the administration of the Marshall Plan was negotiated.[63] He continued to be involved in the development of international economic policy as Secretary-General of the Foreign Ministry from 1949 and as Minister without Portfolio (effectively Deputy Foreign Minister) from 1951.

At stake in the international policy debates about post-war planning and the reconstruction of Europe was the proper role of the state in relation to economic and social matters. While the market had been a privileged object of governmental action in Western political thought from the sixteenth century, economic rationality from Adam Smith onwards had challenged the capacity of the sovereign to regulate the market. For Smith, the sovereign was incapable of mastering the econ-omy because of a lack of knowledge.[64] It was not possible for the sovereign to comprehend the totality of economic processes. From the 1920s onwards, liberal economic thought had intensified this challenge to the capacity of the state to govern the market. For the German ordoliberals of the Freiburg school, and even more markedly for the neoliberal school that developed in the US through the influence of European émigrés such as Friedrich Hayek and Ludwig von Mises, the state had an extremely limited role to play in relation to the market.[65]

---

[62] Appelqvist, 'A hidden duel', p. 22.   [63] Urquhart, *Hammarskjöld*, p. 369.

[64] Adam Smith, *The Wealth of Nations: Books IV–V* (London: Penguin Books, 1999) (first published 1776).

[65] Michel Foucault, *The Birth of Biopolitics: Lectures at the Collège de France 1978–1979*, Michel Senellart (ed.) and Graham Burchell trans. (New York: Palgrave Macmillan, 2008); Keith Tribe, *Strategies of Economic Order: German Economic Discourse, 1750–1950* (Cambridge: Cambridge University Press, 1995).

During and after the Second World War, these schools of economic thought mounted a sustained attack on state planning. The immediate targets of such attacks were the communist states of the Soviet bloc, and the war economies and proposed post-war planned economies of the UK, the US and France. According to the neoliberal view, it was inappropriate for the state to interfere with market mechanisms, attempt to plan the economy or intervene in the process of competition between individuals or enterprises. The process of competition would produce a fair price – the price mechanism was itself the appropriate form of economic regulation. In its most extreme form, as expressed by Hayek, neoliberalism opposed planning to the rule of law. In planning the economy, Hayek argued, state authorities usurped the role of the individual. The clear distinction that could be made between 'the creation of a permanent framework of laws within which the productive activity is guided by individual decisions, and the direction of economic activity by a central authority' was simply 'a particular case of the more general distinction between the Rule of Law and arbitrary government'.[66] If a government is to act in accordance with the rule of law, it must not introduce rules that deliberately seek to fulfil the wants or needs of particular people.[67] The state and the law must therefore remain neutral as between individuals. The state must remain neutral for moral reasons, because to fail to do so would be to take the first step on the road to serfdom and totalitarian rule. The state must also remain neutral for reasons of efficiency, because central authorities were not capable of gaining the knowledge or making the calculations necessary to govern a complex market economy. The state should not intervene in ways that change the economic status quo as between individuals, and could only fail as an agent of planning, control or redistribution. For economists of this ilk, the state thus did not have a role to play in post-war reconstruction except to the extent that social action enabled markets and protected economic freedom.

Hammarskjöld had already indicated his sympathy for liberal economic thinking about the proper role of the state through his commitment to 'neutrality' and price stability as goals of Swedish economic policy. Hammarskjöld's approach to economic and social policy made him an attractive candidate for UN Secretary-General from the

[66] F. A. Hayek, *The Road to Serfdom* (New York: Routledge, 2001) (first published 1944), p. 76.
[67] *Ibid.*, pp. 76–82.

American perspective.[68] Hammarskjöld remained closely aligned with the US on economic and political questions concerning the role of the post-colonial state during his time as Secretary-General. Hammarskjöld was committed to decolonisation and to the equality of the new states, but he was also a believer in economics and the free market. As a result, while Hammarskjöld believed that the UN had a role to play in decolonisation, he thought that the scope of governmental action, whether undertaken by the UN or by decolonised states themselves, was limited.

The idea that the state had a limited role to play in relation to the market was a radical one within post-war Europe. It was an even more radical idea in the context of decolonisation. The decolonised state was confronted with an economic system designed to enable the profitability of colonial enterprises. The US was opposed to the continuation of colonialism as a coercive order premised upon the concentration of ownership and control in the hands of a particular colonial power. It sought to replace this with a regime of open access, free trade, non-discrimination and the international management of resources in the decolonised world. Yet at the same time, in the name of resisting communism, the US prevented attempts to restructure the colonial state and its relation to the broader international economy. Without such restructuring, decolonisation would merely shift the comparative advantage in accessing and controlling resources and labour located in the former colonies. That access and control would no longer be a monopoly of the colonial powers, but would theoretically be open to all states. The UN would come to play a key role in this process of transforming an empire of land appropriation to an empire of economic administration. Central to this process would be the meaning that Hammarskjöld gave to the principle of 'neutrality' in the project of managing decolonisation. The tension between Hammarskjöld's commitment to independence on the one hand, and his faith in liberal economics as the means for development on the other, would inform the practices he introduced for managing decolonisation. The idea that the government should remain neutral in relation to existing political interests would have significant implications for the project of decolonisation.

---

[68] Appelqvist, 'A hidden duel', p. 2, arguing that Hammarskjöld's performance as a Swedish civil servant goes some way to explaining 'why he was nominated and accepted by the representatives of the United States' as UN Secretary-General.

The space of empire: the UN experiment at Suez

Two operations undertaken while Hammarskjöld was in office had particular significance for the consolidation of a new form of international authority. The first was the UN operation at Suez. That operation changed the landscape of international politics in two ways. First, it signalled the end of a particular form of imperialism. Secondly, it introduced a new form of international executive rule and, in the words of US Secretary of State John Foster Dulles, 'the beginning of a world order'.[69] The emergence of peacekeeping as an instrument of UN action was central to that new form of rule and that emergent world order. In a later study of the experience derived from the establishment of UNEF, Hammarskjöld described it as 'a new and in many ways unique experiment by the United Nations in a type of operation which previously it had not been called upon to conduct'.[70]

The nationalisation of the Canal and the material effects of decolonisation

The Suez crisis erupted on 26 July 1956, when Egyptian President Gamal Abdel Nasser issued a decree nationalising the Compagnie Universelle du Canal Maritime de Suez, transferring its assets to the Egyptian Government and declaring martial law in the Canal zone. The Egyptian Government announced that it intended to use the proceeds of the nationalisation to fund the building of the Aswan Dam.[71] For the Egyptian Government, the dam represented the future of Egypt – it would produce the power and irrigation capacity necessary to fuel a massive modernisation project.[72] Nasser had sought initially to fund the dam with aid from Western sources, but the US Secretary of State John Foster Dulles had announced on 19 July 1956 that the US had withdrawn its offer of aid for the dam, with Britain and the World Bank soon following suit.[73]

---

[69] UN GAOR, 1st Emergency Special Sess., 561st Plen. Mtg., Agenda Item 5, UN Doc. A/PV.561, 1 November 1956, para. 151.

[70] UN Secretary-General, 'Summary Study of the Experience Derived from the Establishment and Operation of the Force: Report of the Secretary-General', UN GAOR, 13th Sess., Agenda Item 65, UN Doc. A/3943, 9 October 1958, annex, para. 1.

[71] 'Note: Nationalization of the Suez Canal Company', *Harvard Law Review* 70 (1957), 480.

[72] Urquhart, *Hammarskjöld*, p. 154.

[73] *Ibid.*, p. 155. Urquhart suggests that the decision by the Secretary of State was probably a response to the Egyptian purchase of Russian arms and its recognition of the People's Republic of China.

With the nationalisation of the Canal, the countries of Europe and North America were suddenly confronted with the material effects of decolonisation. Egypt had long been of enormous strategic and commercial importance to European powers, particularly after the Suez Canal had opened to shipping in 1869. The existence of the Canal contributed greatly to the expansion of European world trade, as it allowed ships to travel from Europe to Asia without having to navigate around Africa. By the 1950s, the canal had become central to international commerce. Perhaps more importantly it had become a 'virtual adjunct of the oil industry', with much of Europe's oil transported through the canal.[74] Control over the Canal was particularly key to the commercial and strategic success of Britain's greater 'empire project'.[75] In 1882, Britain had begun what it described as a 'temporary' occupation of Egypt, conducted with the intention of rescuing Egypt from 'disorder' and the threat of a 'military mutiny' (or nationalist movement).[76] That temporary occupation would last for more than seventy years. At the time of Nasser's announcement, Britain was already reeling from the 1951 nationalisation of the Anglo-Iranian Oil Company. The idea that the Suez Canal might also fall victim to the rising tide of Arab nationalism was extremely troubling for British industries and for Britain's sense of its place in the world.

The main international instrument governing the status and operation of the Suez Canal was the 1888 Convention of Constantinople signed between Turkey and the principal European powers of the period.[77] The Convention sought to neutralise the canal by ensuring that it would 'always be free and open, in time of war as in time of peace, to every vessel of commerce or of war, without distinction of flag'.[78] However, it was also agreed that the neutralisation of the canal would not prevent the Sultan and the Khedive taking measures that they might 'find . . . necessary to take for securing by their own forces the defence of Egypt and the maintenance of public order'.[79] At the time the Convention was signed,

---

[74] Keith Kyle, *Suez: Britain's End of Empire in the Middle East* (London: I. B. Tauris, 2001), p. 7.

[75] John Darwin, *The Empire Project: The Rise and Fall of the British World System 1830–1970* (Cambridge: Cambridge University Press, 2009), pp. 590–605.

[76] Afaf Lutfi Al-Sayyid-Marsot, 'The British Occupation of Egypt from 1882' in Andrew Porter (ed.), *The Oxford History of the British Empire: Volume III, The Nineteenth Century* (Oxford: Oxford University Press, 1999), p. 651 at p. 654.

[77] Convention Respecting the Free Navigation of the Suez Maritime Canal, 29 October 1888, *Supplement to the American Journal of International Law* 3 (1909), 123.

[78] *Ibid.*, article 1.   [79] *Ibid.*, article 10.

Britain was already in 'temporary occupation' of Egypt, and the forces whose freedom was carefully preserved by Article 10 were under British command.[80] The British would rely on this provision to control traffic through the canal during the two world wars, but tensions mounted when the Egyptian Government sought to rely on it to deny Israeli ships access to the canal after 1956.[81]

The nationalisation of the Suez Canal posed a major problem for those states that had come to depend upon access to the canal on favourable terms. The nationalisation did not appear to breach the Constantinople Convention, and there was no general principle of international law requiring that resources deemed of vital importance to the international community must be held or managed by private companies or international bodies.[82] The option of invading Egypt to regain control over the canal seemed to have been ruled out by the provisions of the (still relatively new) UN Charter prohibiting the resort to force in international relations. In response to the news, a coalition of canal users therefore took action publicly, particularly through the UN, to find a peaceful solution to the problem. Hammarskjöld also initiated a series of informal meetings with the foreign ministers of the UK, France and Egypt to discuss the future use of the canal and the settlement of claims relating to the Compagnie Universelle. On 12 October, the foreign ministers agreed on a set of six principles for the future operation of the canal, and those principles were subsequently endorsed by the Security Council.[83]

Yet at the same time as these public negotiations were proceeding, the French, Israeli and British governments also secretly formulated plans 'to break the Canal problem by force'.[84] In 1996, the Israeli Government released its copy of the tripartite Protocol of Sèvres, signed on 24 October 1956 by the UK, Israel and France.[85] The Protocol recorded the agreement reached between the three parties that Israeli forces would launch 'a large scale attack' on Egypt on the evening of 29 October 1956, thus providing a pretext for Britain and France to undertake a police action to secure the canal and restore peace. The following day the British and French governments would simultaneously issue 'appeals' to the

---

[80] Darwin, *The Empire Project*, p. 78.   [81] Kyle, *Suez: Britain's End of Empire*, p. 16.
[82] 'Note: Nationalization of the Suez Canal Company', 485.
[83] Urquhart, *Hammarskjöld*, pp. 167–8.   [84] *Ibid.*, p. 160.
[85] Avi Shlaim, 'The Protocol of Sèvres, 1956: Anatomy of a War Plot', *International Affairs* 73 (1997), 509.

Egyptian and Israeli governments requiring them to 'halt all acts of war' and withdraw all troops ten miles from the canal. In addition, the Egyptian Government would be called upon 'to accept temporary occupation of key positions along the Canal'.[86] If Israel or Egypt did not give its consent to the Anglo-French demands within twelve hours, the 'Anglo-French forces would intervene with the means necessary to ensure that their demands are accepted'.[87] The parties agreed that '[t]he arrangements of the present protocol must remain strictly secret'.[88] On 29 October, as agreed, Israeli forces attacked Egypt, and on 30 October, France and the UK delivered their joint ultimatum directed to Egypt and Israel. While the ultimatum merely required Israel to withdraw from territory it had occupied illegally, it required Egypt to withdraw from part of its own territory.[89] As anticipated, Israel quickly accepted the ultimatum while Egypt rejected it. In response, the Anglo-French invasion of Egypt commenced with the launch of air attacks on 31 October.[90] News of the Anglo-French ultimatum became known during a Security Council meeting on 30 October. During that meeting, Britain and France vetoed both a US and a Russian resolution calling for an Israeli withdrawal.[91] In response to the deadlock of the Security Council, the Yugoslav representative invoked the procedure under resolution 377 (V) of the General Assembly, 'Uniting for Peace', and the matter was referred to the General Assembly.[92]

[86] The Protocol of Sèvres, 24 October 1956, articles 1–2, reprinted as the Appendix to Shlaim, 'The Protocol of Sèvres', 530 and as Appendix A to Kyle, *Suez: Britain's End of Empire*, p. 587.
[87] *Ibid.*, article 3.   [88] *Ibid.*, article 6.
[89] Wm. Roger Louis, *Ends of British Imperialism: The Scramble for Empire, Suez and Decolonization* (London: I. B. Tauris, 2006), p. 680.
[90] Urquhart, *Hammarskjöld*, p. 173.
[91] Louis, *Ends of British Imperialism*, p. 682.
[92] *Uniting for Peace*, GA Res. 377(V), UN GAOR, 1st Comm., 5th Sess., 302nd Plen. Mtg., UN Doc. A/RES/377(V), 3 November 1950. The 'Uniting for Peace' resolution was introduced by the US as a means of enabling the UN to take decisions to authorise US-led military action in Korea in the face of the threat of Soviet veto in the Security Council. It represented a dramatic shift in the balance of power between the Security Council and the General Assembly. The resolution states that: 'If the Security Council, because of lack of unanimity of the permanent members, fails to exercise its primary responsibility for the maintenance of international peace and security in any case where there appears to be a threat to the peace, breach of the peace, or act of aggression, the General Assembly shall consider the matter immediately with a view to making appropriate recommendations to Members for collective measures . . .'. The Yugoslav resolution was the first time the Uniting for Peace procedure had been formally invoked at the UN.

The creation of UNEF

At the Emergency Special Session of the General Assembly convened on 1 November to discuss the Suez situation, the Egyptian representative, Omar Loutfi, announced that his country had 'been subjected to bloody aggression', and that Israel had committed a 'premeditated, carefully prepared armed attack for the purpose of occupying part of Egyptian territory and provoking war in that area'.[93] The Franco-British air force had since begun to bomb Egypt and had attacked a military academy, a mosque, a hospital, all Egyptian airports and other sites in Cairo, Ismailia, Port Said, Suez and Alexandria.[94] Loutfi reported that on 30 October, the Commander-in-Chief of the Franco-British forces had declared:

> Aerial bombing will continue until Egypt sees reason. Length of the operation depends on how quickly Egypt accepts our terms. The sooner Egypt sees reason, the less damage will occur. We have considerable strength to deal severe blows.[95]

Loutfi rejected the UK allegation that the intervention was necessary to safeguard the Suez Canal, noting both that there was no danger threatening the canal prior to the intervention and that even if there were a threat to the canal, the 1888 Constantinople Convention gave 'Egypt alone the right to take measures for the defence of the Canal'.[96]

The British Ambassador to the UN, Sir Pierson Dixon, did not know in advance of the decision by the British Government to support the Israelis and invade Egypt, and wrote later that the effort of 'putting a plausible and confident face on the case was the severest moral and physical strain I have ever experienced'.[97] Dixon warned the British Foreign Secretary and Prime Minister that continued bombing 'would make a mockery of our repeated assertions that our intervention was an emergency action confined to the occupation of a few key points along the canal'.[98] Nonetheless, in addressing the General Assembly, Dixon dutifully sought to characterise the Anglo-French intervention as a police action.

[93] UN GAOR, 1st Emergency Special Sess., 561st Plen. Mtg., Agenda Item 5, UN Doc. A/PV.561, 1 November 1956, para. 25.
[94] Ibid., paras. 29–31. [95] Ibid., para. 32. [96] Ibid., para. 38.
[97] Urquhart, Hammarskjöld, p. 175.
[98] Dixon to Foreign Office, Emergency Secret, 3 November 1956, FO 371/121747, cited in Louis, Ends of British Imperialism, p. 687.

> The action which we and the French government have taken is essentially
> of a temporary character, and, I repeat it, designed to deal with a unique
> emergency. Our intervention was swift because the emergency brooked
> no delay. It has been drastic because drastic action was evidently required.
> It is an emergency police action.[99]

Dixon rejected as 'absurd' and 'false' the suggestion that the UK intervention was undertaken as part of a plan agreed to with Israel.[100] As between Egypt and Israel, 'the attitude of Her Majesty's Government remains quite impartial'.[101] The UK had taken action in response to 'a threat to the vital interests of my country, as well as to those many nations which are dependent on free passage through the Canal'.[102] The objectives of the intervention were simply to safeguard the canal and restore peace.[103]

> We do not seek the domination of Egypt or any part of Egyptian territory.
> Our purpose is peaceful, not warlike. Our aim is to re-establish the rule of
> law, not to violate it; to protect and not to destroy. What we have undertaken is a temporary police action necessitated by the turn of events in the
> Middle East and occasioned by the imperative need not only to protect
> the vital interests of my own and many other countries, but also to take
> immediate measures for the restoration of order.[104]

Dixon stressed that British action was not aimed at the 'sovereignty' or the 'territorial integrity' of Egypt. 'By seeking to protect the Suez Canal area, we would only be seeking to protect a vital waterway.'[105] The UK had no interest in Egyptian territory per se.

> It is not of our choice that the police action which we have been obliged to
> take is occurring on Egyptian territory . . . After all, the fighting in which
> Israel is involved is taking place in Egypt, and it is therefore only in Egypt
> that it can be stopped. When two householders have committed a breach
> of the peace, the policeman has no option but to attempt to separate them
> where it is taking place.[106]

Dixon, however, stated in closing that '[i]f the United Nations were willing to take over the physical task of maintaining peace in the area, no-one would be better pleased than we. But police action there must be, to separate the belligerents and to stop the hostilities.'[107]

---

[99] UN GAOR, 1st Emergency Special Sess., 561st Plen. Mtg., Agenda Item 5, UN Doc. A/PV.561, 1 November 1956, para 79.
[100] *Ibid.*, para. 97.   [101] *Ibid.*, para. 98.   [102] *Ibid.*, para. 95.   [103] *Ibid.*, para. 99.
[104] *Ibid.*, para. 101.   [105] *Ibid.*, para. 102.   [106] *Ibid.*, para. 104.   [107] *Ibid.*, para. 111.

In a significant speech marking the clear separation between the interests of the US and old Europe on the issue of how to manage decolonisation, the US Secretary of State John Foster Dulles condemned the resort to force by Israel, France and the UK. In many ways Dulles had precipitated the Suez crisis by withdrawing US funding for the Aswan Dam on ideological grounds, and he was certainly no friend to Nasser. Yet the US did not want to enable a future legal order premised on the old model of informal imperial occupation of territories in the name of police action. British imperial dominance in the Middle East had operated 'through a network of client dynasties that were in the political, military and financial grip of British diplomatic missions, military bases, and oil companies'.[108] From the perspective of the US State Department, those colonial networks of influence were 'outmoded' and 'dangerous to peace'.[109] The US was committed instead to implementing an 'open-door' approach to foreign relations that was built upon freedom of trade, freedom of navigation and non-discrimination.[110] Dulles' opening words to the General Assembly made clear the gap that had emerged between the US and its allies:

> I doubt that any representative ever spoke from this rostrum with as heavy a heart as I have brought here tonight. We speak on a matter of vital importance, where the United States finds itself unable to agree with three nations with which it has ties of deep friendship, of admiration and of respect, and two of which constitute our oldest and most trusted and reliable allies.[111]

While Dulles admitted that there had been a 'long and sad history of irritations and provocations', this did not justify resort to force by Israel, France and the UK.[112]

> If . . . we were to agree that the existence in the world of injustices which this Organization has so far been unable to cure means that the principle of renunciation of force should no longer be respected, that whenever a nation feels that it has been subjected to injustice it should have the right to resort to force in an attempt to correct that injustice, then I fear that we should be tearing this Charter into shreds, that the world again would be a world of anarchy, that the great hopes placed in this Organization and in our Charter would vanish, and that we should again be where we were at the start of the Second World War, with another tragic failure in place of

---

[108] Louis, *Ends of British Imperialism*, p. 469.   [109] *Ibid.*   [110] *Ibid.*
[111] UN GAOR, 1st Emergency Special Sess., 561st Plen. Mtg., Agenda Item 5, UN Doc. A/PV.561, 1 November 1956, para. 132.
[112] *Ibid.*, paras. 137–9.

what we had hoped – as we still can hope – would constitute a barrier to the recurrence of world war, which, in the words of the preamble to the Charter, has twice in our lifetime brought untold sorrow to mankind.[113]

According to Dulles, it was 'still possible for the united will of this Organization to have an impact upon the situation and perhaps to make it apparent to the world, not only for the benefit of ourselves but for all posterity, that there is here the beginning of a world order'.[114]

The meeting concluded with a resolution calling for an immediate cease-fire, a halting of the movement of military forces and arms into the area, the withdrawal of forces behind the armistice lines established in the Israel–Arab armistice agreements and the reopening of the Suez Canal upon the cease-fire being effective.[115] The Canadian representative, Lester Pearson, also proposed that the General Assembly should create 'a United Nations force, a truly international peace and police force' that could keep Egypt and Israel at peace while a political settlement was negotiated.[116] Two days later, Canada submitted a resolution to the General Assembly requesting 'as a matter of priority, the Secretary-General to submit within forty-eight hours a plan for the setting up, with the consent of the nations concerned, of an emergency international United Nations Force to secure and supervise the cessation of hostilities in accordance with all the terms of the aforementioned resolution'.[117]

The plan that Hammarskjöld developed, which would subsequently be acted upon to establish UNEF, set out a number of key principles to guide the establishment and operation of the force. These principles would come to play a significant role in shaping the rationalisation of executive action by the UN over the following decades. Of particular relevance to the question of authority are the principles addressing the issues of independence, impartiality and host-state consent. First, Hammarskjöld proposed that the force should have an international character and be set up under UN command 'on the basis of principles reflected in the constitution of the UN

---

[113] *Ibid.*, paras. 139–40.   [114] *Ibid.*, paras. 151–2.

[115] GA Res. 997 (ES-I), UN GAOR, 1st Emergency Special Sess., Supp. No. 1, UN Doc. A/3354, 2 November 1956.

[116] UN GAOR, 1st Emergency Special Sess., 562nd Plen. Mtg., Agenda Item 5, UN Doc. A/PV.562, 1 November 1956, paras. 307–8.

[117] GA Res. 998 (ES-I), UN GAOR, 1st Emergency Special Sess., Supp. No. 1, UN Doc. A/3354, 4 November 1956. The resolution passed by fifty-seven to zero with nineteen abstentions.

itself.[118] The officer responsible for that force would be 'fully independent of the policies of any one nation'.[119] Hammarskjöld expected UN military personnel to have the same undivided loyalty to the UN as other international civil servants. While military personnel 'are, of course, not under the same formal obligations in relation to the Organization as *staff* members of the Secretariat', they were nonetheless subject to the 'basic rules of the United Nations for international service ... particularly as regards full loyalty to the aims of the Organization and to abstention from acts in relation to their country of origin or to other countries which might deprive the operation of its international character and create a situation of dual loyalty'.[120]

Secondly, the force must be impartial. Hammarskjöld drew the obligation to act impartially from the fact that the force was authorised to operate only for a temporary period and for a confined purpose. The General Assembly had established the force on an 'emergency' basis and had authorised it 'to secure and supervise the cessation of hostilities'.[121] According to Hammarskjöld, the terms of reference made clear that 'there is no intent in the establishment of the Force to influence the military balance in the present conflict and, thereby, the political balance affecting efforts to resolve the conflict'.[122] Thus in establishing the force, 'the General Assembly has not taken a stand in relation to aims other than those clearly and fully indicated in its resolution'.[123] In particular, Hammarskjöld wanted to make clear that the force would not be acting as a proxy for British and French interests in the region. In a subsequent study of the operation, Hammarskjöld stressed that, as a matter of principle: 'United Nations personnel cannot be permitted in any sense to be a party to internal conflicts. Their role must be limited to external aspects of the political situation, as, for example, infiltration or other activities affecting international boundaries.'[124] UNEF had 'functioned under a clear-cut mandate' that 'entirely detached it from involvement in

---

[118] UN Secretary-General, 'Second and Final Report of the Secretary-General on the Plan for an Emergency International United Nations Force Requested in the Resolution Adopted by the General Assembly on 4 November 1956 (A/3276)', UN GAOR, 1st Emergency Special Sess., UN Doc. A/3302, 6 November 1956, para. 4.
[119] *Ibid.*   [120] UN Secretary-General, 'Summary Study of Experience', para. 168.
[121] UN Secretary-General, 'Second and Final Report on the Plan for an Emergency Force', para. 7.
[122] *Ibid.*, para. 8.   [123] *Ibid.*, para. 8.
[124] UN Secretary-General, 'Summary Study of Experience', para. 166.

any internal or local problems, and ... also enabled it to maintain its neutrality in relation to international political issues'.[125]

Thirdly, while the General Assembly acting under the Uniting for Peace resolution could establish an emergency force, consent of the parties was required to the operation or stationing of the force on the territory of a given country.[126] The need for consent flowed from the principle of equality between Members, as decisions about the use of force by foreign troops within a territory went to the heart of political sovereignty.[127] A clear commitment to respecting the sovereign equality of newly independent states such as Egypt was clearly of great importance in a situation where the Secretary-General was seeking to distinguish the use of force by the UN from intervention by former colonial powers.

The Suez operation and the future of the UN

The UN action in the Suez had two major consequences for the future world order. These consequences led in different directions – one towards the goal of sovereign independence, the other towards the expansion of executive rule. On the one hand, the UN action 'vindicated the view that colonialism was an anachronism'.[128] The conduct of the Anglo-French invasion of Egypt, and its comparison with the contemporaneous Soviet invasion of Hungary, meant that 'the British Empire was now denounced as being just as immoral and vicious as the Soviet Empire in Eastern Europe and Central Asia'.[129] While the UN may have 'started out as a mechanism for defending and adapting empire in an increasingly nationalist age',[130] with Suez it seemed that it might yet be transformed into something else – an organisation committed to

---

[125] *Ibid.*, para. 149.
[126] UN Secretary-General, 'Second and Final Report on the Plan for an Emergency Force', para. 9.
[127] Nabil Elaraby, 'United Nations Peacekeeping by Consent: A Case Study of the Withdrawal of the United Nations Emergency Force', *New York University Journal of International Law and Politics* 1 (1968), 149.
[128] Louis, 'The Suez Crisis and the British Dilemma at the United Nations' in Vaughan Lowe *et al.* (eds.), *The United Nations Security Council and War: The Evolution of Thought and Practice since 1945* (Oxford: Oxford University Press, 2008), p. 297.
[129] Louis, *Ends of British Imperialism*, p. 695.
[130] For this view of the ideological origins of the UN, see Mark Mazower, *No Enchanted Palace: The End of Empire and the Ideological Origins of the United Nations* (Princeton and Oxford: Princeton University Press, 2009), pp. 26–7.

realising self-determination and enabling decolonisation. Suez marked a moment at which former European imperial powers were forced to recognise that the preservation of the old colonial system was no longer possible and that they had to adjust to the new US-led world economy while, if possible, maintaining their standing as great powers. The UN offered one solution – a way for progressive Europeans to make clear that they had abandoned the old world of empire and embarked on a new project with the independent states of Asia and Africa as their partners.[131]

> Many of us have had contact with the European world of the fading nineteenth century – the typical attitudes of which have, of course, reached far into our own – and then experienced the breakdown of the European circle of culture, spiritually, politically and geographically, finally seeing at least the beginning of a new synthesis on a universal basis. Depending on temperament and background, reactions to this evolution may vary. One may reach back for the imagined calm of the closed world. One may find one's spiritual home in the very disintegration and its drama. Or, one may reach ahead towards the glimpse of the synthesis, inspired by the dream of a new culture in which there is achieved, on a level encompassing the whole world, what once seemed to have become a regional reality in Europe.[132]

The character of that 'new culture' was not, however, up for negotiation. It was clear after Suez that powerful states would no longer readily be able to secure access to resources or strategic advantage through 'temporary' occupation or land appropriation. Yet it was also clear that newly independent states would not be free to deny foreign access to and control over resources. Instead, Suez signalled the birth of an Americanised global economy, premised upon an openness to investment, free trade, non-discrimination and the international management of resources in the decolonised world. That was the context within which

---

[131] European integration offered another solution. An integrated Europe offered 'a space in which ruling elites were provided an opportunity to trade the grievances over the loss of empire – and all that this would encompass in terms of damaged national pride, international prestige, sense of national direction, and, not the least, the humiliating experience of being defeated by peoples often designated as inferior races – for a new beginning, a new project, and a new national purpose in a "new Europe"'. See Peo Hansen, 'European Integration, European Identity and the Colonial Connection', *European Journal of Social Theory* 5 (2002), 483 at 494.

[132] Dag Hammarskjöld, 'Asia, Africa, and the West' in Wilder Foote (ed.), *The Servant of Peace: A Selection of the Speeches and Statements of Dag Hammarskjöld* (London: The Bodley Head, 1962), p. 212 at p. 214.

the development of UN peacekeeping would take effect. The political implications of that development were therefore ambiguous. At Suez, the interests of the US and of the newly independent states had aligned and shaped the role that the UN would play in resolving the immediate crisis. The US was willing to support the expansion of General Assembly jurisdiction over matters of peace and security because it could rely upon a 'majority of pro-Western allies in the General Assembly'.[133] While the Suez crisis temporarily empowered the parliamentary organ of the General Assembly, it also empowered the international executive in the form of the Secretary-General and the Secretariat.[134] According to Dixon, Hammarskjöld's influence had been significantly increased by his handling of Suez: 'The outcome of this crisis left him more than a symbol or even an executive; he had become a force.'[135] The success of quiet diplomacy as developed in the Chinese negotiations and executive rule as developed at Suez reaffirmed the Secretary-General's belief that dynamic international executive action was to be preferred to static conference diplomacy. As the Secretary-General noted in his plan for UNEF, if 'the Force is to come into being with all the speed indispensable to its success, a margin of confidence must be left to those who will carry the responsibility for putting the decisions of the General Assembly into effect'.[136] At the time of the Suez crisis, that expansion of executive power and the 'margin of confidence' it left to those with decision-making authority was equated with the dilution of Great Power politics and the empowerment of the newly independent states of the decolonised world. Yet the views of newly independent states would not always align with those of the US and the Secretary-General. It was during the Congo operation that the significant problems this raised would become apparent.

---

[133] Dominik Zaum, 'The Security Council, the General Assembly, and War: The Uniting for Peace Resolution' in Vaughan Lowe, Adam Roberts, Jennifer Welsh and Dominik Zaum (eds.), *The United Nations Security Council and War: The Evolution of Thought and Practice since 1945* (Oxford: Oxford University Press, 2008), p. 154 at p. 159.

[134] Edward Johnson, '"The Umpire on Whom the Sun Never Sets": Dag Hammarskjöld's Political Role and the British at Suez', *Diplomacy & Statecraft* 8 (1997), 249 at 268.

[135] Sir Pierson Dixon, 'The Secretary General of the United Nations: Mr Dag Hammarskjöld', Confidential memorandum to Mr Selwyn Lloyd, 16 January 1958, FO371/137002/UN2303/1 (The National Archives, Kew).

[136] UN Secretary-General, *Second and Final Report on the Plan for an Emergency Force*, para. 19.

Protecting life and maintaining order: the United Nations in the Congo

The conduct of the UN Operation in the Congo reveals most clearly what the expansion of international executive rule would come to mean for the process of decolonisation. 1960, the year in which the Congo crisis erupted, was welcomed at the UN as 'the great year of African independence'.[137] It was 'symbolically inaugurated' with the accession to independence on 1 January 1960 of the former French Trust Territory of the Cameroons – the first time a territory previously under UN trusteeship had become an independent state.[138] Seventeen new Member States were admitted to the UN over the course of 1960, sixteen of them from Africa. Suddenly there were a significant number of political communities from the African continent recognised as states, and representatives from those communities sitting in the General Assembly of the UN. Hammarskjöld saw it as the UN's responsibility to support policies 'aiming at independence, not only in a constitutional sense but in every sense of the word, protecting the possibilities of the African peoples to choose their own way'.[139] The Congo operation was the most infamous exercise of that responsibility.

it was not just The SG

History of the crisis

On 12 July 1960, Joseph Kasavubu, the President and Supreme Commander of the National Army of the Republic of the Congo, and Patrice Lumumba, the Prime Minister and Minister of National Defence, jointly wrote to the UN Secretary-General condemning 'the dispatch to the Congo of metropolitan Belgian troops in violation of the treaty of friendship signed between Belgium and the Republic of the Congo on 29 June 1960' and requesting the 'urgent dispatch by the United Nations of military assistance' in order 'to protect the national territory of the Congo from the present external aggression which is a threat to international peace'.[140] The crisis in the Congo began when soldiers of the *Armée Nationale Congolaise* (formerly the *Force*

---

[137] Urquhart, *Hammarskjöld*, p. 382.

[138] UN Secretary-General, *Introduction to the 1960 Annual Report*, p. 1.   [139] *Ibid.*, p. 2.

[140] 'Cable Dated 12 July 1960 from the President of the Republic of the Congo and Supreme Commander of the National Army and the Prime Minister and Minister of National Defence Addressed to the Secretary-General of the United Nations', UN SCOR, 15th Sess., UN Doc. S/4382, 13 July 1960.

Publique) revolted against their Belgian officers soon after Congo's accession to independence.[141] The soldiers demanded immediate appointment of Congolese officers and, along with other public servants, sought higher wages and promotions.[142] The new government responded to the soldiers' demands by agreeing to Africanise the officer corps and raise army wages by 30 per cent. This was interpreted by outside observers as an invitation to 'public employees and the black proletariat in mines and factories to follow the soldiers' lead and consolidate independence with social demands'.[143] Ralph Bunche, the Secretary-General's special adviser in the Congo, wrote to Hammarskjöld: 'Strikes continue and spread, encouraged and triggered originally by successful tactics of army.'[144]

Belgium quite properly saw the Congolese Government's approach to this and related questions as a threat to the future of Belgian power and resources in the Congo. King Leopold II of Belgium had established the Congo Free State as a personal fiefdom and source of income. The production of materials for export from the Congo Free State had depended upon 'the use of force and even of terror'.[145] Once the Belgian state took over the Congo from Leopold, it softened but still continued to use existing forms of political and economic coercion 'to create a labour market and to facilitate the accumulation of capital'.[146] During the colonial period from 1910 until 1960, the foreign minority continued to control the economy and remove the Congolese from their land, thus producing both a dependent labour force and a concentration of resources in the hands of foreign settlers and investors. The colonial administration also intervened directly to prevent the formation of indigenous economies that could compete with Belgian producers and to ensure the continued availability of Congolese labour and materials to entrepreneurs.[147] By the 1920s, 'the density of administration in the Congo was unequalled in

[141] See further Chapter 1 above.
[142] Georges Nzongola-Ntalaja, *The Congo from Leopold to Kabila: A People's History* (London: Zed Books, 2002), p. 89.
[143] Ludo De Witte, *The Assassination of Lumumba*, Ann Wright and Renée Fenby (trans.) (London: Verso, 2001), p. 8.
[144] *Ibid.*
[145] Jean-Philippe Peemans, 'Capital Accumulation in the Congo under Colonialism: The Role of the State' in Peter Duignan and L. H. Gann (eds.), *Colonialism in Africa 1870–1960 (Volume 4): The Economics of Colonialism* (London and New York: Cambridge University Press, 1975), p. 165 at p. 171.
[146] *Ibid.*, p. 180. [147] *Ibid.*, pp. 167, 172.

Africa'.[148] 'No Congolese, rural or urban, could have failed to perceive that he was being administered.'[149] This was true both of those living in the urban centres and those living in rural areas – 'what differentiated the Belgian system from others in Africa was the extent of its occupation and organization of the countryside'.[150] Colonial policies supported the recruitment of labour for the mines, plantation and army, as well as halting the rural exodus and preserving the health of the workforce through public immunisation and other health programmes. The administration severely limited the union activity, political organisation, education and free speech of the Congolese through to the mid-1950s.

Until independence the Congo remained a major source of profit for Belgian firms. While Belgian firms in general averaged returns of 8 to 9 per cent during the 1950s, those operating in the Congo averaged 20 per cent.[151] By 1958, although the foreign minority represented 'only 1 per cent of the population, [it] controlled 95 per cent of the assets, 88 per cent of private savings and 82 per cent of all the firms'.[152] The most powerful group within that foreign minority were the high- and middle-level managers of the major Belgian companies, plus the major industrialists and settlers.[153] While many of those managers did not directly own resources, they organised and controlled production in the Congo.[154] The Belgian and Congolese governments thus had competing interests in the future of an independent Congo. Belgium's economic stake in its former colony 'motivated Brussels' post-independence efforts to retain its economic lock on the Congo's economy'.[155] In contrast, if decolonisation were to be meaningful for the Congolese people, it required the redistribution of property, power and control over the economy.

It was that promise of redistribution that was at stake in the aftermath of the post-independence revolt of the Congolese military. On 10 July, the Congolese Government sought assistance from the UN in the reorganisation and retraining of the army. The same day, before the request for assistance from the UN could be granted, Belgium invaded,

---

[148] Crawford Young, *Politics in the Congo: Decolonization and Independence* (Princeton: Princeton University Press, 1965), p. 10.
[149] *Ibid.*, p. 11.   [150] *Ibid.*
[151] Carole J. L. Collins, 'The Cold War Comes to Africa: Cordier and the 1960 Congo Crisis', *Journal of International Affairs* 47 (1993), 243 at 251.
[152] Peemans, 'Capital Accumulation in the Congo under Colonialism', p. 181.
[153] *Ibid.*   [154] *Ibid.*   [155] Collins, 'The Cold War Comes to Africa', 251.

claiming its action was a 'humanitarian intervention' undertaken 'with the sole purpose of ensuring the safety of European and other members of the population and of protecting human lives in general'.[156] The Belgian intervention began in the resource-rich province of Katanga, which declared independence the day after Belgian forces arrived.

Belgian support for the Katangese secessionists posed a serious threat to the political stability and economic viability of an independent Congo. In part this was due to the economic and fiscal effects of the attempted secession. Prior to independence, control over the economy of the Belgian Congo had been exercised in Brussels. After independence, direct taxes on companies operating both in the Congo and in Belgium continued to be collected in Brussels, and those taxes accounted for more than one-third of the revenues of the Congo.[157] Government of the Belgian Congo had been conducted through a large number of publicly owned but privately administered 'para-statal institutions', including financial agencies such as the central bank and the savings bank, as well as agencies providing basic services such as electricity, housing and transport in the Congo.[158] Management of these institutions had also been based in Brussels, and no agreement had been reached as to the transfer of authority over those institutions by the time of independence.[159] After the Katangese secession, Belgian mining companies paid taxes and export duties levied by the central government to the government of the State of Katanga.[160] Those revenues, which would otherwise have formed the basis of the Congolese economy, were then used to form, train and equip the armed forces of Katanga. Secessionist forces seized local branches of para-statal institutions such as the central bank, further limiting the capacity of the central government to exercise 'the chief economic control instruments of the state'.[161] The Belgian intervention also obviously shifted the military balance of power in favour of Katanga. While Belgian forces in other parts of the Congo were instructed to 'intervene when Belgian lives are threatened', in Katanga they were instructed to occupy 'all centres of importance'.[162] Belgian troops in Katanga rounded up and neutralised the *Force Publique*, attacked troops

---

[156] UN SCOR, 15th Sess., 873rd Mtg., UN Doc. S/PV.873, 13–14 July 1960, paras. 183, 197.
[157] Robert L. West, 'The United Nations and the Congo Financial Crisis: Lessons of the First Year', *International Organization* 15 (1961), 603.
[158] *Ibid.*, 605.   [159] *Ibid.*
[160] Conor Cruise O'Brien, *To Katanga and Back: A UN Case History* (New York: Simon and Schuster, 1962), p. 87.
[161] West, 'The United Nations and the Congo Financial Crisis', 612.
[162] Georges Abi-Saab, *The United Nations Operation in the Congo 1960–1964* (Oxford: Oxford University Press, 1978), p. 41.

loyal to the central government in their barracks and trained the Katangese *gendarmerie*.[163]

In their cable to the Secretary-General, Kasavubu and Lumumba characterised the 'unsolicited' Belgian military action 'as an act of aggression against our country' and claimed that the 'colonialist machinations' of the Belgians were the 'real cause of most of the disturbances' experienced since independence. Kasavubu and Lumumba claimed that the Belgian Government had 'carefully prepared the secession of Katanga with a view to maintaining a hold on our country' and declared that the Congolese Government, 'supported by the Congolese people, refuses to accept a "fait accompli" resulting from a conspiracy between Belgian imperialists and a small group of Katanga leaders'. The cable specified that the 'essential purpose of the requested military aid is to protect the national territory of the Congo against the present external aggression which is a threat to international peace'.[164]

The Security Council debate and the characterisation of the crisis

The following evening, the Security Council met to consider the Secretary-General's report concerning the request of the Congolese Government for UN assistance. The colonial powers of Belgium, France and the UK all spoke at the meeting in defence of the Belgian intervention. Belgium claimed that the *Force Publique* had 'ceased to be an instrument of order in the hands of the new Congolese state' and the state was therefore 'no longer in a position to ensure the safety of the inhabitants'.[165] Belgium declared that its troops could only be withdrawn once 'security has been genuinely established and properly assured by a responsible authority'.[166] France and the UK supported the Belgian intervention, with the UK representative declaring that 'these Belgian troops have performed a humanitarian task for which my Government is grateful, and for which, we believe, the international community should be grateful'.[167] According to the French representative, the Belgian 'mission of protecting lives and property is the direct result of the failure of the Congolese authorities and is in accord with a recognized principle of international law, namely, intervention on humanitarian grounds'.[168]

---

[163] *Ibid.*   [164] 'Cable dated 12 July 1960', 13 July 1960.
[165] UN SCOR, 15th Sess., 873rd Mtg., UN Doc. S/PV.873, 13–14 July 1960, para. 183.
[166] *Ibid.*, para. 194.   [167] *Ibid.*, para. 130.   [168] *Ibid.*, para. 144.

In contrast, the representative of the USSR supported the Congolese claim that 'the real cause of the present disturbances in the country can be found in the machinations to which the colonialists have resorted in their unwillingness to accept defeat'.[169] Statements 'about the necessity of protecting the lives and property of United States, United Kingdom, Belgian and French citizens in the Congo' were simply attempts 'to find a "legal basis" to justify aggression against the Republic of the Congo'. All such 'talk about the need for protecting "the lives of residents" and restoring "order" in other countries' was merely 'a well-worn device which was used on more than one occasion during the nineteenth and early twentieth centuries to conceal armed intervention by the colonial Powers in the countries of Asia, Africa and Latin America'.[170] The USSR thus called upon the Security Council to 'take effective action to halt the aggression against the Republic of the Congo, to check any attempts to interfere in its domestic affairs and to extend the necessary material assistance to the young State'.[171] The US representative also argued that 'the speediest possible United Nations assistance' was 'impera-tive'.[172] While the US concluded that 'no aggression has been committed' by the Belgians, it nonetheless called for the UN to support 'the efforts of the Government of the Congo to restore peace, security and tranquillity in the country' so that it could 'get on with the job of building a great new modern State in the very heart of Africa'.[173] It was left to the representa-tive of Tunisia to raise the issue of lawful authority. The Tunisian representative declared that 'the Government of the Congo, as the Government of an independent and sovereign State, is the sole judge of the advisability of [military] assistance'.[174] Tunisia therefore took the view that the UN 'must, as an act of general solidarity', assist the Congo 'in the great task of reorganization and peace'.[175] According to the Tunisian representative, however, it was 'understood that this United Nations military assistance will cease on the day that the Congolese Government considers the objectives of the assistance to have been accomplished'.[176]

In his report to the Security Council, Hammarskjöld was careful to avoid any legal characterisation of the situation in the Congo and thus was able to avoid alienating Western states by labelling the Belgian intervention as aggression or alienating African states and the USSR by labelling the intervention humanitarian. Instead, he argued that if the

---

[169] *Ibid.*, para. 100.   [170] *Ibid.*, para. 103.   [171] *Ibid.*, para. 107.   [172] *Ibid.*, para. 95.
[173] *Ibid.*, para. 98.   [174] *Ibid.*, para. 89.   [175] *Ibid.*, para. 90.   [176] *Ibid.*

UN were authorised to perform the functions that Belgium had claimed for itself, the Belgian presence in the Congo would no longer be necessary. Hammarskjöld noted that 'the Belgian government has in the Congo troops stated by the Government to be maintained there in protection of life and for the maintenance of order'.[177] Although he took the view that it was 'not for the Secretary-General to pronounce on this action and its legal and political aspects', Hammarskjöld concluded that 'the presence of these troops is a source of internal, and potentially also of international, tension'.[178] He therefore proposed that the UN should accede to the Congolese Government's request for military assistance. Hammarskjöld made clear that 'were the United Nations to act as proposed' and as a result 'the national security forces are able to fully meet their tasks', it was understood that the Belgian Government would then 'see its way to a withdrawal'.[179]

Hammarskjöld told the Security Council that if he were given a mandate to act, he intended to base his actions on principles derived from the recent UN intervention in the Suez. In particular, Hammarskjöld undertook that the proposed UN force would 'not take any action which would make them a party to internal conflicts in the country'.[180] The members of the Security Council did not reach agreement on the formal question of how the Belgian intervention should be characterised. However, because Hammarskjöld had put before the members a plan on which they could agree, the competing characterisations of the situation were 'reduced from the main battle ground to a mere registration of positions'.[181]

The UN and the Katangese secession

The Security Council authorised 'the Secretary-General to take the necessary steps, in consultation with the Government of the Republic of the Congo, to provide the Government with such military assistance as may be necessary'.[182] The Secretary-General was thus given wide discretion to determine what steps were 'necessary' in order to provide the Congo Government with military assistance. He did not, however, appear to have been given discretion to decide which actors to liaise with in the Congo. According to the Security Council resolution, the Secretary-General was to take action in consultation with the

[177] *Ibid.*, para. 26.   [178] *Ibid.*   [179] *Ibid.*   [180] *Ibid.*, para. 28.
[181] Abi-Saab, *The United Nations Operation in the Congo*, p. 12.
[182] SC Res 143, UN SCOR, 15th Sess., 873rd Mtg, UN Doc S/4387, 14 July 1960.

Government of the Republic of the Congo. Nonetheless, the UN was quickly confronted by the question of which competing claimants to lawful authority in the Congo it should recognise. That question initially arose in the context of the challenge posed by Belgian-backed secessionists to the authority of the central government.

In his first report to the Security Council on the conduct of the Congo operation, Hammarskjöld spelt out his interpretation of the mandate he had been given. According to Hammarskjöld, 'it was the breakdown of those instruments of Government, for the maintenance of law and order which had created a situation which through its consequences represented a threat to peace and security'.[183] It was the threat to peace and security posed by the breakdown of law and order that justified UN intervention 'on the basis of the explicit request of the Government of the Republic of the Congo'.[184] The question of whether there was also a 'conflict between two parties' was therefore 'legally not essential for the justification of the action'.[185] ONUC was 'limited to assisting the Government in the maintenance of law and order' and 'would have no direct functions in relation to the withdrawal of Belgian troops, though indirectly it would provide Belgium with a way out'.[186]

Belgium, however, refused to withdraw its troops from Katanga and the Katangese authorities refused to allow UN troops to enter the province. On 20 July, Hammarskjöld made a statement to the Security Council affirming that the resolution of the Security Council applied to the territory of the Congo as a whole, thus implicitly making clear that Belgian forces were required to withdraw from Katanga. However, he also restated his view that 'the United Nations Force cannot be a party to any internal conflict nor can the United Nations Force intervene in a domestic conflict'.[187] In a report of 6 August to the Security Council, Hammarskjöld made clear his view that the attempted secession of Katanga was an internal conflict. Hammarskjöld stated that the case of Katanga 'does not have its root in the Belgian attitude' and therefore

[183] UN Secretary-General, 'First Report of the Secretary-General on the Implementation of Security Council Resolution S/4387 of 14 July 1960', UN SCOR, 15th Sess., UN Doc. S/4389, 18 July 1960, para. 5.
[184] Ibid.   [185] Ibid.   [186] Abi-Saab, The United Nations Operation in the Congo, p. 17.
[187] Andrew W. Cordier and Wilder Foote (eds.), Public Papers of the Secretaries-General of the United Nations, Volume V: Dag Hammarskjöld 1960–1961 (New York: Columbia University Press, 1975), p. 43.

was 'an internal political problem to which the United Nations as an organization obviously cannot be a party'. [188]

On 9 August 1960, the Security Council passed a resolution specifically addressing the situation in Katanga. The resolution called upon the Belgian Government 'to withdraw immediately its troops from the province of Katanga'.[189] Yet it also included a paragraph proposed by Hammarskjöld as a means of giving Belgium and Katanga an 'assurance that the deployment of the UN Force in Katanga would not affect the outcome of the political controversy between Katanga and the Central Government'.[190] Paragraph 4 reaffirmed 'that the United Nations Force in the Congo will not be a party to or in any way intervene in or be used to influence the outcome of an internal conflict, constitutional or otherwise'.

On 12 August, Hammarskjöld made a controversial visit to Elisabethville, the capital of Katanga, to meet with Katangese President Moise Tshombé and his government. On the way, Hammarskjöld drafted a memorandum setting out his interpretation of paragraph 4 of the 9 August resolution for use in his talks with Tshombé.[191] That memorandum dealt in detail with the question of how the UN would relate to the competing claimants for authority within Congo. According to Hammarskjöld, the UN could only be 'directly concerned with the attitude taken by the provincial government of Katanga to the extent that it may be based on the presence of Belgian troops, or as being, for its effectiveness, influenced by that presence'.[192] Hammarskjöld then explicitly characterised the situation in Katanga in light of what he described as principles and doctrines developed in earlier UN 'precedents'.

> In the application of operative paragraph 4, as seen in the light of precedents, it can be concluded that if the Belgian troops were withdrawn and if, pending full withdrawal, a Belgian assurance were given to the Secretary-General that the Belgian troops would in no way 'intervene in or be used to influence the outcome of the conflict between the provincial government and the central government – that is to say, that they would remain completely inactive during the phasing out – the question between the provincial government and the central government would

---

[188] UN Secretary-General, 'Second Report by the Secretary-General on the Implementation of Security Council Resolution S/4387 of 14 July 1960 and S/4405 of 22 July 1960', UN SCOR, 15th Sess., UN Doc. S/4417, 6 August 1960, para. 10.

[189] SC Res. 146, UN SCOR, 15th Sess., 886th Mtg., UN Doc. S/4426, 9 August 1960, adopted by nine votes with two abstentions (France and Italy).

[190] Abi-Saab, *The United Nations Operation in the Congo*, p. 33.

[191] Cordier and Foote, *Public Papers, Volume V*, p. 84.   [192] *Ibid.*, p. 87.

be one in which the United Nations would in no sense be a party and on which it could in no sense exert an influence.[193]

Hammarskjöld acknowledged that it might be thought that the UN should support the central government, but UN precedents militated against that conclusion.

> It might be held that the United Nations is duty bound to uphold the Fundamental Law as the legal constitution and, therefore, should assist the central government in exercising its power in Katanga. However, the United Nations has to observe that, *de facto*, the provincial government is in active opposition – once a Belgian assurance of nonintervention and withdrawal has been given – using only its own military means in order to achieve certain political aims.

Thus for Hammarskjöld the contention 'that the United Nations should support the central government, as it functions under the provisional Fundamental Law, and as it is the party which has asked for assistance', was 'contradicted' by the position taken by the UN in earlier operations where it had only assisted in preventing outside actors from supporting insurgents but had otherwise not favoured either the government or rebels.[194] Hammarskjöld concluded 'that the United Nations Force cannot be used on behalf of the central government to subdue or to force the provincial government to a specific line of action' or 'to transport civilian or military representatives, under the authority of the central government, to Katanga against the decision of the Katanga provincial government'.[195] In addition, the UN could not 'protect civilian or military personnel representing the Central Government, arriving in Katanga, beyond what follows from its general duty to maintain law and order'.[196]

Hammarskjöld's determination that the UN should not assist the central government in regaining control over Katanga marked a turning point in the relation between the UN and the central government. In a heated exchange of letters with Hammarskjöld, Lumumba rejected Hammarskjöld's interpretation of the Katangese secession as an internal matter, accused him of behaving improperly in travelling to Elisabethville to meet Tshombé without consulting with the central government and argued that it was clear from the initial Security Council resolution that the UN was 'not to act as a neutral organisation' but was 'to place all its resources at the disposal of my government'.[197]

---

[193] *Ibid.*   [194] *Ibid.*   [195] *Ibid.*, p. 88.   [196] *Ibid.*

[197] De Witte, *The Assassination of Lumumba*, p. 14; Cordier and Wilde, *Public Papers, Volume V*, p. 97.

Given the refusal of the UN to provide military assistance to the central government in its attempt to defeat the Belgian-backed secession, the government decided to accept Russian military assistance of 100 trucks and 16 planes to transport troops to the secessionist provinces in order to stage a military campaign against the insurgents.[198] The receipt of Russian aid, together with an attack on civilians by Congolese troops, confirmed Hammarskjöld's view that the UN should not support the central government. In addition, Hammarskjöld stated to the Security Council on 9 September that any support to the central government by outside actors was also an illegal interference in the internal affairs of the Congo. In making that argument, Hammarskjöld again equated the authority of the central government with that of the insurgents in Katanga:

> I have already referred to Belgian assistance in Katanga. But the Belgians are not alone. There are others who follow a similar line, though they justify their policy by reference to the fact that assistance is given to the constitutional government of the country. Admittedly, there is a difference ... I think, however, it should be recognized that this is no longer a question of form and legal justification, but a question of very hard realities, where the use to which the assistance is put is more important than the heading in an export list under which it is registered, or the status of the one to whom it is addressed.[199]

For the USSR, in contrast, the status of the one to whom assistance was addressed was the key question. The UN had no authority to 'control the relation between the Republic of the Congo and other states'.[200] Neither the UN Charter nor the Security Council gave 'any United Nations administrative officer, whoever he may be, the right to intervene in relations between sovereign States unless they request his intervention'.[201]

Executive rule versus the Congolese Parliament

It was in that context of deteriorating relations between the government of Lumumba and the UN that the constitutional crisis in the Congo

---

[198] Abi-Saab, *The United Nations Operation in the Congo*, p. 54.

[199] Cordier and Wilde, *Public Papers, Volume V*, p. 169.

[200] 'Note Verbale dated 5 September 1960 from the Secretary-General of the United Nations to the Delegation of the Union of Soviet Socialist Republics and Note Verbale dated 10 September 1960 from the Delegation of the Union of Soviet Socialist Republics to the Secretary-General of the United Nations', UN SCOR, 15th Sess., UN Doc. S/4503, 11 September 1960.

[201] *Ibid.*

erupted in early September. While the doctrine of impartiality required UN officials to avoid intervening in internal political conflicts, UN officials could not avoid making decisions about which of the competing claimants to authority they would recognise as exercising de facto control.

The actions of the American Andrew Cordier were of particular significance during that period. Cordier worked for the UN from its inception until 1961. He was Hammarskjöld's executive assistant from 1952 until Hammarskjöld's death, and for three key weeks in September 1960 Cordier filled in as the Secretary-General's interim special representative to the Congo.[202] The declassification of UN and US documents relating to the period has made clear that Cordier was liaising and collaborating with US diplomats concerning Congo policy.[203] Whether or not Cordier's actions were taken under instruction from the US Government, his choices had a decisive influence upon the Congo situation.

On 3 September, Cordier was asked to attend a meeting with Kasavubu at his residence.[204] Kasavubu there told him that he intended to dismiss Lumumba. Cordier later wrote to a friend that 'he welcomed the move', but refused Kasavubu's request for UN assistance with the plan.[205] Following the meeting, Cordier consulted Hammarskjöld in New York to see what he should do if Kasavubu proceeded with his plan. Hammarskjöld told Cordier: 'If you have to go ahead time may be more important than our comments . . . At any time you may face the situation of complete disintegration of authority that would put you in a situation of emergency which in my view would entitle you to greater freedom of action in protection of law and order. The degree of disintegration thus widening your rights is a question of judgment.'[206] Two days later, Kasavubu advised Cordier that he was going to dismiss Lumumba that evening. Kasavubu requested that ONUC provide protection for the Presidential residence, deny Lumumba the use of the radio station and close the airport to planes bringing pro-Lumumba troops to Leopoldville.[207]

---

[202] Collins, 'The Cold War Comes to Africa', 245–6.
[203] Ibid., 254–6; Madeleine G. Kalb, The Congo Cables: The Cold War in Africa – From Eisenhower to Kennedy (New York: Macmillan, 1982).
[204] Urquhart, Hammarskjöld, p. 440.
[205] Ibid.; Collins, 'The Cold War Comes to Africa', 260.
[206] Urquhart, Hammarskjöld, p. 441.   [207] Ibid., p. 442; Kalb, The Congo Cables, p. 73.

At 8.15pm on 5 September, in a brief speech broadcast from the Leopoldville radio station, Kasavubu announced that he was dismissing the Prime Minister, Patrice Lumumba, 'because he had "betrayed his trust", deprived "numerous citizens of their fundamental liberties", and involved the country in an "atrocious civil war"'.[208] He also told his audience that he had dismissed six other ministers and had asked the President of the Senate, Mr Ileo, to form a new Cabinet.[209] Less than an hour later, Lumumba responded with a broadcast stating that 'Kasavubu had no power to dismiss a Prime Minister who enjoyed the confidence of the Parliament and that by doing so he had defied the Parliament and the people'.[210] He declared that, subject to the approval of the Parliament, Kasavubu was 'stripped of his office of President of the Republic and his functions were to be exercised by the Central Government'.[211] Lumumba concluded that his dispute with Kasavubu was an internal matter and that no outside power had a right to interfere in it.[212]

Hammarskjöld immediately sent general instructions to Cordier, designed to strengthen him against pressures from 'the various Congolese factions' as well as pressures from foreign embassies.[213] Hammarskjöld's advice was that the UN could continue to take action for the maintenance of law and order, provided it was in accordance with the principles of the UN and the mandate of the Security Council. Such action could be undertaken in consultation with the government, and for those purposes the UN must regard the President as 'the only unquestioned constitutional authority'.[214] Hammarskjöld then allowed himself to make what he described as an 'irresponsible observation': 'In such a situation, responsible people on the spot might commit themselves to what the Secretary-General could not justify doing himself – taking the risk of being disowned when it no longer mattered.'[215]

In the wake of the radio broadcasts, Cordier ordered the closure of all airports and the radio station in Leopoldville. While the actions were neutral in that everyone but the UN was denied access to the airports and to the Leopoldville radio station, the effect was to strengthen the position of the President and the Katangese secessionists, and weaken that of the Prime Minister. Kasavubu's support base was in Leopoldville while Lumumba's supporters were in Stanleyville and Luluabourg and could

---

[208] Kalb, *The Congo Cables*, p. 71.
[209] Abi-Saab, *The United Nations Operation in the Congo*, p. 59.   [210] *Ibid.*, pp. 59–60.
[211] *Ibid.*, p. 60.   [212] *Ibid.*   [213] Urquhart, *Hammarskjöld*, p. 443.
[214] *Ibid.*, p. 444.   [215] *Ibid.*

only reach Leopoldville by plane.[216] Lumumba was not able to move his troops to the secessionist provinces while the airports were closed. In addition, Lumumba was a particularly effective speaker (or a 'far more effective demagogue', to use the language of one UN official), so that depriving Lumumba of the use of the radio denied him a significant political advantage.[217] Through his alliance with President Fulbert Youlou of Congo-Brazzaville, Kasavubu had access to the transmitters of Radio Brazzaville just across the river, and was soon broadcasting to the Leopoldville area from that radio station. While Cordier may not have been aware that closing the airport and the radio station would work to the disadvantage of Lumumba, the fact that Kasavubu had requested these actions might have suggested the propriety of consulting with Lumumba before carrying them out. Instead, Cordier made himself 'unavailable' when Lumumba sought to meet with him on the morning of 6 September.[218]

On 7 and 8 September, Lumumba won the overwhelming support of both houses of the Congolese Parliament, which voted to reinstate him as Prime Minister. Nonetheless, in his speech to a meeting of the Security Council on 9 September, Hammarskjöld asked 'to register the fact that, according to the constitution, the president has the right to revoke the mandate of the prime minister and that his decisions are effective when countersigned by constitutionally responsible ministers', while 'the constitution does not entitle the prime minister under any circumstances to dismiss the chief of state'.[219] Given the conflict between 'the chief of state whom the United Nations must recognize' and 'a cabinet which continued in being, but the chief of which put himself in sharp opposition to the chief of state', the only response available to UN representatives in the Congo was 'to avoid any action by which, directly or indirectly, openly or by implication they would pass judgement on the stand taken by either one of the parties in the conflict'.[220] For that reason, in making decisions about emergency action the UN representatives were effectively unable to consult any Congolese.

> With whom could the United Nations representatives consult in this situation without taking sides? In the light of what I have said, the answer

---

[216] Kalb, *The Congo Cables*, p. 75.
[217] Abi-Saab, *The United Nations Operation in the Congo*, p. 66; Urquhart, *Hammarskjöld*, p. 445.
[218] Collins, 'The Cold War Comes to Africa', 261.
[219] Cordier and Foote, *Public Papers, Volume V*, p. 164.   [220] *Ibid.*

is obvious: they had to act on their own responsibility, within their general mandate, in order to meet the emergency which they were facing. Let me repeat it, there was nobody, really nobody, with whom they could consult without prejudging the constitutional issue.[221]

In response to Hammarskjöld's statement, Kasavubu expressed his 'gratitude', while Lumumba considered it a 'confirmation' of 'the flagrant interference of the United Nations in the internal affairs of the Congo'. According to Lumumba, Hammarskjöld's interpretation 'runs counter to the sovereign decisions taken by the Congolese Parliament, which has annulled by two separate votes, each by a large majority, Mr Kasavubu's illegal decree'. He concluded that: 'It is not for the Secretary-General of the United Nations to interpret the Fundamental Law; that is the responsibility of the Congolese Parliament.'[222]

Despite Hammarskjöld's claim that it was both possible and necessary for the UN to remain impartial, in practice the UN could not avoid recognising particular authorities as collaborators. For example, after the constitutional crisis had erupted, UN officials had to decide which Congolese authorities should be given the $US1 million the UN had available to fund the food and wages of the Congolese army. The payment of those funds was a priority, as a hungry and discontented army was considered a threat to the safety of civilians and to law and order. Cordier authorised the payment of that money to Colonel Mobutu. That decision allowed Mobutu, who had just been appointed chief-of-staff by Kasavubu, 'to win credit for paying the soldiers their past-due salaries, to buy their loyalty for Kasavubu and himself and to pave the way for his coup attempt a few days later'.[223] On 14 September, Mobutu announced that 'he was neutralizing the Chief of State, the two rival governments, and the Parliament until the end of the year and would meanwhile call in "technicians" to run the country'.[224] ONUC officials then had to decide which Congolese authorities they would liaise with in order to administer the country. From September onwards, ONUC officials 'decided to collaborate, as far as civilian operations were concerned, with the *de facto* authorities'.[225] These de facto authorities were the 'technicians' appointed by Mobutu, described by ONUC's Financial Adviser as

[221] *Ibid.*, 165.
[222] 'Communication dated 10 September 1960 from the Prime Minister of the Republic of the Congo Addressed to the Secretary-General of the United Nations', UN SCOR, 15th Sess., UN Doc. S/4498, 10 September 1960.
[223] Collins, 'The Cold War Comes to Africa', 262.   [224] Urquhart, *Hammarskjöld*, p. 451.
[225] West, 'The United Nations and the Congo Financial Crisis', 608.

'non-political' commissioners who 'undertook to reactivate the administrative machinery of the state'.[226] Once Mobutu had come to power, Lumumba remained under virtual house arrest until his escape and subsequent murder by Belgian officers and Katangese leaders in January 1961.

Cordier made clear that his choices were based on his opposition to Lumumba. Cordier dismissed Lumumba as a Communist sympathiser, and 'seemed only bemused by the fact that Lumumba was the democratically elected and legitimate leader of the Congo government, who had received significantly more votes than Kasavubu in the May elections and commanded predominant support in the Congo parliament'.[227] For Cordier, and indeed for other Western UN officials, Lumumba was a dangerous influence who needed to be 'neutralised'.[228] In a letter written to a close confidante during that period, Cordier claimed:

> There is really no such thing as a Congolese Government. Several weeks ago I sent a cable to Dag suggesting that he see someone in the Government about a certain matter. He replied, 'But who can I see?' There is a cabinet, but Lumumba uses it as his tool. Some members of the Cabinet share his vision and lust for power, while the few moderates . . . are understandably fearful to take any positive line.[229]

'But who can I see?' The UN and the recognition of authority in the Congo

Reflecting on this period a year later, Hammarskjöld would comment that 'the unanimous resolution authorizing assistance to the Central Government of the Congo offered little guidance to the Secretary-General when that Government split into competing centres of authority, each claiming to be the Central Government and each supported by different groups of Member States within and outside the Security Council'.[230] Hammarskjöld concluded that the situation in the Congo had clearly revealed 'the special possibilities and responsibilities of the Organization in situations of a vacuum'.[231] Great Powers and other interests from outside Africa had 'seen in the Congo situation a possibility of developments with strong impact on their international position'.[232] They had been able to influence developments in the country 'by

---

[226] *Ibid.*, 608.   [227] Collins, 'The Cold War Comes to Africa', 258.   [228] *Ibid.*, 258.
[229] *Ibid.*   [230] Hammarskjöld, 'The International Civil Servant', p. 344.
[231] UN Secretary-General, *Introduction to the 1961 Annual Report*, p. 4.   [232] *Ibid.*, p. 7.

supporting this or that faction or personality'.[233] The UN, in contrast, truly represented the people of the Congo.

> True to its principles, the United Nations has had to be guided in its operation solely by the interest of the Congolese people and by their right to decide freely for themselves, without any outside influences and with full knowledge of facts.[234]

Neither Congolese officials – dismissed nonchalantly in Hammarskjöld's reference to factions and personalities – nor their international sponsors could claim the authority to rule in Congo. It was the UN that represented the interests of the Congolese people and guarded their right to choose their future. The UN had therefore 'refused – what many may have wished – to permit the weight of its resources to be used in support of any faction so as thereby to prejudge in any way the outcome of a choice which belonged solely to the Congolese people'.[235]

Yet the UN was not, and could not be, neutral in the Congo. It was there as an actor and its action shaped the political situation. The presence of a large military force in the Congo necessarily changed the internal balance of power: in such circumstances 'every act or omission by the Force had a potential effect on the internal situation'.[236] More significantly, it could not be impartial because those with whom it chose to deal gained advantages. The recognition of authority by the UN and other international actors had significant effects on the politics of the Congo. Hammarskjöld asked 'who can I see?' He gave no account of how such choices should be made. Yet he clearly did make choices and those choices were necessarily based on an implicit theory of recognition. He chose efficiency and order over parliamentary support or self-determination. He also sought to support actors whom he thought would act responsibly – 'the best and most responsible elements of all countries of the continent'.[237] He had a clear sense of the proper role of public authority in relation to economic matters. That sense was well illustrated by the following statement to the Security Council, presented at the height of the constitutional crisis and just a little over two months after Congo had gained its independence:

> Members will have gathered from the report that, in spite of the great natural resources of the country, the financial situation is one of bankruptcy. True, there are financial assets, but they are hopelessly

---

[233] *Ibid.*   [234] *Ibid.*   [235] *Ibid.*   [236] Abi-Saab, *The UN Operation in the Congo*, p. 65.
[237] UN Secretary-General, 'Introduction to the 1960 Annual Report', p. 2.

insufficient. And with a complete disruption of civilian and economic life, where are the new revenues, where the foreign exchange, where the taxes, where the customs duties? We face a nation with a budget with all the necessary outlays and nothing to cover them . . .

In this situation spokesmen of the central government speak about the assistance rendered by the international community through the United Nations as if it were an imposition and treat the Organization as if they had all rights and no obligations. They seem to believe that the independence of the Republic of the Congo, in the sense of the international sovereignty of the state which everybody respects, means independence also in a substantive sense of the word which, in our interdependent world of today, is unreal even for a country living by its own means and able to provide for its own security and administration.

A government without financial means is dependent on those who help it to meet its needs. It may depend financially on another state, or group of states, and thereby tie its fate to that of the donors. Or it may depend on the international community in its entirety, represented by the United Nations, and so remain free. There is no third alternative this side of a complete breakdown of the state through inflation or a speedy disintegration of all social and economic services.

. . . These are the hard facts which should be remembered when the relations of the United Nations with the central government are discussed.[238]

This indictment of the Lumumba government was premised upon economic thinking. Hammarskjöld did not suggest that the Congo was no longer sovereign in a formal sense, or that its rulers were political opponents or even evil tyrants who should be punished. Instead, Hammarskjöld simply dismissed the Lumumba government as 'a clumsy, inadequate government that does not do the proper thing'.[239] He was for neutrality in the economic sphere and against redistribution. He was committed to 'bringing the underdeveloped countries into the world market in the proper way'.[240]

Hammarskjöld offered a way of thinking about UN intervention that assumed it was possible, and indeed desirable, to avoid deciding which competing interests or 'factions' to recognise as lawful authorities. The UN, like the state before it, should aim only to act as an impartial arbiter between positions. It should take no role itself in planning, except to the extent of creating the conditions in which individual actors can take their own decisions and thus shape the future. Hammarskjöld offered no developed account of why power should vest with the UN rather than

[238] Cordier and Foote, *Public Papers, Volume 5*, p. 163.
[239] Foucault, *The Birth of Biopolitics*, p. 10.   [240] Urquhart, *Hammarskjöld*, p. 376.

the peoples of decolonised states. He offered no formal explanation as to why the UN executive, rather than other actors within or beyond the UN system, was the appropriate institution to exercise authority over life and death in the decolonised world or to decide when and why preventing conflict takes precedence over other goods (such as redistributing property, realising justice or attacking evil). The insistence upon impartiality as the core principle of executive rule meant that UN officials also had no adequate account of the basis upon which they should choose one set of internal actors rather than another as the appropriate parties with which to engage in practical tasks. As international executive rule became more expansive, the idea that it was a temporary exercise of power that could avoid having any internal political effect or any consequences in terms of consolidating particular forms of authority began to seem increasingly inadequate and implausible.

The master texts of executive action

The Suez and Congo operations initiated a set of practices aimed at 'the maintenance of order in the country and the protection of life' that rapidly expanded during the era of decolonisation. The concepts of preventive diplomacy, peacekeeping and territorial administration are not found in the UN Charter, but have their origin in Hammarskjöld's innovations and the UN's 'operating experiences'.[241] Those practices have continued to be developed on the basis of a very broad mandate to the executive, guided by a minimalist set of principles.

Hammarskjöld deliberately sought to avoid formal questions about status and authority whenever such questions might pose a barrier to achieving support for the mandates he sought. Returning to New York from Cairo on 19 November 1956 after lengthy negotiations with the Egyptian Government, Hammarskjöld reported to the Advisory Committee that the arrangements for the deployment of the UN force were 'becoming almost metaphysical in their subtlety. I have no complaint about that because if, from the beginning of this operation, we had attempted to be specific, we would not have had an operation at all.'[242]

[handwritten marginal note: peace + security & disaster did not come to picture until Somalia]

---

[241] Michael G. Schechter, 'Possibilities for Preventive Diplomacy, Early Warning and Global Monitoring in the Post-Cold War Era; or, the Limits to Global Structural Change' in W. Andy Knight (ed.), *Adapting the United Nations to a Postmodern Era: Lessons Learned* (Hampshire: Palgrave, 2001), p. 52, at p. 55.

[242] Urquhart, *Hammarskjöld*, p. 192.

In seeking a mandate to intervene in the Congo, Hammarskjöld avoided the controversial question of how the Belgian intervention should be characterised in order to gain support for a concrete plan of action to restore order and protect life. Hammarskjöld did not cultivate informality because he sought power and influence for himself. Rather, he believed in the mission of the UN, as did his colleagues. As one former UN official from the Congo noted:

> I did not, it is true, feel personally very happy about the wide spans of ambiguity, the underlying contradictions, in the resolutions which we were supposed to implement. I knew, however, that to Mr Hammarskjöld such ambiguities were the breath of his nostrils, the medium in which he had his being. The greater the ambiguity in a Security Council decision, the wider was the Secretary-General's margin of appreciation. Through ambiguities resolved, through margins skilfully used, the office of Secretary-General had grown in stature and authority far beyond what the framers of the Charter seem to have envisaged at San Francisco . . . To most good 'United Nations people', like myself, this growth seemed entirely healthy. The strengthening of the office was also the strengthening of the international community, the strengthening of the defences of peace . . . We even, I think, found something slightly intoxicating in the paradox of equivocation being used in the service of virtue, the thought of a disinterested Talleyrand, a Machiavelli of peace.[243]

Hammarskjöld persistently characterised intervention as a temporary measure and administration as a form of rule with no effect on internal politics. He rejected any attempts at formalising the outcome of those experiments or creating something permanent out of what he saw as temporary expedients. Hammarskjöld saw the development of international executive rule as a practical or experimental process.

> [T]he value of speculation about what should be the ultimate constitutional form for international cooperation is obviously limited. Those who advocate world government, and this or that special form of world federalism, often present challenging theories and ideas, but we, like our ancestors, can only press against the receding wall which hides the future. It is by such efforts, pursued to the best of our ability, more than by the construction of ideal patterns to be imposed by society, that we lay the basis and pave the way for the society of the future.[244]

---

[243] O'Brien, *To Katanga and Back*, p. 47.
[244] Dag Hammarskjöld, 'The Development of a Constitutional Framework' in Wilder Foote (ed.), *The Servant of Peace: A Selection of the Speeches and Statements of Bag Hammarskjöld* (London: The Bodley Head. 1962), p. 252.

For Hammarskjöld, that sense of the UN as an experiment also gave 'a broader and more organic sense of the role of law – again I use the word in its broadest sense, including not only written law but the whole social pattern of established rules of action and behaviour'.[245] In the aftermath of Suez, Hammarskjöld gave a similar account 'of how we work in the United Nations'.[246]

> The Force was created in an emergency situation, and for that reason we had to improvise. We had to improvise in the field of international law, in the field of military organization, in various fields where usually one does not like to jump into cold water and start swimming without having learned how best to swim. That means that the Force, as established, cannot, in my view, serve as a good foundation on which to build anything permanent of the very same form. But it does serve as an extremely useful and valuable experiment. We have learned very much. And, in the Secretariat, I have started a study which will digest our experiences, work out some kind of blueprint, master texts of the kind needed for this kind of operation. That means that, if another operation of a similar type should arise, where the same need would be felt, we would not have the Force but we would have everything ready in such a way that we would not again improvise . . . I think that the counsel of wisdom is, in the first instance, to digest the experience, to work out what I call the blueprints, the master texts for agreements, for orders, and so on and so forth . . . to get that firmly in hand, and then work with that as the emergency arrangement.[247]

As that passage suggests, while Hammarskjöld rejected the idea that past precedents should be used as the basis for the creation of 'anything permanent of the very same form', he nonetheless considered it necessary to produce 'some kind of blueprint' or a set of 'master texts of the kind needed for this kind of operation'. These master texts would be addressed to the executive itself, and would ensure that civil servants 'would not again improvise'. According to Hammarskjöld, the Congo operation revealed the value of having the necessary master texts in place to enable executive action to be undertaken swiftly when the need arose.

> The value of such preparedness can be seen from the fact that the organization of the United Nations Force in the Congo was considerably facilitated by the fact that it was possible for the Secretary-General to

---

[245] Ibid., p. 252.
[246] Dag Hammarskjöld, 'The Uses of Private Diplomacy' in Wilder Foote (ed.), The Servant of Peace: A Selection of the Speeches and Statements of Dag Hammarskjöld (London: The Bodley Head, 1962), p. 170.
[247] Ibid., p. 173.

> draw on the experience of the United Nations Emergency Force in Gaza and on the conclusions regarding various questions of principle and law which had been reached on the basis of that experience. The Congo operation being far more complicated and far bigger than the Gaza operation, it is likely that it will lead to a new series of valuable experiences which should be fully utilized by the United Nations, by appropriate informal planning within the administration.[248]

It was through 'appropriate informal planning within the administration', rather than through the attempt to create something 'permanent' or formal, that executive action would proceed. Hammarskjöld systematically digested the principles and lessons to be learned from past operations, and transmitted these as 'master texts' or instruction manuals for emergency governance. As the Congo case illustrated, Hammarskjöld himself referred to previous operations as 'precedents' and treated the principles that arose from them as constraints on his freedom of action.

The development of executive action was thus accompanied by a persistent tendency to avoid offering a public and formalised account of UN authority on the one hand, while systematically developing and codifying the principles gained from practice on the other. That combination of external informality and internal formality would shape the management of decolonisation over the next fifty years. Digests of practice and principle were passed on through UN culture in the form of lessons-learned reports, mandates, studies and rules of engagement. Through the systematisation of these practices of protection and the principles derived from past experience, a new form of international authority took shape. Neutrality, impartiality and independence were to continue as the primary form of self-description used by UN officials to explain their actions to themselves. These minimalist principles did not define in any detail the ends of international executive rule, the constraints on that power or any limitations on the means by which executive power would be exercised.

The expansion of executive rule and the challenge to international authority

The role of the UN in the post-Cold War world

Hammarskjöld had developed his model of preventive diplomacy in the context of the Cold War. The aim was to fill the kind of post-colonial

---

[248] UN Secretary-General, 'Introduction to the 1960 Annual Report', p. 4.

political vacuum that Hammarskjöld detected in Congo, in order to prevent superpower intervention that could exacerbate the immediate conflict and increase Cold War tensions. With the end of the Cold War, the concept of security, and thus the ends to which the conflict prevention machinery of the UN was to be put, became more ambitious. The expansive apparatus of techniques developed at the UN for conflict-prevention, peacekeeping and civil administration would no longer be limited to filling a political, economic, social or military vacuum. Instead, they would be used for detecting possible causes of conflict and acting early to prevent disputes arising.

The Security Council signalled its adoption of a broader meaning of 'threats to the peace' in a 1992 statement issued after the first Council meeting at the level of heads of state and government. The members of the Security Council declared that the 'absence of war and military conflicts amongst States does not in itself ensure international peace and security', and that 'non-military sources of instability in the economic, social, humanitarian and ecological fields have become threats to peace and security'.[249] In an influential 1992 report entitled 'An Agenda for Peace' then Secretary-General Boutros Boutros-Ghali indicated the expansive role to be played by conflict prevention in such an environment:

> The most desirable and efficient employment of diplomacy is to ease tensions before they result in conflict – or, if conflict breaks out, to act swiftly to contain it and resolve its underlying causes.[250]

Conflict prevention and resolution required 'early warning based on information gathering and informal or formal fact-finding', as well as 'preventive deployment and, in some situations, demilitarized zones'.[251] Boutros-Ghali stated that prevention 'must be based upon timely and accurate knowledge of the facts'.[252] The facts required by the UN 'now must encompass economic and social trends as well as political developments that may lead to dangerous tensions'.[253] Thus there was a need for 'an increased resort to fact-finding ... initiated either by the

---

[249] President of the Security Council, 'Note by the President of the Security Council', UN SCOR, 47th Sess., UN Doc. S/23500, 31 January 1992, p. 3.

[250] UN Secretary-General, 'An Agenda for Peace: Preventive diplomacy, peacemaking and peace-keeping, Report of the Secretary-General pursuant to the statement adopted by the Summit Meeting of the Security Council on 31 January 1992', A/47/277-S/24111, 17 June 1992, para. 23.

[251] Ibid.   [252] Ibid., para. 25.   [253] Ibid.

Secretary-General, to enable him to meet his responsibilities under the Charter, including Article 99, or by the Security Council or the General Assembly'.[254] More broadly the UN needed to develop proper integrated systems for gathering and interpreting information relating to the risk of conflict.

> In recent years the United Nations system has been developing a valuable network of early warning systems concerning environmental threats, the risk of nuclear accident, natural disasters, mass movements of populations, the threat of famine and the spread of disease. There is a need, however, to strengthen arrangements in such a manner that information from these sources can be synthesized with political indicators to assess whether a threat to peace exists and to analyze what action might be taken by the United Nations to alleviate it.[255]

As the conception of security and the ends of conflict prevention grew more expansive, 'unprecedented demands' for diplomacy, peace operations, refugee protection and administration began to be placed on the Secretariat and UN agencies.[256] The UN was asked to respond to natural disasters, warn of impending crises, establish inquiries and fact-finding missions, appoint special representatives, conduct peacekeeping operations in situations of civil war and conflict and set up war crimes tribunals. The forms of executive rule initiated by Hammarskjöld thus came to play an increasingly significant role in the administration of life in decolonised states in the post Cold-War era.

During the 1990s, the scale of international executive action increased dramatically. For example, the mandates granted to UN peacekeeping forces extended beyond the traditional task of monitoring ceasefires to include 'the full spectrum of peacebuilding activities, from providing secure environments to monitoring human rights and rebuilding the capacity of the state'.[257] The number of peacekeepers deployed by the UN increased from around 10,000 at the end of 1990 to more than 78,000 by July 1993.[258] Peacekeeping became established as a core technique of international rule in the aftermath of the Cold War – by the end of 2009,

---

[254] *Ibid.*   [255] *Ibid.*, para. 26.

[256] Schechter, 'Possibilities for Preventive Diplomacy', p. 53.

[257] Victoria Holt and Glyn Taylor with Max Kelly, *Protecting Civilians in the Context of UN Peacekeeping Operations: Successes, Setbacks and Remaining Challenges*, Independent study jointly commissioned by the Department of Peacekeeping Operations and the Office for the Coordination of Humanitarian Affairs (New York: United Nations, 2009).

[258] United Nations, *United Nations Peace Operations 2009: Year in Review* (New York: United Nations, 2010).

the UN Department of Peacekeeping Operations (DPO) could claim that it led 'the world's second largest deployed military force (after that of the US)'.[259]

UN civilian operations also became significantly more ambitious in scope and scale during the 1990s. It was during this period that the UN took on responsibility for the plenary administration of Kosovo and East Timor. While international organisations had long been involved in territorial administration, administrators in Kosovo and East Timor had to 'face challenges and responsibilities that are unique among UN field operations'.[260] Administrators were authorised, inter alia, to 'set and enforce the law, establish customs services and regulations, set and collect business and personal taxes, attract foreign investment, adjudicate property disputes and liabilities for war damage, reconstruct and operate all public utilities, create a banking system, run schools and pay teachers, and collect the garbage'.[261]

Similarly, during the post-Cold War period UN agencies in the humanitarian field began to exercise an increasing range of governmental powers in order to provide services and protection to populations throughout the decolonised world. To take one example, by the end of 2008 the UN High Commission for Refugees, the UN agency with responsibility for providing protection and support to refugees, asylum-seekers and internally displaced people, estimated that it was responsible for a total population of 34.4 million.[262] In addition, other international institutions such as the International Monetary Fund and the World Bank increasingly took up the task of determining social policy and shaping the administration of life in African, Asian, Latin American and Eastern European states.

Over that period, humanitarian action undertaken by NGOs also expanded significantly. The amount of overseas development aid directed to humanitarian assistance increased from just over $US2 billion in 1990 to $US4.6 billion in 1991.[263] By 2007, international funding from

[259] Ibid., pp. 3, 5.

[260] Panel on United Nations Peace Operations, 'Report to the United Nations Secretary-General', UN GAOR, 55th Sess., Provisional Agenda Item 87; UN SCOR, 55th Sess., UN Doc. A/55/305-S/2000/809, 21 August 2000, para. 77.

[261] Ibid.

[262] UNHCR, 2008 Global Trends: Refugees, Asylum-seekers, Returnees, Internally Displaced and Stateless Persons, 16 June 2009, www.unhcr.org/4a375c426.html.

[263] Development Initiatives, Global Humanitarian Assistance 2000 (Geneva: The Inter-Agency Standing Committee, 2000), p. 1.

official (governmental and UN) and public (charitable and corporate) sources devoted to humanitarian assistance amounted to $US15 billion.[264] Almost one-third of that was channelled through NGOs. International humanitarian action gave rise to 'a set of institutions, a business and an industry' that provided employment for hundreds of thousands of people.[265] Many of those employed by the humanitarian sector were nationals of countries to which assistance was directed, but there was also an influential minority of staff from Western countries, who 'set the standards and terms for the functioning of the enterprise'.[266]

Executive rule and the rise of managerialism

The expansion of the practices of fact-finding, peacekeeping and administration in the immediate post-Cold War period consolidated executive and military rule in the decolonised world. Peace operations and territorial administrations, such as those undertaken by the Interim Administration Mission in Kosovo (UNMIK) and the United Nations Transitional Administration in East Timor (UNTAET), created new legal orders, in which the decrees and regulations passed by international administrators prevailed over the laws in force prior to the international administrations or subsequently passed by local parliaments.[267] In territories under international control, judicial independence was routinely subordinated to executive rule. To take one example, UNMIK closely controlled 'the appointment and removal of judges and prosecutors from office'.[268] Judges were appointed as UNMIK employees for short terms and UNMIK retained a wide margin of appreciation regarding the decision to dismiss a judge or prosecutor. UNMIK rejected criticisms of its practice, stating:

These are temporary arrangements

> Administrative independence and security of tenure are essential for the justice system which UNMIK must build for Kosovo's future, but the [international judges and prosecutors] are not part of that future. They are a special force for intervention to enable UNMIK to administer impartial justice at this early phase, when the local judiciary is too weak

---

[264] Development Initiatives, *Global Humanitarian Assistance Report 2009* (Wells: Development Initiatives, 2009), p. 1.

[265] Antonio Donini, 'The Far Side: The Meta Functions of Humanitarianism in a Globalised World', *Disasters* 34 (2010), S220 at S221.

[266] *Ibid.*, S232.

[267] Carsten Stahn, *The Law and Practice of International Territorial Administration: Versailles to Iraq and Beyond* (Cambridge: Cambridge University Press, 2008), p. 664.

[268] *Ibid.*, p. 702.

to be able to withstand the societal pressures on it in the aftermath of the conflict. Their appointment and deployment is therefore highly tactical, and must be under the United Nations' direct control.[269]

UN civilian and military officials increasingly authorised executive detention of those considered to pose a threat to public peace and order. For example, officials of the United Nations Operation in Somalia (UNOSOM) II decided that suspects could be detained 'when the public authorities [had] reasonable grounds to believe that the detainee represents a threat to public order'.[270] UNMIK authorised the temporary detention, or restriction on the freedom of movement, of individuals who pose a 'threat to public peace and order', including those who pose a threat to 'a safe and secure environment' or to 'public safety and order'.[271] UNMIK explained its use of executive detentions for security reasons in the following terms:

> The situation in Kosovo is analogous to emergency situations envisioned in the human rights conventions. We emphasise that UNMIK's mandate was adopted under Chapter VII, which means that the situation calls for extraordinary means and force can be used to carry out the mandate. Any deprivation of liberty by an Executive Order is temporary and extraordinary, and its objective is the effective and impartial administration of justice.[272]

International actors exercised these expansive executive powers while enjoying wide-ranging privileges and immunities. The UN as a legal person has absolute immunity under the UN Convention on Privileges and Immunities of 13 February 1946 (the General Convention), and UN officials are granted immunity 'in respect of words spoken or written and all acts performed by them in their official capacity'.[273] The head of the mission and other senior officials enjoy diplomatic privileges and immunities in addition to their functional immunity.[274] Military personnel generally enjoy criminal immunity and functional immunity under Status of Forces Agreements negotiated between the UN and the host state.[275] In addition, the international administrations themselves have passed regulations granting expansive immunity and privileges to personnel. The practice of granting broad-ranging privileges and immunities to international actors was designed to protect the UN and peacekeepers from 'interference by the government of the territory in which they operate'.[276]

[269] *Ibid.*, p. 703.   [270] *Ibid.*, p. 692.   [271] *Ibid.*, p. 693.   [272] *Ibid.*, p. 507.
[273] *Ibid.*, p. 582.   [274] *Ibid.*   [275] *Ibid.*, p. 584.   [276] *Ibid.*, p. 581.

The tendency towards executive rule was intensified by the managerial structure adopted by many of the NGOs that depended upon donor governments for funding. The 1990s saw a growing tendency for donor countries to integrate development aid and humanitarian assistance programmes with foreign and security policy.[277] Many NGOs perceived the politicisation of aid as a major challenge to their humanitarian mandate.[278] Yet just as significant was the new managerial culture required of NGOs seeking to prove their reliability to government donors.[279] NGOs seeking government funding and contracts developed an increasingly professionalised and centralised leadership and a managerial culture of efficiency and accountability.[280] Funds were earmarked for specific projects decided upon by bureaucrats in donor countries rather than the parliaments of states under administration.

As in Hammarskjöld's era, the exercise of executive rule during the 1990s continued to be justified as temporary and apolitical, and was accompanied by a minimalist set of operating principles rather than a developed account of international authority. The UN continued to rely upon a set of principles inherited from Hammarskjöld to explain and guide the conduct of peace and humanitarian operations. These principles were transmitted through directives, guidelines, standard operating procedures, manuals and training materials produced by the Secretariat. Peace operations were organised around the principles of impartiality, neutrality, consent and the limited use of force first articulated in relation to UNEF. In 2000, a UN report on the future of peace operations referred to consent, impartiality and the use of force in self-defence as the 'bedrock principles' of peacekeeping.[281] Scholars argued that these principles had 'acquired constitutional status' and defined 'the essence of peacekeeping'.[282] The authors of a 2008 UN report that aims 'to codify the major lessons learned from the past six decades of United Nations

[277] Development Initiatives, *Global Humanitarian Assistance 2000*, p. x.   [278] *Ibid.*, p. xi.
[279] See generally Sadhvi Dar and Bill Cooke (eds.), *The New Development Management: Critiquing the Dual Modernization* (London: Zed Books, 2008).
[280] James Heartfield, 'Contextualising the Anti-capitalism Movement in Global Civil Society' in Gideon Baker and David Chandler (eds.), *Global Civil Society: Contested Futures* (London: Routledge, 2005), pp. 87, 96.
[281] Panel on United Nations Peace Operations, 'Report to the Secretary-General', UN GAOR, 55th Sess., Provisional Agenda Item 87, UN Doc. A/55/305-S/2000/809, 21 August 2000, para. 48.
[282] Nicholas Tsagourias, 'Consent, Neutrality/Impartiality and the Use of Force in Peacekeeping: Their Constitutional Dimension', *Journal of Conflict and Security Law* 11 (2009), 465 at 466.

peacekeeping experience' comment that while over that period peace-keeping had evolved into 'a complex, global undertaking', it had been guided 'by a largely unwritten body of principles'.[283] The report confirms that the 'three basic principles' of peacekeeping continue to be consent of the parties, impartiality and non-use of force except in self-defence or the defence of the mandate.[284] UN operations must be implemented 'without favour or prejudice to any party'.[285]

Executive rule and the question of authority

The authority of the UN to exercise increasing amounts of executive power had continued to be explained in terms of the minimalist principles of neutrality, independence and impartiality. Those principles were increasingly unable to offer either operationally useful or ideologically satisfying answers to questions about authority that arose as a result of the growth of the power of the international executive. Those questions took two main forms.

The first set of questions about authority concerned issues of recognition. With which local actors should the UN engage? Was impartiality an appropriate or useful principle to draw upon in answering that question? International humanitarians, as well as their critics, increasingly felt that it was not. In *Sovereignty as Responsibility*, Francis Deng described the approach that international actors took to dealing with de facto authorities:

> [I]t is not always easy to determine the degree to which the government of a country devastated by civil war can be said to be truly in control, when, as is often the case, sizable portions of the territory are controlled by rebel or opposing forces . . . Indeed, the international community modifies its traditional ideas of sovereignty when it finds civilian populations in areas of states controlled by insurgent groups. Then the international community sometimes deals directly with those populations and insurgent movements. Increasingly, humanitarian agencies have been establishing dialogues with nongovernmental actors in order to reach persons on all sides of conflict situations.[286]

---

[283] United Nations, *United Nations Peacekeeping Operations: Principles and Guidelines* (New York: United Nations, 2008), pp. 7–8.

[284] *Ibid.*, p. 31.   [285] *Ibid.*, p. 33.

[286] Francis M. Deng *et al.*, *Sovereignty as Responsibility: Conflict Management in Africa* (Washington DC: The Brookings Institution Press, 1996), p. 16.

As in Congo, international executive action necessarily involved controversial decisions about which local actors to recognise as collaborators, whether on the basis of pragmatic decisions about who could effectively exercise control in a region or more legalist decisions about who could properly claim to represent the people. The political issues raised by the decision to engage with de facto leaders became an issue of pressing concern during the 1990s for humanitarians working in the refugee camps of eastern Zaire and Tanzania following the Rwandan genocide. *Génocidaires* had taken control of many of those camps, dividing them into prefectures, killing and threatening people who disobeyed them and using the camps as a base to launch raids into Rwanda.[287] While the UN High Commissioner for Refugees (UNHCR) and other humanitarian agencies had 'developed speedy and sophisticated mechanisms to deliver medicine, food, sanitation, and shelter to refugees in crisis',[288] the *génocidaires* 'manipulated the aid system to entrench their control over the refugees and diverted resources to finance their own activities'.[289] The UNHCR special envoy to the Great Lakes commented: 'The UNHCR emergency field manual said, "Find the natural leaders and get them to help you distribute relief" . . . We didn't think this through, but it meant: Give the genocidal leaders more power.'[290] The French section of Médecins Sans Frontières (MSF) took the view that aid was contributing to the conflict, that the distribution of resources was creating a vehicle for control over the population that could be abused by the *génocidaires* and consequently took the controversial decision to withdraw their assistance from the camps.[291] It became increasingly difficult to argue that humanitarian action could be neutral or impartial in a strong sense.

Some administrators were comfortable taking a partisan position in relation to internal conflicts between authorities. Indeed, from Cordier in the Congo onwards, there were numerous international officials who considered that it was necessary to sideline those local leaders or elected officials who were resistant to implementing the policies decided by the international community. In Bosnia-Herzegovina, for example, the High Representative used his authority to impose legislation drafted by international actors but rejected by democratically elected state and entity

---

[287] Samantha Power, *Chasing the Flame: Sergio Vieira de Mello and the Fight to Save the World* (London: Penguin Books, 2008), p. 192.

[288] *Ibid.*, p. 192.

[289] Fiona Terry, *Condemned to Repeat?: The Paradox of Humanitarian Action* (New York: Cornell University Press, 2002), p. 2.

[290] Power, *Chasing the Flame*, p. 193.   [291] Terry, *Condemned to Repeat?*, pp. 1–16.

bodies, to ban political parties, and to dismiss 'obstructive' elected and appointed officials.[292] The former High Representative, Wolfgang Petritsch, made clear that this capacity to dismiss officials, ban parties and impose legislation extends to situations where parliamentarians refuse to pass legislation drafted by the international community implementing far-reaching economic reforms.[293] In an interview with *Slobodna Bosna* in November 2001, Petritsch explained that elected politicians do not have the right to reject legislation imposing radical economic reform:

> I want to see the immediate adoption of the laws which are pending before the State Parliament. That is the first thing they have to do. If some representatives are concerned about the content of some laws, from the professional point of view, they can discuss it. However, it will not be acceptable whatsoever to reject the laws with the argument that they are unacceptable or that they do not want to deal with these laws at all. The laws concerning economic reform and development are essential, and they simply have to be passed. In case this does not happen, you can be sure that I will not hesitate to exercise my powers.[294]

International administrators also took steps to prevent such situations arising, by delaying the holding of elections until the outcomes could be managed properly. The experience gained in preparing countries for transition to democracy led to a shift in policy in UN administration during the 1990s.[295] In Cambodia, for instance: 'Some of the very laws and regulations that had been enacted by the UN administration were reversed.'[296] As a result, the UN adopted the policy of 'no exit without strategy'. It was felt that elections should only be held once there are 'follow-up strategies', because 'elections do not *per se* suffice to manage successful transitions'.[297] 'It must be sufficiently clear at the outset of the mission what shall follow after the elections.'[298] If not, the post-administration period could see 'a return to previous customs and power configurations'. The goal is for the ends of the administrators to become the ends of the local people as well. If not, 'local actors' may 'lose the

---

[292] Anne Orford, *Reading Humanitarian Intervention: Human Rights and the Use of Force in International Law* (Cambridge: Cambridge University Press, 2003), pp. 127–39.
[293] 'Interview: Wolfgang Petritsch, the High Representative in BiH: "What message I got across to the SDS"', 9 November 2001, www.ohr.int/ohr-dept/presso/pressi/ (accessed 13 November 2001).
[294] *Ibid.*
[295] Stahn, *The Law and Practice of International Territorial Administration*, p. 728.
[296] *Ibid.*   [297] *Ibid.*, p. 726.   [298] *Ibid.*, p. 729.

willingness to implement standards' and perhaps even 'fail to develop a sense of responsibility for the management of "their" affairs'.[299] The UN was also willing to design electoral rules in order to ensure that parties or individuals deemed unsuitable from an international perspective were not elected. For example, during the administration of East Timor, UNTAET passed a regulation decreeing that elections to the newly created Constituent Assembly would be conducted on the basis of pro-portional representation, 'a choice made in order to reduce the influence of the major party (FRETILIN)'.[300]

The second set of issues about international authority concerned questions of jurisdiction. Why should the UN, rather than the people of a territory, have the authority to decide who should govern? Why did the UN, rather than other external claimants to authority such as the North Atlantic Treaty Organization (NATO), have the authority to determine and defend international values? Why should the executive rather than the parliamentary organs of the UN have power to shape the meaning given to peace and security in the post-Cold War world? The East Timorese, for example, were shocked when on 25 October 1999 the Security Council took decision-making about East Timor 'out of Timorese hands'.[301] Security Council Resolution 1272 announced the establishment of the UN Transitional Administration in East Timor and endowed it 'with overall responsibility for the administration of East Timor' and the power 'to exercise all legislative and executive authority,

(handwritten marginalia: But this has not happened)

---

[299] *Ibid.*, p. 730.

[300] The reasons for the UN's attempt to reduce the influence of FRETILIN are unclear. FRETILIN (*Frente Revolucionária do Timor-Leste Independente* or Revolutionary Front for an Independent East Timor) was the most popular of the groups contesting power during the preparations for Timorese independence in 1974. On 28 November 1975, in the context of repeated cross-border attacks by Indonesian special forces seeking to provoke civil war and thus provide an alibi for intervention, FRETILIN declared Timor's independence. A little over a week later, on 7 December 1975, Indonesia launched a general invasion of Timor, carried out with the knowledge and tacit support of the US, UK and Australian governments. This support was motivated by issues of regional security, concern that an independent Timor might align itself with China and, in the case of Australia, the desire to secure access to Timor Sea oil and gas. In the democratic elections for the Constituent Assembly held in 2001, FRETILIN won 57 per cent of the vote, and its Secretary-General Mari Alkatiri became Chief Minister. See further Anne Orford, 'What Can We Do to Stop People Harming Others? Humanitarian Intervention in Timor-Leste (East Timor)' in Jenny Edkins and Maja Zehfuss (eds.), *Global Politics: A New Introduction* (London and New York: Routledge, 2009), p. 427.

[301] Power, *Chasing the Flame*, p. 299.

including the administration of justice'.[302] José Ramos-Horta commented: 'Imagine a transition in South Africa, where Mandela wasn't given the ultimate authority. Imagine if some UN official were given all the power and told it was up to him whether he felt like consulting Mandela or not.'[303]

Many of the debates and concerns about the reality and desirability of the UN commitment to impartiality came to a head in 1999. 1999 was the year in which NATO circumvented the UN Security Council to intervene in Kosovo. While some states and commentators saw the NATO intervention as illegal and ineffective, others asserted that there was strong 'moral or humanitarian justification for the action' and welcomed the intervention as 'a long overdue internationalization of the human conscience'.[304] 1999 was also the year in which the reports of two UN inquiries were published – one into the responsibility of the UN for allowing genocide to unfold in Rwanda in 1994 and the other into the responsibility of the UN for the failure to protect the inhabitants of the UN-created safe haven of Srebrenica from genocide in 1995.[305] In the aftermath of those genocides, both internal and external critics questioned the viability of the long-standing commitment to impartiality and neutrality on the part of UN peacekeepers and humanitarian agencies in situations of mass atrocity. In the words of a major UN report into the future of UN peace operations, although impartiality should remain one of the 'bedrock principles' of peacekeeping, there are cases where 'local parties consist not of moral equals but of obvious aggressors and victims'.[306] In such situations, 'continued equal treatment of all parties by the United Nations can in the best case result in ineffectiveness and in the worst may amount to complicity with evil'.[307]

---

[302] SC Res. 1272, UN SCOR, 54th Sess., 4057th Mtg., UN Doc. S/RES/1272, 25 October 1999, para. 1.

[303] Power, *Chasing the Flame*, p. 300.

[304] ICISS, *The Responsibility to Protect* (Ottawa: International Development Research Centre, 2001), p. vii.

[305] UN Secretary-General, 'Report of the Secretary-General pursuant to General Assembly Resolution 53/35: The Fall of Srebrenica', UN GAOR, 54th Sess., Agenda Item 42, UN Doc. A/54/549, 15 November 1999; 'Report of the Independent Inquiry into the Actions of the United Nations during the 1994 Genocide in Rwanda', UN SCOR, 54th Sess., UN Doc. S/1999/1257, 15 December 1999, annex.

[306] Panel on United Nations Peace Operations, 'Report to the United Nations Secretary-General', pp. ix, 9.

[307] *Ibid.*, p. ix.

For many NGOs and for the UN, the initial answer was found in the new rights-based humanitarianism. Many UN officials and other humanitarian actors responded to the perceived need to become more political and less impartial through the turn to human rights. The abandonment of impartiality and neutrality, and the concomitant embrace of human rights as a basis for taking sides in a conflict or determining which people to assist, ushered in the 'new humanitarianism'.[308] By the late 1990s, many humanitarian relief agencies and NGOs had embraced human rights and values as the basis for their action, and accepted the resulting creation of a new distinction between deserving and undeserving victims. The UN had moved away from the austere ethics of the 'humanitarian imperative' and towards a commitment to prosecuting evil and refusing to negotiate with tyrants. It was in this context that Kofi Annan famously asked the members of the General Assembly: 'if humanitarian intervention is, indeed, an unacceptable assault on sovereignty, how should we respond to a Rwanda, to a Srebrenica – to gross and systematic violations of human rights that affect every precept of our common humanity?'[309] He warned that the UN had to earn its place as the 'greatest tribune' of the 'collective conscience of humanity'.[310] If international actors cannot be neutral, then they must embrace transcendental rights or values rather than politics as the basis for their choice as to which authorities to recognise within a territory. Yet abandoning impartiality did not resolve questions about authority – it merely raised them in a different form. The principle of impartiality had at least made the basis for engaging in international action clear in theory: the international executive must assist 'all in need and in proportion to that need'.[311] To focus upon fighting evil required political decisions 'about rightness and just causes'.[312]

---

[308] Fiona Fox, 'New Humanitarianism: Does It Provide a Moral Banner for the 21st Century?', *Disasters* 25 (2001), 275.

[309] UN Secretary-General, 'We the Peoples: The Role of the United Nations in the 21st Century', UN GAOR, 54th Sess., Agenda Item 49(b), UN Doc. A/54/2000, 27 March 2000, p. 48.

[310] UN, 'Secretary-General Presents His Annual Report to General Assembly', UN Press Release SG/SM/7136 GA/9596, 20 September 1999, www.un.org/News/Press/docs/1999/19990920.sgsm7136.html.

[311] Nicholas Leader, 'Proliferating Principles; or How to Sup with the Devil without Getting Eaten', *Disasters* 22 (1998), 288.

[312] *Ibid.*

In many conflicts all or most civil structures will be to some extent politicised and co-opted into the conflict. Although in some conflicts the 'just cause' is clear, in most this is not the case. If the principle of impartiality is rejected, who is to judge which is which?[313]

The responsibility to protect and the legacy of Hammarskjöld

The responsibility to protect concept offers a response to those questions about authority that had arisen with the expansion of international executive action in the decolonised world. It seeks to consolidate and systematise the practices initiated by Hammarskjöld, and to offer a coherent account of authority through which international officials can interpret their role to themselves and to those they govern. The turn to protection can be seen as an attempt to address growing questions about the legitimacy of international humanitarianism. It has strengthened the idea that the UN has the responsibility and the capacity to maintain peace in the decolonised world, and to coordinate international functions of law-making, discipline and security.

The techniques of protection

At a practical level, the responsibility to protect concept focuses upon expanding the institutional capacity of the UN to respond to protection challenges through creating coordinated systems of early warning and information analysis. It offers a framework to guide analysis and decision-making. The responsibility to protect concept thus builds upon and systematises the practices of executive rule initiated by Hammarskjöld. According to the ICISS report, the responsibility to protect encompasses a responsibility to prevent conflict, to react to conflict and to rebuild after conflict.[314] Although that sounds like a temporal description, it is in fact better understood as a way of thinking about groups of techniques – techniques for prevention such as surveillance, techniques for reaction such as the use of force and techniques for rebuilding such as administration, security sector reform and economic development. The focus of the responsibility to protect concept is upon consolidating and streamlining the existing practices of protection that have developed and been institutionalised since the late 1950s, such as administration, surveillance, fact-finding, quiet diplomacy, management, capacity-building and policing.

[313] *Ibid.*   [314] *Ibid.*, pp. 19, 29, 39.

The types of action needed to achieve protection may include military intervention. But the report also lists many other potential actions that may be designed to achieve this end, including the provision of development assistance or support for 'local initiatives to advance good governance, human rights, or the rule of law',[315] the deployment of 'good offices missions' or 'mediation efforts to promote dialogue or reconciliation',[316] monitoring and reporting on human rights abuses,[317] receiving and analysing 'sensitive information from member states',[318] promoting better terms of trade for developing economies,[319] reforming the military and state security services[320] or prosecuting 'perpetrators of crimes against humanity' before the International Criminal Court (ICC).[321] According to ICISS, the responsibility to protect also brings with it a responsibility on the part of the international community 'to build a durable peace' in the aftermath of military intervention.[322] That may require 'staying in the country for some period of time after the initial purposes of the intervention have been accomplished'.[323]

The General Assembly accepted this broad vision of the kinds of techniques that might be authorised as an exercise of the responsibility to protect.[324] UN members undertook to help states build 'capacity to protect their populations', assist 'those which are under stress before crises and conflicts break out' and support the UN to establish 'an early warning capability'.[325] In addition, states undertook 'to use appropriate diplomatic, humanitarian and other peaceful means . . . to help to protect populations' and to take 'collective action, in a timely and decisive manner, through the Security Council, in accordance with the Charter' in situations where 'peaceful means' prove inadequate and 'national authorities are manifestly failing to protect their populations from genocide, war crimes, ethnic cleansing and crimes against humanity'.[326] The World Summit Outcome 'puts relatively little weight on military or coercive responses' and gives 'priority attention' to a 'raft of less coercive measures'.[327] Thus although the scope of the responsibility to protect concept is narrow, being limited to 'the four crimes and violations agreed

---

[315] *Ibid.*, p. 19. [316] *Ibid.* [317] *Ibid.*, pp. 20–1. [318] *Ibid.*, p. 22. [319] *Ibid.*, p. 23.
[320] *Ibid.* [321] *Ibid.*, p. 24. [322] *Ibid.*, p. 39. [323] *Ibid.*
[324] '2005 World Summit Outcome', GA Res. 60/1, UN GAOR, 60th Sess., 8th Plen. Mtg., Agenda Items 46 and 120, Supp. No. 49, UN Doc. A/RES/60/1, 24 October 2005 (adopted 16 September 2005), para. 139.
[325] *Ibid.*, paras. 138–9. [326] *Ibid.*
[327] Edward C. Luck, *The United Nations and the Responsibility to Protect* (Muscatine: Stanley Foundation Policy Analysis Brief, August 2008), pp. 5–6.

by the world leaders in 2005', the techniques for its implementation are broad.[328] According to Secretary-General Ban Ki-moon, those techniques involve 'utilizing the whole prevention and protection tool kit available to the United Nations system, to its regional and subregional and civil society partners, and not least to the Member States themselves', with the aim of 'integrating the system's multiple channels of information and assessment'.[329]

The implementation phase of the responsibility to protect project has also been understood to involve much more than responding to conflicts through force, and to extend to preserving life and protecting populations through prevention, punishment, development and post-conflict administration. The Secretary-General's 2009 Report on Implementing the Responsibility to Protect makes clear that the responsibility to protect concept is not intended to create new practices of protection but rather to offer a 'unifying perspective' that 'would facilitate system-wide coherence'.[330] The UN's approach to implementing the responsibility to protect rests upon three 'pillars'. Pillar one involves 'the protection responsibilities of the State'.[331] Meeting that responsibility requires states to build 'institutions, capacities and practices for the constructive management of the tensions so often associated with the uneven growth or rapidly changing circumstances that appear to benefit some groups more than others', and engage in 'self-reflection' and 'periodic risk assessment' to ensure that they are not vulnerable to mass atrocities.[332] Pillar two involves international assistance and capacity-building. States can be assisted to protect their populations either through 'persuasive measures' such as diplomacy or preventive deployment of peacekeepers, or through 'positive incentives' such as development assistance.[333] In addition, 'military assistance to help beleaguered States deal with armed non-state actors threatening both the State and its population' could be encompassed within pillar two.[334] For Ed Luck, this will require 'inter-agency cooperation on key cross-sectoral issues, such as conflict

---

[328] UN, 'Secretary-General Defends, Clarifies "Responsibility to Protect" at Berlin Event on "Responsibility to Protect: International Cooperation for a Changed World"', UN Press Release SG/SM/11701, 15 July 2008, www.un.org/News/Press/docs/2008/sgsm11701. doc.htm.

[329] Ibid.

[330] UN Secretary-General, 'Implementing the Responsibility to Protect: Report of the Secretary-General', UN GAOR, 63rd Sess., Agenda Items 44 and 107, UN Doc. A/63/677, 12 January 2009, p. 32.

[331] Ibid., p. 8.   [332] Ibid., pp. 10, 13.   [333] Ibid., p. 15.   [334] Ibid.

prevention, rule of law assistance, security sector reform, human rights promotion, and gender equality'.[335] Implementing this pillar of the responsibility to protect will be helped by 'the wide-ranging efforts to build, rebuild, or bolster institutional capacity in fragile states being undertaken by the UN peace-building and development entities, as well as by bilateral donors and international financial institutions'.[336] Pillar three involves engaging in a 'timely and decisive' response if a state proves unable or unwilling to protect its population. The Secretary-General's report suggests that the UN executive has particular authority to undertake such action:

> While the first and enduring responsibility resides with each State to meet its obligations relating to the responsibility to protect, when it manifestly fails to do so the Secretary-General bears particular responsibility for ensuring that the international community responds in a 'timely and decisive manner', as called for in paragraph 139 of the Summit Outcome ... The Secretary-General must be the spokesperson for the vulnerable and the threatened when their Governments become their persecutors instead of their protectors or can no longer shield them from marauding armed groups.[337]

The responsibility to protect as a rationalisation of executive rule

In its engagement with the process of systematising and integrating executive action, the responsibility to protect concept can thus be seen to build on the legacy left by Hammarskjöld. Yet the responsibility to protect concept also represents a departure from that legacy in its attempt to offer a normative account of international authority.

As Chapter 3 will show, the responsibility to protect concept offers an account of how to recognise lawful authority. That was the question that Hammarskjöld systematically avoided answering in either abstract or doctrinal terms. Hammarskjöld used notions of impartiality and neutrality to avoid addressing such questions. Nevertheless, in practice Hammarskjöld and the UN officials who came after him needed a working account of which local actors they would recognise and who could be counted as the 'responsible elements' within a population. The responsibility to protect concept attempts to make that working account explicit.

---

[335] Luck, *The United Nations and the Responsibility to Protect*, p. 6.   [336] *Ibid.*
[337] UN Secretary-General, 'Implementing the Responsibility to Protect', p. 26.

As Chapter 4 will show, the responsibility to protect concept also addresses the question of authority in a second sense. The turn to protection as the grounds of authority leaves open the question of which concrete institution should decide when a government is manifestly failing to protect its population. The responsibility to protect concept answers that question by reasserting the central role to be played by the state and by the UN in making such decisions. The responsibility to protect concept claims a specific responsibility to protect for the international community acting through the UN. At the heart of the responsibility to protect concept is the idea that the legitimacy of international humanitarian action through the UN is founded upon the capacity of international actors to offer protection in situations where the state is struggling to do so.

In offering a basis for consolidating and explaining disparate practices of rule, the responsibility to protect concept in many ways resembles the arguments made in early modern Europe to rationalise the practices of rule now associated with the state. In his influential reinterpretation of the emergence of the modern state form in Europe, Michel Foucault argued that the state did not appear first as an elaborated concept or idea – rather, its origin lay in the development of governmental practices and their subsequent transformation into concepts like sovereignty or statehood. The state was not a 'kind of natural-historical given' or a 'cold monster', but 'the correlative of a particular way of governing'.[338] Foucault argued that in order to understand the emergence of the state, it was necessary to analyse 'how it appears and reflects on itself, how at the same time it is brought into play and analyzes itself, how, in short, it currently programs itself'.[339] The choice to start with governmental practice is 'obviously and explicitly a way of not taking as a primary, original, and already given object, notions such as the sovereign, sovereignty, the people, subjects, the state, and civil society'. Instead, by starting from governmental practice and the ways in which 'it reflects on itself and is rationalised', it is possible to 'show how certain things – state and society, sovereign and subjects, etcetera – were actually able to be formed'.[340] The shift from a form of political order organised around the personal rule of the monarch to one organised around an impersonal administrative entity distinct from the ruler did not simply occur as a matter of shifts in language or because certain intellectual preconditions (that there can be only one supreme authority in a territory, or that the state exists solely for political purposes) developed incrementally. The

---

[338] Foucault, *Birth of Biopolitics*, p. 6.   [339] *Ibid.*, p. 78.   [340] *Ibid.*, p. 3.

state as a 'theoretical construct' would not simply have appeared 'regardless of the historical appearance of any political institution or system resembling the modern state itself'.[341] The emergence of the singular conception of the state was the result of the correspondence of certain material preconditions (such as the centralisation of authority, the growth of bureaucracies and the consolidation of territories with defined boundaries) with the development of new ways of rationalising and speaking about power.[342]

This chapter has suggested that a similar process is taking place in relation to the forms of rule established by Hammarskjöld in the early years of decolonisation. The responsibility to protect concept is an attempt, both institutionally and conceptually, to consolidate the new forms of authority that have emerged in the decolonised world through the expansion of executive action. The idea that there exists an international community with the responsibility to protect populations at risk does not simply emerge because the time is right for humanity to realise its own law, or because a set of intellectual preconditions happen to have coalesced in the twenty-first century to produce the responsibility to protect concept. Instead, the emergence of the responsibility to protect concept is part of a protracted process in which power is being reorganised. Those who champion the responsibility to protect concept seek to integrate a set of governmental practices into a coherent theoretical account of international authority. What will it mean for UN officials to tell themselves that their authority to rule is based upon their responsibility to protect? What political possibilities are opened up – and what possibilities foreclosed – by conceptualising international authority in those terms? These are the questions to which I turn in Chapter 3.

[341] Cary J. Nederman, *Lineages of European Political Thought: Explorations Along the Medieval/Modern Divide from John of Salisbury to Hegel* (Washington DC: Catholic University of America Press, 2009), p. 20.
[342] Ibid., pp. 13–23.

3

How to Recognise Lawful Authority: Hobbes, Schmitt and the Responsibility to Protect

Civil war and the turn to protection

This chapter explores the implications of the basic claim at the heart of the responsibility to protect concept – that the authority of states and of the international community is grounded on the capacity to provide protection. During his tenure as Secretary-General, Dag Hammarskjöld transformed the UN into an instrument of executive action in order to fill the dangerous 'power vacuums' that were arising as the colonial system was being 'liquidated'.[1] The responsibility to protect concept has sought to consolidate and rationalise those practices of executive action as a response to the challenge of creating political order in situations of 'internal war, insurgency, repression or state failure'.[2] In that sense, the responsibility to protect concept can be seen as part of a long tradition of political thought that has sought to explain how to distinguish between competing claimants to authority during times of civil war or revolution. In particular, the turn to protection as the solution to the problem of civil war was championed by two political and legal theorists who wrote during periods of civil war and revolution in Europe – Thomas Hobbes and Carl Schmitt. Both Hobbes and Schmitt argued that the capacity to guarantee protection grounds lawful authority. The tendency of their arguments to support an agenda that is at once revolutionary and authoritarian gives a sense of the potential promises and dangers inherent in the linking of authority, responsibility and protection.

In his classic treatise *Leviathan*, Hobbes sought to explain why it was rational to submit to an absolute political authority capable of containing

---

[1] UN Secretary-General, 'Introduction to the Annual Report of the Secretary-General on the Work of the Organization', UN GAOR, 16th Sess., Supp. No. 1A, UN Doc. A/4800/Add.1, 1961, p. 7.

[2] ICISS, *The Responsibility to Protect* (Ottawa: International Development Research Centre, 2001), p. xi.

[handwritten margin notes:] The problem concerns not how to distinguish, but the willingness occupying to intervene

the warring religious factions threatening the continued existence of the commonwealth.[3] He did so at a time in which the legitimacy of public authority had become a serious question. The wars of religion that had been waged throughout Europe had undermined appeals to a universal and shared set of values that might ground political and legal authority.[4] Appeals to the truth of competing religious beliefs and the post-sceptical spirit of the new sciences were everywhere shaking the foundations of established political orders.[5] When Hobbes wrote *Leviathan*, it was still uncertain how the fundamental divisions between political and religious groups within European states, and particularly within England, would ever be bridged, or which if any values and political forms would emerge triumphant. In *Leviathan*, Hobbes therefore did not seek to ground authority upon inheritance, or conformity with custom or precedent, or upon a shared set of moral values or some authentic relationship with God or the people to be governed. Rather, he argued that the creation of a political order depended upon the establishment of a common power with the capacity to protect its subjects.

The attempt to ground the legitimacy of authority upon the responsibility to protect was explicitly revived in the twentieth century by Carl Schmitt.[6] Schmitt was writing at a time when Germany, and indeed Europe more generally, was struggling to come to terms with the

---

[3] Thomas Hobbes, *Leviathan*, J. C. A. Gaskin (ed.) (Oxford: Oxford University Press, 2006) (first published 1651).

[4] See Richard Tuck, 'The "Modern" Theory of Natural Law' in Anthony Pagden (ed.), *The Languages of Political Theory in Early-Modern Europe* (Cambridge: Cambridge University Press, 1987), p. 99 at p. 118.

[5] *Ibid.*, p. 117. Hobbes was writing in a tradition of seventeenth-century European philosophy, particularly that of the Mersenne school, which sought to transcend the anti-scientific scepticism of the previous generation of humanists. The aim was to provide a new method for the production of true and systematic knowledge, without falling back upon discredited Aristotelian accounts of the fundamental correctness of human perceptions of the world. That philosophical project was strongly influenced by developments in physics and optics, where new, non-Aristotelian accounts of the relation between observation and reality were emerging. This new science inspired philosophers to explore whether it might be possible to produce systematic moral science that could accommodate, rather than seek to deny, 'the multiplicity of possible beliefs and customs to which the relativist pointed'. For discussions of the influence of these broader European schools of thought on the models developed by Hobbes, see Noel Malcolm, *Aspects of Hobbes* (Oxford: Oxford University Press, 2002), pp. 200–29; Richard Tuck, *Hobbes* (Oxford: Oxford University Press, 1989), pp. 1–27.

[6] See particularly Carl Schmitt, *The Concept of the Political*, George Schwab trans. (Chicago and London: University of Chicago Press, 1996) (first published 1932), pp. 52–3; Carl Schmitt, *The Leviathan in the State Theory of Thomas Hobbes: Meaning and Failure of a Political Symbol*, George Schwab and Erna Hilfstein trans. (Westport: Greenwood Press, 1996) (first published 1938). Schmitt's fascination with the late sixteenth and early

devastation of the First World War and with 'the swell of revolutions and class-based civil wars that ran all across the continent from 1918 to 1923' in the aftermath of the Russian revolutions.[7] Schmitt agreed with Hobbes that 'the factual, current accomplishment of genuine protection is what the state is all about'.[8] However, the end of protection for Schmitt was neither the fulfilment of the needs of individuals nor the procurement of the material well-being of the population. Rather, for Schmitt the author-ity of the state as protector was premised upon its capacity to defend the will of an 'indivisibly similar, entire, unified people'.[9] That capacity in turn depended upon the existence of a sovereign who could distinguish between friends and enemies. The lawful authority, for Schmitt, was the one ready and able to defend a unified people against its enemies in order to guarantee the security of those within the state. Schmitt elevated the general interest into which the freedom of the individual was incorpo-rated above the material interests or needs of any given individual or group.

The responsibility to protect concept builds on this tradition, to argue that the existence of a worldly power with the capacity to protect its subjects is the solution to the problem of civil war. As Chapter 2 showed, that idea has shaped the way in which the UN has understood its role as the maintainer of international peace and security since 1960. For those who have advocated the need for new forms of authority in the decolon-ised world, it is axiomatic that 'a diffuse desire for peace rarely serves to guarantee it'.[10] Something more is needed to realise the desire for peace on earth. Where for Hobbes that something more was the absolutist state, and for Schmitt that something more was executive rule, for contemporary lawyers and philosophers that something more has become international authority.[11] This chapter suggests that attention

seventeenth centuries is reflected not only in his repeated reworkings of the writing of Hobbes and other theorists of absolute sovereignty such as Jean Bodin, but also in his interest in Shakespeare. See further Victoria Kahn, 'Hamlet or Hecuba: Carl Schmitt's Decision', *Representations* 83 (2003), 67.

[7] Eric D. Weitz, 'Foreword to the English Edition' in Pierre Broué, *The German Revolution 1917–1923*, John Archer trans. (Chicago: Haymarket Books, 2006) (first published 1971), p. xi.

[8] Schmitt, *Leviathan in the State Theory of Thomas Hobbes*, p. 34.

[9] Carl Schmitt, *Legality and Legitimacy*, Jeffrey Seitzer trans. (Durham and London: Duke University Press, 2004) (first published 1932), p. 28.

[10] Steven R. Ratner, *The New UN Peacekeeping: Building Peace in Lands of Conflict after the Cold War* (New York: St Martin's Press, 1995), p. 4.

[11] *Ibid.* ('The resources offered by outside actors have become essential to preserving the peace.')

to earlier moments at which authority and protection have been linked can help to reveal the stakes of the turn to protection as the justification for international authority today. Much of the attention in internationalist literature to date has been on the ways in which the responsibility to protect concept justifies the expansion of international authority in situations where a state has failed to protect its population. There has been less attention paid in that literature to articulating the proper limits to the jurisdiction or actions of such an international protective authority. Yet as the history explored in this chapter suggests, to represent power in terms of an office or responsibility to protect is potentially dangerous. If the absolutist potential inherent in the turn to protection is to be avoided, the institutionalisation of the responsibility to protect concept must involve not only legitimising new forms of authority, but also marking out the proper limits to the interests of such authorities in the lives (and deaths) of their subjects.[12] It is those questions of the limits and ends of protective authority that those advocating the embrace of the responsibility to protect concept are yet to address.

Thomas Hobbes, natural law and the preservation of life

Protection, representation and the state

How are people to recognise authority during a time of civil or religious war, when authority is no longer guaranteed by tradition, ritual or God? What makes a person recognisable as the representative of a sovereign to be obeyed, rather than an enemy to be fought or an occupier to be resisted? This was a live question in the England of Hobbes – let alone Ireland or Scotland. The answer was not altogether obvious if we think about the competing claims to authority at play in the English civil wars or the Irish rebellion. Those conflicts had made a pressing issue of 'the subject's duty when two or more legitimate authorities were competing to claim his allegiances at the sword's point'.[13] According to Hobbes, the lawful authority was recognisable

---

[12] See Shaun McVeigh, 'Subjects of Jurisdiction: The Dying, Northern Territory, Australia, 1995–1997' in Shaun McVeigh (ed.), *Jurisprudence of Jurisdiction* (Oxon: Routledge-Cavendish, 2007), p. 202 (arguing for the contemporary relevance of a civil jurisprudence organised around the notion of office).

[13] J. G. A. Pocock, 'Introduction' in James Harrington, *The Commonwealth of Oceana and A System of Politics* (Cambridge: Cambridge University Press, 1992), p. xiv.

as the one capable of procuring the safety of the people.[14] The creation of a political order in conditions of civil war depended upon the establishment of a common power with the capacity to protect its subjects. Somehow the first principle of natural law – the 'commandment to make peace' – had to 'be transformed into a law that can be satisfied by concrete execution'.[15] Yet during civil war it is not possible to determine 'unequivocally what is good and what is evil' and under such conditions 'the wish for peace is not itself sufficient to cause a flagging of the will to power'.[16] The problem in a situation of civil war was thus how 'to develop a legality' that would allow natural law to become reality.[17] Hobbes attempted to solve this problem of authority by introducing the state as the political form that could guarantee compliance with the commandment to make peace. Hobbes argued that an earthly power was needed to bring into being a condition in which the right of each man to self-preservation could be realised.[18] According to Hobbes, men would covenant as equals to bring about such a condition.[19] The marker of the state's authority was thus its capacity to guarantee peace and in so doing to protect the security and welfare of its subjects according to the terms of the covenant.

According to Hobbes, 'during the time men live without a common power to keep them all in awe, they are in that condition which is called war; and such a war, as is of every man, against every man'.[20] In this state of nature, there is no *civil* law, because such law 'depends for its existence upon a 'common power'.[21] But it is important to note that this does not mean that for Hobbes the state of nature was a lawless space. According to Hobbes, men in the state of nature were governed by the laws of nature – that is, by divine law.[22] The 'first and fundamental law of nature' was '*to seek peace, and follow it*'.[23] As long as the state of nature prevailed, there could be no peace or security.[24] In part this was because the laws of nature had no settled meaning. The unwritten laws of nature were not reliably available to men – men differed in their interpretation of Scripture, they claimed to have experienced miracles or to have received divine inspiration that could not be verified. This was a messy state of affairs in which there was no reliable and agreed earthly judge of what the

---

[14] Hobbes, *Leviathan*, p. 222.
[15] Reinhart Koselleck, *Critique and Crisis: Enlightenment and the Pathogenesis of Modern Society* (Cambridge: The MIT Press, 1988).
[16] *Ibid.*   [17] *Ibid.*   [18] Hobbes, *Leviathan*, p. 87.   [19] *Ibid.*, p. 114.   [20] *Ibid.*, p. 84.
[21] *Ibid.*, pp. 84–5.   [22] *Ibid.*, p. 215 (equating the laws of nature and divine law).
[23] *Ibid.*, p. 87.   [24] *Ibid.*, p. 87.

laws of nature required or meant in any given situation. There could also be no security in the state of nature because there was no common power to enforce the law.[25] As nature created men equal, in mind and body, no man could ever really gain a permanent advantage over another.[26] Men in such a condition lived in 'continual fear, and danger of violent death'.[27] For these reasons, Hobbes argued that the creation of political order depended upon the establishment of a common power – a commonwealth. The authority of such an earthly power would be grounded on its capacity to guarantee protection, understood as the realisation and fulfilment of the laws of nature on earth.[28]

Hobbes argued that it is therefore immaterial to questions of authority whether the sovereign is constituted through institution or acquisition. A commonwealth comes into existence by *institution* where a 'real unity' is created among the members of the multitude through a covenant.[29] A commonwealth comes into existence by *acquisition* 'where the sovereign power is acquired by force'. Yet even in the situation of forceful acquisition, Hobbes argued that the legitimacy of public authority derives from the rational calculation and consent of those subject to that authority. According to Hobbes, the act of submission to an invading force out of fear can still be understood as a choice. 'It is not therefore the victory, that giveth the right of dominion over the vanquished, but his own covenant'.[30] For that reason, 'the imperfect generation' of any given commonwealth is irrelevant to the rightful authority of the civil sovereign. The right of the sovereign does not depend on the means by which its 'power was at first gotten', but on the possession of power.[31] After all, Hobbes comments, 'there is scarce a commonwealth in the world, whose beginnings can in conscience be justified'.[32]

It is not that Hobbes did not make a question of political authority – the whole of *Leviathan* is such a question. However, he refused to treat the question of authority as a question about the lawfulness of acquisition, or about an authentic relationship or common history linking ruler and ruled. In *Leviathan* 'the public realm confronts us without *raising the question* of its authorization and authorship'.[33] Hobbes' approach is thus very different to that of the revolutionaries of his age, and it is also very

---

[25] *Ibid.*, p. 111.   [26] *Ibid.*, p. 83.   [27] *Ibid.*, p. 84.

[28] David Dyzenhaus, 'Hobbes' Constitutional Theory' in Ian Shapiro (ed.), *Leviathan* (New Haven: Yale University Press, 2010), p. 453.

[29] Hobbes, *Leviathan*, p. 114.   [30] *Ibid.*, p. 135.   [31] *Ibid.*, p. 470.   [32] *Ibid.*

[33] Tracy B. Strong, 'How to Write Scripture: Words, Authority and Politics in Thomas Hobbes', *Critical Inquiry* 20 (1993), 128 at 155.

different to the arguments for the lawfulness of authority that we are used to seeing in international law today, based on Kantian notions of self-determination. For Hobbes, *nothing of importance* turns on the nature of the link between ruler and ruled, or on whether the territory of the commonwealth was acquired through conquest or otherwise unlawfully.

In making that argument, Hobbes was responding to contemporary Protestant challenges to earthly power and authority. Protestant reformists challenged papal authority with the argument that there was no '*humanly available presence of the authorizing deity*'.[34] God could be known only through Scripture – not through the Pope, not through priests, not through the teachings of any person, but through the written word that was available to the priesthood of all believers. Just as for the Protestant reformists there was no available presence of the authorising deity, so too for Hobbes there was no available presence of the authorising creator(s) of the commonwealth. Hobbes equated the position of God and the position of the authors of the commonwealth in the very first paragraphs of *Leviathan*. According to Hobbes, the covenants by which the commonwealth is made 'resemble that *fiat*, or the *let us make man*, pronounced by God in the creation'.[35] Man creates the commonwealth in the same gesture as God creates the world. For the Protestants of seventeenth-century Europe, God then disappears from the world – and in a structurally similar way so do the people who make the artificial man of the commonwealth. According to Hobbes, the intentions or will of the people could be known only through their representative, the sovereign. For Hobbes there is no third term that stands between the commonwealth and its authors.[36]

> A multitude of men, are made *one* person, when they are by one man, or one person, represented: so that it be done with the consent of every one of that multitude in particular. For it is the *unity* of the represeter, not the *unity* of the represented, that maketh the person *one*. And it is the represeter that beareth the person, and but one person: and *unity*, cannot otherwise be understood in multitude.[37]

---

[34] *Ibid.* [35] Hobbes, *Leviathan*, p. 7.
[36] Istvan Hont, *Jealousy of Trade: International Competition and the Nation-State in Historical Perspective* (Cambridge, Massachusetts and London: The Belknap Press, 2005), p. 130; Ernst H. Kantorowicz, *The King's Two Bodies: A Study in Medieval Political Theology* (Princeton: Princeton University Press, 1957), pp. 207–32.
[37] Hobbes, *Leviathan*, p. 109.

Hobbes thus portrayed the sovereign as a 'text of which each individual is the author'.[38] Yet this 'is a text for which the author is no longer available'.[39]

Hobbes as a counter-revolutionary theorist

The disappearance of the people, and of the past, had multiple effects. Many of those effects were conservative and absolutist. Hobbes' arguments were conservative because they denied a particular set of questions about the relationship between the origins of the state and the legitimacy of authority. Hobbes based his defence of power on its present efficacy rather than the validity of its origins. This was a theory that spoke to conditions of conquest and of civil war. Hobbes argued that the continual debate about the legitimacy of the conditions under which authority was first constituted was radically destabilising and ultimately irresolvable. In doing so, Hobbes was taking a position in the highly charged debate about the implications of the Norman Conquest of England for seventeenth-century titles to rule and to land. The Norman Conquest had become a live political issue – revolutionaries argued that the rule of the aristocracy, the king and indeed all property relations were 'invalidated by the fact of the Conquest'.[40] The disparaging of the 'Norman Yoke' was the language of many seeking to challenge the absolutism of James I and his advisers.[41] According to the arguments made by the Levellers and others, the fact of the conquest marked 'a state of nonright that invalidates all the laws and social differences that distinguish the aristocracy, the property regime, and so on'.[42] Hobbes was answering that claim when he argued that it does not matter how a commonwealth was erected, nor the form that its government takes. The rights and

---

[38] Strong, 'How to Write Scripture', 157.   [39] Ibid.

[40] Michel Foucault, *Society Must Be Defended: Lectures at the Collège de France, 1975–76*, David Macey trans. (London: Penguin Books, 2004) (first published 1997), p. 108.

[41] See, for example, Richard Overton with William Walwyn's collaboration, 'A Remonstrance of Many Thousand Citizens, 7 July 1646' in Andrew Sharp (ed.), *The English Levellers* (Cambridge: Cambridge University Press, 1998), p. 33 at p. 45: 'we remain under the Norman yoke of an unlawful power, from which we ought to free ourselves, and which ye ought not to maintain upon us, but to abrogate'. See further the discussion in Christopher Hill, *Puritanism and Revolution: Studies in Interpretation of the English Revolution of the 17th Century* (New York: St Martin's Press, 1997), pp. 46–111; George Garnett, *Conquered England: Kingship, Succession, and Tenure 1066–1166* (Oxford: Oxford University Press, 2007), p. 353.

[42] Foucault, *Society Must Be Defended*, p. 107.

consequences of sovereignty are not altered by the status of a territory or the means of institution of the commonwealth – *both* inherited and acquired territories are subject to whatever laws the sovereign decided to introduce.

Hobbes' approach to authority was also conservative in terms of what it meant for the relation between law, property and the state. Hobbes argued that laws were binding, not because of their customary or traditional nature, but because they were a manifestation of the will of the sovereign. For Hobbes, there could be no property or dominion in a state of nature – such institutions only come into existence in the civil state brought into being through the sovereign.[43] The power to distribute materials for the nourishment of the commonwealth belonged to the sovereign power, and the first law for this distribution was 'for the division of land itself'.[44] Where a people came into possession of land through war, they might allow the 'ancient inhabitants' to continue to hold their estates, 'yet it is manifest that they hold them afterwards as of the victors' distribution; as the people of England held all theirs of William the Conqueror'.[45] Thus Hobbes sought to do away with customary rights to land and also with other forms of allegiance shaped by feudal or communal relations to land. This had implications for the important contemporary debate about whether (and if so, why) the system of title derived from the Norman Conquest was legitimate. Hobbes' approach to law meant that the creation of a common power became the legal basis for private property. His focus upon promoting the welfare of the people meant that this distribution of property was to be undertaken in the interests of the broader good. Indeed, this was the way in which the Parliament of the interregnum approached the project of agrarian reform, with the state intervening to confiscate and sell Church and Crown lands, oversee the mass foreclosing on mortgages and enclose forests and other commons.[46] Adam Smith was later to explain such practices in terms inherited from Hobbes – it was 'for the interest of the society' or the commonwealth to 'divide' Crown land 'among the people', so as to free up the revenue that these lands represented.[47] However, by

---

[43] Hobbes, *Leviathan*, pp. 84, 163–5.   [44] *Ibid.*, p. 164.   [45] *Ibid.*, p. 165.

[46] Hill, *Puritanism and Revolution*, pp. 138–77; Harold J. Berman, *Law and Revolution II: The Impact of The Protestant Reformations on the Western Legal Tradition* (Cambridge and London: The Belknap Press, 2003), pp. 330–48.

[47] Adam Smith, *The Wealth of Nations, Books IV–V* (London: Penguin Books, 1999) (first published 1776), p. 415. See the discussion of Smith's argument in Hill, *Puritanism and Revolution*, pp. 140–1.

linking law and the state in this way, Hobbes left no place for the more radical arguments of groups like the Levellers and the Diggers, who had sought to defend the right of the people to land in the face of enclosures and other forms of dispossession.[48]

By arguing that the intention of the people could only be known through their representative the sovereign, Hobbes 'pulled the rug out' from under arguments based on the nation as a 'platform for resistance' to tyranny or misrule.[49] The idea of the 'freeborn people' as an active subject of politics that existed separately from the state emerged in England during the revolutionary period of the civil wars. That idea animated the radicalisation of the parliament and justified the regicide of Charles I.[50] It took its most radical form in the arguments of the Levellers, who had proposed a written constitution authorised by an 'agreement of the people', as well as 'abolition of the legislative powers of the king and the House of Lords, much of the king's executive power, and all of the ancient royal prerogative power in foreign affairs'.[51] The 'represented' would also have the right to choose their religion – thus challenging the existence of a centrally controlled state church.[52] Both London civilians and some soldiers were committed to this idea of the rights of the people – 'many at least of the Parliamentary soldiers knew what they were fighting for, and it was for a fundamental change to the constitution'.[53] The more radical aspects of the Levellers' claims, and particularly the 'idea that the consent of the people or even of any organized people like the General Council could constitute a structure of government' were dismissed by New Model officers and by Cromwell, who argued that this could lead to 'anarchy'.[54] Yet when Charles I was charged with treason and with maintaining 'a cruel War in the Land, against the Parliament and Kingdom', the effect was to give legitimacy to the idea that sovereignty might vest somewhere other than the king's person.[55] As treason was a crime against the sovereign, 'in order to try the

---

[48] Hill, *Puritanism and Revolution*, pp. 139–77; Christopher Hill, *The World Turned Upside Down: Radical Ideas during the English Revolution* (London: Penguin Books, 1984).

[49] Hont, *Jealousy of Trade*, p. 130.

[50] Ian W. Duncanson, 'Reading for Law and the State: Theaters of Problematization and Authority', *International Journal of the Semiotics of Law* 22 (2009), 321.

[51] Andrew Sharp, 'The Levellers and the End of Charles I' in Jason Peacey (ed.), *The Regicides and the Execution of Charles I* (Hampshire: Palgrave MacMillan, 2001), p. 181.

[52] *Ibid.*, p. 182. [53] Duncanson, 'Reading for Law and the State', 340.

[54] Sharp, 'The Levellers and the End of Charles I', p. 183.

[55] D. Alan Orr, 'The Juristic Foundation of Regicide' in Jason Peacey (ed.), *The Regicides and the Execution of Charles I* (Hampshire: Palgrave MacMillan, 2001), p. 126.

king for treason the locus of sovereignty had to be relocated with the people as a perpetual popular corporation'.[56]

On the one hand, for Hobbes to say that the state was an 'artificial' person was to accept the juristic decoupling of public authority and the king's natural person – a decoupling that had been dramatically performed by the regicide of Charles I.[57] His model uneasily incorporated the notion that the sovereign is in effect merely entrusted with power as some sort of senior magistrate for so long as he acts for the good of the people. Yet on the other hand, by arguing that the people had no existence beyond that of the common power they had brought into being, Hobbes rejected the argument that the people were the locus of sovereignty and deflected the revolutionary potential inherent in his model.

Finally, the disappearance of the author of the covenant also legitimised absolutism. Through a fictitious original covenant, subjects could be said to have authorised the absolute rights of the sovereign and their own subjection. According to Hobbes, subjects had an obligation to obey the sovereign (provided such obedience 'was not repugnant to the laws of God'),[58] while nothing that 'the sovereign representative' could 'do to a subject', for whatever reason, could 'properly be called injustice'.[59] A representative of the sovereign could not justly be punished or put to death, for if hurt is 'inflicted on the representative of the commonwealth', this was not properly understood as punishment but was rather 'an act of hostility'.[60] This was a clear challenge to the idea behind the regicide that the sovereign existed to further the good of the people and could be punished for crimes against the people.

If such moves were conservative in Hobbes' time, they are in many ways even more conservative to a twenty-first-century audience who are used to thinking about questions of legitimacy in terms of a romantic or nationalist notion of self-determination. Yet something similar is being staged with the turn to protection as the basis of international authority today. The linking of authority and protection is presented as a solution to the problem of creating political order in situations where such order is non-existent or under threat due to 'internal war, insurgency, repression or state failure'. Those supporting an expansion of international authority argue that 'most of the dreadful human rights abuses of the early to middle 1990s were being done by the anarchic

---

[56] *Ibid.*, p. 127.   [57] *Ibid.*, p. 122.   [58] Hobbes, *Leviathan*, pp. 134, 235.   [59] *Ibid.*, p. 141.
[60] *Ibid.*, pp. 118, 207.

forces of fractured states like Serbia and Rwanda, or were taking place in a civil war with mutual atrocities as in Bosnia, or were perpetrated by warlords and tribes that lacked any government as in Somalia'.[61] The problem is specifically portrayed in terms of the recognition of authority: 'If the UN Secretary-General or the OHCHR sent a special representative to Burundi, with whom should he negotiate?'[62] The answer, at least according to the responsibility to protect concept, is that the lawful authority is recognisable as the one capable of protecting populations at risk.

The responsibility to protect concept thus does not conceptualise the legitimacy of authority in relation to a third term, whether that be the people, the nation or the *Volk*. So whether or not the representatives of the international community should, say, be present in Iraq, Kosovo or Darfur, will not be answerable in terms of the legitimacy of the initial acquisition of control over the territory in question, or in terms of whether international authority was constituted in accordance with the will of the people. By focusing upon de facto authority, the responsibility to protect concept implicitly asserts not only that an international community exists, but that its authority to govern is, at least in situations of civil war and repression, superior to that of the state. The turn to protection works to delegitimise appeals to de jure authority, whether that be the authority of the Holy Roman Empire or the principles of sovereign equality, territorial integrity and self-determination that have been significant limiting factors to foreign rule under the UN Charter.

Recognising lawful authority

Despite the many conservative and absolutist implications of the model of authority championed in *Leviathan*, the authority of the sovereign was nonetheless constrained in one important respect. For Hobbes, the sovereign is recognisable to its subjects and other sovereigns – that is, successfully created – only to the extent that this artificial creature has certain attributes.[63] For Hobbes, 'sovereignty is artificial and owes its existence to an authorization that each individual has to make to each

---

[61] Paul Kennedy, *The Parliament of Man: The Past, Present and Future of the United Nations* (New York: Vintage, 2007), p. 199.

[62] *Ibid.*, p. 200.   [63] Dyzenhaus, 'Hobbes' Constitutional Theory'.

other'.[64] The sovereign is the one who acts according to this authorisation and brings into being a situation in which the laws of nature, and
principally the right to self-preservation, can be realised. The sovereign is
recognisable to its subjects and to other sovereigns as the one who fulfils
the terms of the covenant. While covenants, without the sword, are but
words, it is still the case that 'they would not be covenants were they not
words (as opposed, say, simply to being force)'.[65] Authors do not authorise absolutely anything – they authorise to certain ends. According to
Hobbes:

> The office of the sovereign, (be it a monarch or an assembly,) consisteth
> in the end, for which he was trusted with the sovereign power, namely the
> procuration of *the safety of the people*, to which he is obliged by the law of
> nature ... [B]y safety here, is not meant a bare preservation, but also all
> other contentments of life, which every man by lawful industry, without
> danger, or hurt to the commonwealth, shall acquire to himself.[66]

Hobbes' reference to the covenant as the vehicle through which subjects
would bring the sovereign into being was central to the sense he gave
that sovereign authority was constrained. The political crisis of the civil
war had brought into 'explosive contact' the covenant theology of
Protestants such as John Preston and contractual accounts of natural
law such as that developed by Hugo Grotius.[67] The result was a widespread debate about the conditional nature of political obligation
couched in the twinned languages of covenant and contract. For the
inhabitants of seventeenth-century England, and for Europe more
generally, the question of the subject's duty when multiple authorities
claimed allegiance 'at the sword's point' was a practical one.[68] Ideas
drawn from covenant theology and from natural law theories were
relevant to the resolution of this question. The Engagement controversy of 1650 gives a good example of this. In the aftermath of the
execution of Charles I, the monarchy and the House of Lords were
abolished and the Commonwealth of England was proclaimed. The
new Parliament passed an act on 2 January 1650 requiring all adult men
to 'declare and promise' that they would be 'true and faithful to the
Commonwealth of England, as it is now established, without a King or

---

[64] Strong, 'How to Write Scripture', 157.   [65] *Ibid.*, 131.   [66] Hobbes, *Leviathan*, p. 222.
[67] Victoria Kahn, *Wayward Contracts: The Crisis of Political Obligation in England, 1640–
1674* (Princeton: Princeton University Press, 2004).
[68] Pocock, 'Introduction', p. xiv.

House of Lords'.[69] For many Englishmen, the question of whether to take this Engagement required them both to make a judgment about the legitimacy of de facto authority and to resolve whether in good conscience they could swear an oath which seemed to violate previous obligations.[70] The Engagement controversy thus raised a question of private conscience for those who had sworn oaths to earlier rulers. For Anglicans, it raised the question of whether the Engagement was compatible with the oath of allegiance, by which they had promised to defend the king and his successors 'to the uttermost of my power against all conspiracies and attempts whatsoever'.[71] For Presbyterians the issue was whether this new oath was compatible with the Solemn League and Covenant of September 1643, by which they had promised to defend 'the King's Majesty's person and authority, in the preservation and defence of the true religion and liberties of the kingdoms'.[72]

The practice of requiring oaths or covenants of obedience was a well-established one during the wars of religion, and had led to the growth of an accompanying tradition of moral theology that sought to explain how and why such oaths might be conditional. This tradition was mobilised in England during the Engagement controversy. Pamphleteers and divines argued that it was possible to subscribe to the Engagement and swear an oath of loyalty to the commonwealth, where the commonwealth was understood to refer to the English nation rather than any existing authority.[73] Or perhaps, as one pamphleteer argued, the earlier Solemn League and Covenant was no longer binding, because it had been conditional upon the King's continued 'preservation and defence of the true religion and liberties of the kingdoms'.[74]

It was that sense of conditional authority that Hobbes invoked in his use of the covenant in *Leviathan*. According to Hobbes: 'The obligation of subjects to the sovereign, is understood to last as long, and no longer, than the power lasteth, by which he is able to protect them.'[75] The frightening power of the Leviathan was directed to realising the ends of

---

[69] S. R. Gardiner, *The Constitutional Documents of the Puritan Revolution, 1625–1660*, 3rd edn (Oxford: Clarendon Press, 1906), p. 391.

[70] Edward Vallance, 'Oaths, Casuistry, and Equivocation: Anglican Responses to the Engagement Controversy', *The Historical Journal* 44 (2001), 59.

[71] Glenn Burgess, 'Usurpation, Obligation and Obedience in the Thought of the Engagement Controversy', *The Historical Journal* 29 (1986), 515 at 516.

[72] Vallance, 'Oaths, Casuistry and Equivocation', 66.

[73] Burgess, 'Usurpation, Obligation and Obedience', 516.

[74] Vallance, 'Oaths, Casuistry and Equivocation', 66.   [75] Hobbes, *Leviathan*, p. 147.

the covenant. The sovereign represented the unified will of the people, but that will was constrained by the terms upon which the sovereign was created. The representatives of the sovereign could not act in their own private interest or declare war against the people. Nonetheless, the power of the sovereign was absolute, and the subject had no right to resist that which he had covenanted to create – 'in the act of our *submission*, consisteth both our *obligation*, and our *liberty*'.[76] Hobbes made very clear the tension between authority and freedom that is embodied in the form of the state.

Hobbes also softened the conservative implications of his theory of authority through his attention to the work of mediation involved in interpreting the will of the sovereign. Hobbes argued that the sovereign is to achieve protection through the making of good laws, where law is understood as 'properly . . . the word of him, that *by right hath command over others*'.[77] It is through 'the word' that the sovereign is able to communicate his authority and his command:

> the law is a command, and a command consisteth in declaration, or manifestation of the will of him that commandeth, by voice, writing, or some other sufficient argument of the same.[78]

For Hobbes, this again raises the question of how to recognise particular words as law. For Hobbes, words were tricky things: 'words are wise men's counters, they do but reckon by them: but they are the money of fools, that value them by the authority of an Aristotle, a Cicero, or a Thomas, or any other doctor whatsoever, if but a man'.[79] So again, the question that arises for Hobbes is one of knowledge: it is necessary to consider 'what arguments, and signs be sufficient for the knowledge of what is the law; that is to say, what is the will of the sovereign'.[80] Those 'arguments, and signs' were the 'material circumstances' that had to exist 'for obligation to arise'. According to Hobbes, these material circumstances included the requirement that law must 'be written, and published',[81] and that there be 'manifest signs' that this written law 'proceedeth from the will of the sovereign'. According to Hobbes: 'it is of the essence of law, that he who is obliged, be assured of the authority of him that declareth it'.[82] In addition, in order for there to be 'knowledge of what is the law', an 'authentic interpretation' of the law was necessary.

[76] *Ibid.*, p. 144.   [77] *Ibid.*, p. 106.   [78] *Ibid.*, p. 179.   [79] *Ibid.*, p. 24.   [80] *Ibid.*, p. 180.
[81] *Ibid.*, p. 181.   [82] *Ibid.*, p. 189.

> For it is not the letter, but the intendment or meaning; that is to say, the authentic interpretation of the law (which is the sense of the legislator,) in which the nature of the law consisteth.[83]

That 'authentic interpretation' of the law could not be found by seeking out the law's original authors. Rather, Hobbes argued that it was necessary to look to the judges appointed as representatives of the sovereign for an authentic interpretation of the law. For Hobbes, the will of the sovereign was always manifested through and mediated by the written text and its institutional interpreters. His attention to words and their interpretation by worldly authorities meant that there could never be perfect or unmediated access to the pure will of the sovereign.

The process of interpretation of positive law in turn required conformity with natural or divine laws. While Hobbes introduced empirical questions about effectiveness into his science of government, we have seen that *Leviathan* did not abandon questions of right as relevant to the recognition of authority. The commonwealth was created to enable the realisation of the first principle of natural law – to seek peace and follow it. That out of which the commonwealth emerges is not a legal void. The representatives of the sovereign must therefore judge in accordance with the laws of nature because the 'scope and purpose' of the 'person of the commonwealth, is to be supposed always consonant to equity and reason'.[84] As a result, judges must assume that the law is to be interpreted in accordance with the pre-existing obligations of 'the eternal law of God', even if that requires them to depart from the precedents set by previous judges.[85]

Authority as fact and right

Hobbes thought about authority both as a matter of right and as a matter of fact, a matter of natural law and of worldly politics. In *Leviathan*, Hobbes made visible the interrelationship between law, theology and politics in grounding the legitimacy of state authority. Authority was legitimate, according to *Leviathan*, only if it was effective. Authority was effective if it could preserve the safety and well-being of the population. The core responsibility of the sovereign was to protect the subjects of the commonwealth. This was then an empirical claim – authority is recognisable as such on the basis of the fact of its capacity to guarantee

---

[83] *Ibid.*, p. 182.   [84] *Ibid.*, p. 181.   [85] *Ibid.*, p. 184.

protection. Yet protection itself had a normative value – the common-wealth was the form in which the obligations of natural law could best be realised. The power of the commonwealth was thus limited both by the obligations that pre-existed its existence, and by the terms of the cove-nant by which it was created.

Hobbes mediated the repressive effects of the turn to protection by making clear the problems involved in determining whether or not protection had in fact been realised. This fact of protection was not simply available to human knowledge – whether or not the state was effective at guaranteeing protection was a matter for judgment and interpretation. For Europeans of Hobbes' generation, who had experi-enced the wars of religion and the rise of sceptical reason, it was evident that individual judgments about such worldly matters could differ. The sovereign was created in conditions of civil war precisely to enable the question of judgment to be resolved.[86] Hobbes advocated submission to the authority of the commonwealth as a way of substituting public for private judgment in those areas that fell within the office of the sovereign (that is, the responsibility to protect), unless and until the common-wealth ceased to function effectively. It is through the claim to represent a general interest or a common wealth that the state will continue to confront the individual 'as a priority and as a *demand*' – in particular, as a demand for obedience.[87] For Hobbes, 'in the act of our *submission*, consisteth both our *obligation*, and our *liberty*'.[88] Hobbes makes very clear the tension between authority and freedom that is embodied in the form of the state. That tension was decisively resolved in favour of authority when Carl Schmitt, in developing his state law theory, returned to Hobbes and to the idea of a link between authority and protection.

Carl Schmitt, the European order and protection as war

Civil war and the European order

In order to explore further the stakes of the linking of authority with a responsibility to protect, I want now to turn to the writings of Schmitt.

---

[86] See generally Quentin Skinner, 'The Study of Rhetoric as an Approach to Cultural History: The Case of Hobbes' in Willem Melching and Wyger Velema (eds.), *Main Trends in Cultural History: Ten Essays* (Amsterdam: Rodopi, 1994), p. 17.

[87] Herbert Marcuse, *A Study on Authority*, Joris De Bres trans. (London: Verso, 2008) (first published 1936), p. 43.

[88] Hobbes, *Leviathan*, p. 144.

Weimar Germany, like seventeenth-century England, was faced with what some call constitutional crisis, and others call revolution. In the immediate post-war period, the German state was faced with significant external challenges to its authority. It had suffered substantial territorial and financial losses under the terms of the Treaty of Versailles – a treaty that Schmitt saw as an illegitimate interference with the authority of the German state.[89] In addition, the German Government faced serious internal challenges to its authority. The communist revolutionaries of Russia and Germany had politicised the claim that the state existed to further the general interest of the collective.[90] The rise of the German Communist Party saw a wave of mass strikes and armed struggles for 'possession of the streets and factories',[91] while the creation in 1925 of the SS, the right-wing paramilitary force loyal to Hitler, tested the capacity of the new republic to maintain a monopoly on the legitimate use of force. Throughout the post-war period, the government had to manage the effects on unemployment of the move from a war to a peace economy while faced with periodic economic crises, including the hyper-inflation of the early 1920s and the mass unemployment and banking collapse that accompanied the global financial crisis of 1929. The institutions of the German state were transformed as a result of these internal and external pressures, economic and political relations within the state were subject to violent contest, and alliances between political parties were in constant flux.[92] The nature of authority as a political relationship focused upon the state, and as an economic relationship focused upon the workplace, was under constant challenge in both theory and practice.

It was in the context of these ongoing political and economic upheavals that Schmitt would turn to the work of Hobbes, as well as to the writings of counter-revolutionary philosophers such as Joseph de Maistre and Juan Donoso Cortés, in order to fashion an account of authority that he saw as capable of responding effectively to the challenges facing the German state. The link between protection and authority articulated by

[89] Carl Schmitt, *The* Nomos *of the Earth in the International Law of the* Jus Publicum Europaeum, G. L. Ulmen trans. (New York: Telos Press, 2003) (first published 1950), pp. 260–80.

[90] Vladimir Lenin, *The State and Revolution*, Robert Service trans. (London: Penguin Books, 1992) (first published 1918). On the revolutionary situation in Weimar Germany, see generally Pierre Broué, *The German Revolution 1917–1923*, John Archer trans. (Chicago: Haymarket Books, 2006) (first published 1971).

[91] Weitz, 'Foreword', p. xii.

[92] See generally Theo Balderston, *Economics and Politics in the Weimar Republic* (Cambridge: Cambridge University Press, 2002).

Hobbes was at the heart of the state law theory developed by Schmitt during the 1920s and 1930s. Schmitt applauded what he described as Hobbes' efforts 'to restore the natural unity' of the state.[93] Schmitt continued, in terms strikingly reminiscent of the language of the responsibility to protect concept:

> it must be taken into consideration that the totality of this kind of state power always accords with the total responsibility for protecting and securing the safety of citizens and that obedience as well as the renunciation of every right of resistance that can be demanded by this god is only the correlate of the true protection that he guarantees.[94]

For Schmitt, the state emerges out of something very like that which Hobbes called the state of nature. Hobbes had described the state of nature as a state of war, which 'consisteth not in actual fighting; but in the known disposition thereto'.[95] Schmitt described the concept of the political in very similar terms:

> The political does not reside in the battle itself, but in the mode of behaviour which is determined by this possibility, by clearly evaluating the concrete situation and thereby being able to distinguish correctly the real friend and the real enemy.[96]

The existence of a sovereign capable of taking such a decision, and properly distinguishing between friend and enemy, was the necessary condition of the existence and preservation of the state. Where for Hobbes the sovereign was brought into being so that men could escape the 'miserable and hateful state' of war,[97] for Schmitt the sovereign was the name given to the 'decisive entity' that was essential to the existence of the state in a world oriented 'toward the possible extreme case of an actual battle against a real enemy'.[98] Indeed, this propensity to do battle defined 'the concept of the political' for Schmitt. In this sense, 'Schmitt restores the Hobbesian state of nature to a place of honor'.[99]

Yet for Schmitt, unlike Hobbes, that out of which the state emerges – the political or the state of nature – is a legal vacuum: 'Looked at

[93] Schmitt, *Leviathan in the State Theory of Thomas Hobbes*, pp. 85, 96.
[94] *Ibid.*, p. 96.   [95] Hobbes, *Leviathan*, p. 84.
[96] Schmitt, *The Concept of the Political*, p. 37.
[97] Thomas Hobbes, *On the Citizen* (Cambridge: Cambridge University Press, 1998) (first published 1642), p. 12.
[98] Schmitt, *The Concept of the Political*, p. 39.
[99] Leo Strauss, 'Notes on Carl Schmitt, The Concept of the Political' in Schmitt, *The Concept of the Political*, p. 90.

normatively, the decision emanates from nothingness.'[100] The sovereign decision brings into being the 'normal everyday frame of life' to which law 'can be factually applied'.[101] The essence of the legal form thus 'lies in the concrete decision'.[102] Schmitt argued that in times of emergency or civil war, the preservation of the legal and political order depended upon the existence of a sovereign who could restore the legal form, that is, make a decision and impose it. It is this capacity to make the decision that provides Schmitt's answer to the question of how to recognise lawful authority. As Schmitt wrote in perhaps his most famous sentence: 'Sovereign is he who decides on the exception.'[103] To the extent that a sovereign exists who can and does make such decisions, the law that such a sovereign makes is valid.

Within the state, the capacity to secure peace and guarantee order depended upon the existence of one superior authority that could create unity and command loyalty. Like Hobbes, Schmitt thought that the existence of competing obligations and multiple allegiances could only lead to conflict and potentially to civil war. Schmitt was thus opposed to any attempt to 'negate not only the state as the supreme comprehensive unity but also, first and foremost, its ethical demand to create a different and higher order of obligation than any of the other associations in which men live'.[104] For Schmitt, at stake in any theory of the state was the way in which unity could be created in a situation of conflicting claims for loyalty, fidelity and recognition. According to Schmitt, sovereignty is the name given to the 'political unity' that is capable of creating the normal situation out of that potential for civil war.

> Political unity is the highest unity – not because it is an omnipotent dictator, or because it levels out all other unities, but because it decides, and has the potential to prevent all other opposing groups from dissociating into a state of extreme enmity – that is, into civil war. Where a political unity exists, the social conflicts among individuals and social groups can be decided, so that an order – that is, a normal situation – is maintained.[105]

[100] Carl Schmitt, *Political Theology: Four Chapters on the Concept of Sovereignty* (George Schwab trans., Chicago and London: University of Chicago Press, 2005) (first published 1922), p. 32.
[101] *Ibid.*, p. 13. [102] *Ibid.*, p. 34. [103] *Ibid.*, p. 5.
[104] Carl Schmitt, 'Ethic of State and Pluralistic State' in Chantal Mouffe (ed.), *The Challenge of Carl Schmitt* (London: Verso, 1999), p. 196.
[105] *Ibid.*, p. 203.

To the extent that a sovereign exists who can and does make such decisions, the law that such a sovereign makes is valid. For Schmitt, the question as to whether a decision or a measure is a 'valid law in the formal sense' is thus an 'essentially political' question.[106] Answering it involves determining whether the law has been made by the sovereign – that is, by the one able in fact to make the decision and guarantee security and order. Schmitt dismissed the argument, made by contemporaries such as Hans Kelsen, that the validity of law could be derived from a formal inquiry, or that there could exist a pure legal theory that 'wants only to cognize, not to want; only to be scholarship, not politics'.[107] According to Schmitt, one could only submit to the rule of law, and to accepting 'a purely formal concept of law, independent of all content', where certain political conditions were in place.[108] For the decisions of a legislative state such as Weimar Germany to be legitimate, there must be only one lawmaker, and that lawmaker must be 'the final guardian of all law, ultimate guarantor of the existing order, conclusive source of all legality, and the last security and protection against injustice'.[109] In addition, for a '"formal" concept of law' to be 'conceivable and acceptable', there must be 'congruence between the parliamentary majority and the will of the homogenous people'.[110]

Underpinning this conception was the assumption that 'every democracy rests on the presupposition of the indivisibly similar, entire, unified people'.[111] For Schmitt, the link between legitimacy and democracy had as its precondition that the parliament represented the will of a unified people. If parliament did not do so, respect for legislation would descend into sterile formalism. In making such arguments, Schmitt was intervening in an ongoing debate about the propriety of the President using the emergency powers of the new Weimar constitution.[112] For Schmitt, the President was the guarantor of the constitution, as it was the President who represented the will of the people in its purest form. Schmitt argued that it made no sense to obey statutes passed by a (socialist) parliament simply on the grounds that as a matter of formal process they had been

---

[106] Schmitt, *Legality and Legitimacy*, p. 17.

[107] Hans Kelsen, 'Legal Formalism and the Pure Theory of Law' in Arthur J. Jacobson and Bernhard Schlink (eds.), *Weimar: A Jurisprudence of Crisis* (2000) (first published 1929), p. 76 at p. 78.

[108] Schmitt, *Legality and Legitimacy*, p. 20.   [109] *Ibid.*, p. 19.   [110] *Ibid.*, p. 24.

[111] *Ibid.*, p. 28.

[112] See David Dyzenhaus, *Legality and Legitimacy: Carl Schmitt, Hans Kelsen and Hermann Heller in Weimar* (Oxford: Oxford University Press, 1997), pp. 17–37.

passed by a democratically elected assembly. If the parliament had ceased to represent the will of an 'indivisibly similar, entire, unified people', then the sovereign lawmaker who could act as guarantor of the legal order would have to be found elsewhere.

For Schmitt, this question of who is able to guarantee protection is the core question of politics. Protection involves deciding on the exception and restoring order. Who or what has the capacity to do this is always a factual rather than a normative question. It cannot be answered mechanically, for example by assuming that any law passed by a parliament is valid. But nor can political or legal theory avoid offering a normative account of authority, as economic thinking, pluralism and positivism in their different ways sought to do. In the context of Weimar, Schmitt argued that in order to achieve political unity and social integration, it was necessary to question the treatment of parliament as the locus of political authority and the source of law in the democratic state. Schmitt advocated instead the expansion of executive rule. He argued that under the Weimar Constitution, the President was the one capable of guaranteeing political order. This required decisive action and the capacity to protect against enemies both within and beyond the state.

> Every actual democracy rests on the principle that not only are equals equal but unequals will not be treated equally. Democracy requires, therefore, first homogeneity and second – if the need arises – elimination or eradication of heterogeneity ... A democracy demonstrates its political power by knowing how to refuse or keep at bay something foreign and unequal that threatens its homogeneity.[113]

Protection and the capacity to distinguish friend from enemy

Schmitt, like Hobbes, was interested in the transfer that takes place 'from theology to the theory of the state'.[114] Schmitt understood theology and politics as linked through a chain of 'systematic and methodological analogies'.[115] In a system of that kind, that which 'is found at the beginning of a chain of things, is always found in a similar form at its

---

[113] Carl Schmitt, *The Crisis of Parliamentary Democracy*, Ellen Kennedy trans. (Cambridge, Massachusetts: The MIT Press, 1988) (first published 1934), p. 9.

[114] Schmitt, *Political Theology*, p. 36.

[115] *Ibid.*, p. 37. On the structure of the transfer from theology to politics in Schmitt's writing, see Anselm Haverkamp, 'Richard II, Bracton, and the End of Political Theology', *Law & Literature* 16 (2004), 313 at 314.

end'.[116] According to Schmitt, it was the Catholic counter-revolutionary philosophers who had recognised the substantial identity of the claims that 'the relevance of the state rested on the fact that it provided a decision' and that 'the relevance of the Church' rested 'on its rendering of the last decision that could not be appealed'.[117] Just as a state that cannot make the decision between friend and enemy is no longer sovereign, so too a theology that does not distinguish between friend and enemy ceases to be a true theology.

> A theologian ceases to be a theologian when he no longer considers man to be sinful or in need of redemption and no longer distinguishes between the chosen and the nonchosen.[118]

For Schmitt, the capacity to distinguish between friend and enemy was thus a key marker of authority. Jurisprudence no longer properly understood that in order to be representative, authority must be capable of making such distinctions.[119] An institution requires both 'political thinking and political form' in order to be representative.[120] An abstract idea without a concrete institution to give it expression has no effect in the world.[121] On the other hand, a concrete institution that has 'a sufficient minimum of form "to establish order"' and yet represents nothing beyond that order has no real claim 'to a unique power and authority'.[122]

According to Schmitt, this was the fate that had befallen the *jus publicum Europaeum* at the end of the nineteenth century. With the recognition of the Congo Free State, European international law had become 'purely positivistic' and 'lost any sense of ... the essential and specific distinctions in soil statuses in international law'.[123] European international law had depended for its meaning upon a spatial order premised upon the 'notion that European soil or soil equivalent to it had a different status in international law from that of uncivilized or non-European peoples'.[124] Once that was abandoned, European international

---

[116] Jens Bartelson, *A Genealogy of Sovereignty* (Cambridge: Cambridge University Press, 1995), p. 109.

[117] Schmitt, *Political Theology*, p. 55.   [118] Schmitt, *The Concept of the Political*, p. 64.

[119] Carl Schmitt, *Roman Catholicism and Political Form*, G. L. Ulmen trans. (Westport: Greenwood Press, 1996) (first published 1923), p. 26.

[120] *Ibid.*, p. 25.

[121] Carl Schmitt, *Political Theology II: The Myth of the Closure of Any Political Theology*, Michael Hoelzl and Graham Ward trans. (Cambridge: Polity Press, 2008) (first published 1970), p. 114.

[122] Schmitt, *Roman Catholicism*, p. 30.   [123] Schmitt, *Nomos of the Earth*, p. 220.

[124] *Ibid.*, p. 230.

law 'changed into a universal international law lacking any distinctions'.[125] Once it ceased to be capable of making such distinctions it ceased to be meaningful – the 'dissolution into general universality simultaneously spelled the destruction of the traditional global order of the earth'.[126] By implication, because international law could no longer properly distinguish between friend and enemy, it was no longer relevant, at least to Germany. Schmitt did think it possible to imagine a version of contemporary international law that would have worldly authority. It would have to be a form of international law that was represented by a concrete institution and capable of distinguishing between friend and enemy. His vision of an authoritative international legal order bears a marked resemblance to the form of international executive rule over the decolonised world that is being formalised through the implementation of the responsibility to protect. Schmitt wrote:

> The power to decide who is sovereign would signify a new sovereignty. A tribunal vested with such powers would constitute a supra-state and supra-sovereignty, which alone could create a new order if, for example, it had the authority to decide on the recognition of a new state. Not a Court of Justice but a League of Nations might have such pretensions. But in exercising them, it would become an independent agent. Together with the function of executing the law, managing an administration, etcetera ... it would also signify something in and of itself. Its activity would not be limited to the application of existing legal norms ... It would also be more than an arbiter, because in all decisive conflicts it would have to assert its own interests ... it would have to decide on the basis of its own power what new order and what new state is or is not to be recognized ... Such a tribunal would not only represent the idea of impersonal justice but a powerful personality as well.[127]

In his turn to protection as the grounds of authority, Schmitt was concerned with conjuring up the figure of an all-powerful sovereign who could restore order and issue commands that would be obeyed. That figure both enabled and represented the general will. Law, to be worthy of the name, must be created by such a sovereign – an authority both willing and able to distinguish between friend and enemy, the chosen and the non-chosen, the civilized and the uncivilized, Europe and its others. Any law that 'would not dare reach a decision on this question' or 'that forgoes imposing a substantive order, but chooses

---

[125] *Ibid.*, p. 231. [126] *Ibid.*, p. 227. [127] Schmitt, *Roman Catholicism*, pp. 30–1.

instead to give warring factions, intellectual circles, and political programs the illusion of gaining satisfaction legally . . . would end by destroying its own legality and legitimacy'.[128] The responsibility to protect demanded not police action but war.

International executive rule and the politics of protection

This chapter has offered a history of the linkage of protection and authority during times of revolution or civil war – in other words, when the notion of war is used to shape understandings of civil life within a state or where there are competing claimants to legitimate rule. The turn to protection has worked in such situations to discredit populist arguments that authority should be grounded on right, or on an authentic or historical relation between governors and governed. Hobbes' argument that the capacity to provide protection was the marker of legitimate authority was a way of pulling the rug out from under revolutionary claims for a rejection of the Norman yoke. His turn to protection privileged de facto authority over appeals to popular sovereignty, the ancient constitution, the will of the people or the obligations of history. Schmitt's return to the notion of protection, and his reclamation of the political theory of Hobbes as inspiration for a new totalitarian state theory, allowed him to deny all that came after the early modern period – the centuries of challenges to the absolutist state in the form of revolutionary, romantic or cosmopolitan accounts of the relation between ruler and ruled.

Grounding authority on the capacity to protect does tend to privilege certain kinds of institutions and certain forms of action over others. For example, the turn to protection functions to privilege de facto over de jure authority, or fact over right. To characterise a situation as one of civil war or anarchy is to register the absence of some preconceived form of integrative force.[129] The turn to protection focuses upon conjuring up that integrative force, and thus moves towards creating institutions that privilege coherence, control and centralisation. This has long been the framework within which the need for international authority in the decolonised world has been explained. Dag Hammarskjöld looked at the newly independent states of Africa and saw a vacuum that needed

---

[128] Schmitt, *Legality and Legitimacy*, p. 94.
[129] Keith Tribe, *Strategies of Economic Order: German Economic Discourse 1750–1950* (Cambridge: Cambridge University Press, 1995), p. 199.

to be filled by a decisive international executive. The advocates of the responsibility to protect concept look at the decolonised world and see a manifest failure to protect and the need for a form of international rule that is coherent, unified and integrated. In each case, the claim that self-determination, popular sovereignty or parliamentary rule should be the marker of legitimacy is marginalised. In that respect, authority justified in terms of its capacity to guarantee protection has a tendency to become authoritarian. The deprivations of liberty in the absolutist states of early modern Europe, the police actions of colonial powers and the terror inflicted by the security forces of fascist Germany were all explained as exercises in institutionalising protection. It might seem extreme to suggest that there could be any relation between those forms of authoritarian rule and the benign ambitions of the responsibility to protect concept. Yet while the responsibility to protect concept challenges the tyranny of states or insurgents in the name of the people, it does not propose to vest the power wrested from the state in the people, or at least not immediately. Instead, it posits the international community as the champion of the people's right to protection. This international community appears to date to be largely unlimited in terms of the actions it can take to achieve its universal mission.[130]

But now almost ½ y int'l Community are Those decolonized world

Yet this is not to say that the turn to protection has a predetermined political effect. To argue that the capacity to protect grounds authority is itself a normative claim. De facto authority, the capacity to protect in fact, is only perceived as giving legitimacy to power where protection is already invested with a normative value. Differences in the nature of that normative claim give rise to important differences in the project of creating institutions that can realise protection in this world. For Hobbes, the normative foundation of authority derives from natural

---

[130] See *Behrami and Behrami v. France*, App. No. 71412/01, *Saramati v. France, Germany, and Norway*, App. No. 78166/01, European Court of Human Rights Grand Chamber, Decision on Admissibility (31 May 2007) (where the Grand Chamber of the European Court of Human Rights held that operations established by Security Council resolutions, such as that conducted in Kosovo, are 'fundamental to the mission of the UN to secure international peace and security' and that to subject the actions carried out under UN authority to the scrutiny of the European Court of Human Rights would 'interfere with the fulfilment of the UN's key mission in this field including, as argued by certain parties, with the effective conduct of its operations'). For a discussion of these admissibility decisions and the way in which they relate to international rule, see Anne Orford, 'The Passions of Protection: Sovereign Authority and Humanitarian War' in Didier Fassin and Mariella Pandolfi (eds.), *Contemporary States of Emergency: The Politics of Military and Humanitarian Interventions* (New York: Zone Books, 2010), p. 335.

law – the sovereign exists to realise the commandment to make peace. By linking authority and protection, Hobbes prefigured at least three traditions that would be taken up in the centuries to follow, and that are potentially directions in which the responsibility to protect concept might be taken today. First, he prefigured an individualist or liberal tradition, in which 'the "generality" into which the freedom of the individual was incorporated was meant at least in theory to fulfil the values and needs of individuals'.[131] Secondly, he prefigured a revolutionary tradition that would politicise the tension between the general interest (properly conceived) and the particular interest of the ruling class that could masquerade as the general interest because the ruling class controlled the state. Thirdly, he prefigured a long line of counter-revolutionary theorists who would move away from the position 'that the state originates from the "material" interests and needs of individuals'.[132] Those theorists would instead elevate the general interest of the unified will of a people or a nation above the interests and needs of particular individuals. It was that latter move that was performed by Schmitt in his argument for the executive as the form that could best realise the will of the people in the twentieth-century democracies of Europe. For Schmitt, the normative foundation of authority was grounded upon the ability to defend the inherent values of the European order. Peace and protection depended upon the existence of a sovereign that was capable of distinguishing between friend and enemy, and defeating that which threatened homogeneity and unity.

To justify authority on the basis of the capacity to protect and to guarantee peace can thus lead to quite different political projects. Hobbes and Schmitt both claimed that the political forms they sought to bring into being would procure the welfare of the people. Yet so too did Rousseau, Lenin and Lumumba. Debates about the meaning of the commitment to maintaining peace and protecting life have haunted international intervention over the past six decades. For example, as Chapter 2 showed, when Dag Hammarskjöld advocated the need for international executive action in the Congo and elsewhere, it was on the grounds that the UN was guided solely by the interests of the people and was capable of maintaining order and protecting life. In the name of peace and protection, he systematically developed a form of emergency rule that would fill the vacuum left by departing imperial powers, prevent the expansion of the Cold War, enable the security of investment and

---

[131] Marcuse, *A Study on Authority*, p. 72.   [132] *Ibid.*, p. 55.

prevent civil war. Yet Lumumba's vision of the future of the Congo could equally plausibly be described as a means of procuring the welfare of the people. His was a vision premised upon ending imperial aggression and destabilisation, building economic independence, redistributing resources and creating nationalist unity built on political solidarity rather than ethnic identity. The visions of peace and protection for the Congo held by Hammarskjöld and Lumumba proved irreconcilable.

Like Hammarskjöld, and like Hobbes and Schmitt before him, those advocating the responsibility to protect concept call for the consolidation of executive rule in order to protect the people. Most of the attention in the responsibility to protect literature to date has been on the ways in which the need for protection justifies the expansion of international authority in situations where a state has failed to protect its population. That literature has been concerned with ensuring the international community is empowered to prevent mass atrocity, to react in a timely and decisive fashion if atrocities are occurring and to rebuild after atrocity. In terms of the responsibility to prevent mass atrocities, the UN and humanitarian actors have focused upon creating more efficient early warning capabilities and enhanced fact-finding mechanisms.[133] The prospect of increased surveillance of foreign populations has been welcomed as a contribution to realising the promise that never again will genocide be allowed to occur, rather than seen as a threat to civil liberties or self-determination.[134] In terms of the responsibility to react, activists have to date focused most of their energy on arguing for increased military intervention and criminal prosecution, calling for decisions about the use of force to be made quickly and for military forces engaged in protection operations to be strengthened.[135] In terms of the responsibility to rebuild, there is an echo of 1930s Europe in the way in which international administration post-intervention is conducted and envisaged.[136] Authoritarian theorists of the state such as Schmitt argued that the function of law was to further social goals on behalf of the will of a

---

[133] *Ibid.*, pp. 31–3.

[134] For an insight into the way in which the widespread US counter-insurgency surveillance conducted in foreign states can be characterised as a form of genocide prevention, see Barbara Harff, 'How to Use Risk Assessment and Early Warning in the Prevention and De-Escalation of Genocide and Other Mass Atrocities', *Global Responsibility to Protect* 1 (2009), 506.

[135] For a critique of this tendency, see Alex de Waal, 'Darfur and the Failure of the Responsibility to Protect', *International Affairs* 83 (2007), 1039.

[136] See further the discussion in Chapter 2 above.

unified people. They aimed to diminish the potential for parliamentary participation and expand the potential for executive governance in the name of achieving social and economic integration.[137] This has also been the nature and effect of post-conflict governance in the aftermath of international interventions.[138] During the 1990s, humanitarian intervention was routinely followed by the creation and legitimation of strong international administrations, marked by an apparent distrust of local parliamentary democracy, an absence of constraints on international executive decisions and the prioritisation of economic liberalisation as a policy goal.[139] The ICISS report continues to treat international administration as a technical project, concerned with 'protection tasks' such as security sector reform, the facilitation of repatriation, the 'pursuit of war criminals' and 'the recreation of markets'.[140] The Secretary-General's report on implementing the responsibility to protect continues to focus upon systematising, integrating and expanding international executive authority. Overall, much of the responsibility to protect literature assumes that in times of emergency, such as is experienced by people caught up in civil war, protection can only be guaranteed where there exists an authority capable of distinguishing between friends and enemies, and taking the decision necessary to restore the normal situation in which the law can function. There is little discussion to date of the legal limits to the actions that the international community might take in the name of protecting populations at risk. It is to that question of limits that those who are institutionalising the responsibility to protect must turn if the authoritarian tendencies inherent in the appeal to de facto protective authority are to be avoided.

But who is the int'l community.

Yet although the literature endorsing the responsibility to protect concept has exhibited authoritarian tendencies, the political implications of the contemporary turn to protection as the ground of authority remain uncertain. The history of attempts to ground authority upon protection shows that much will depend upon who interprets what protection or the safety of the people means in a particular time and place, and who decides whether and how it will be achieved. Hobbes vested the capacity to judge what protection would mean with the representatives of the

---

[137] Alexander Somek, 'Austrian Constitutional Doctrine 1933 to 1938' in Christian Joerges and Navraj Singh Ghaleigh (eds.), *Darker Legacies of Law in Europe* (Oxford and Portland: Hart Publishing, 2003), p. 361.

[138] Anne Orford, *Reading Humanitarian Intervention: Human Rights and the Use of Force in International Law* (Cambridge: Cambridge University Press, 2003), pp. 126–43.

[139] *Ibid.*   [140] ICISS, *The Responsibility to Protect*, pp. 43, 65.

commonwealth. Schmitt vested the capacity to decide what protection required with the representative of the unified nation. The responsibility to protect concept vests the capacity to determine that a state has 'manifestly' failed to guarantee protection with the 'international community'. In 2009, Ban Ki-moon declared that: 'The Secretary-General must be the spokesperson for the vulnerable and the threatened when their Governments become their persecutors instead of their protectors or can no longer shield them from marauding armed groups.'[141] Yet there remain many other actors who claim the responsibility to judge the conduct of rulers, to represent the people of the decolonised world and to guarantee peace. The turn to protection opens up the questions of who can rightly claim to speak in the name of the 'international community' in a given situation, what vision of protection the international community will seek to realise and on whose behalf the responsibility to protect will be exercised. These questions are unavoidably political. Answering them involves deciding upon the normative commitments that will shape the institutionalisation of protection and how these commitments will be achieved. Should implementing the responsibility to protect mean the attempt to control all aspects of life within securitised states in order to defeat the enemies of international peace? Should it mean the adoption of pacification techniques aimed at insurgent groups? Should it mean the implementation of liberal policing to manage the tensions between wealthy and poor inherited from colonialism and entrenched by an international division of labour? Or should it mean the development of new forms of action that are shaped by the communities being policed? Which authority, representing which normative commitments and acting on behalf of which people, will have the jurisdiction to state what protection means and which claimant to authority is capable of delivering it? As Hobbes himself recognised, questions about who decides and who interprets are fundamental to an account of authority premised upon the capacity to protect. Those questions are taken up in Chapter 4.

---

[141] UN Secretary-General, *Implementing the Responsibility to Protect: Report of the Secretary-General*, UN GAOR, 63rd Sess., Agenda Items 44 and 107, UN Doc. A/63/677, 12 January 2009, p. 26.

4

Who Decides? Who Interprets?: Jurisdiction, Recognition and the Institutionalisation of Protection

> Until the Day of Judgement, the Augustinian teaching on the two kingdoms will have to face the twofold open question: *Quis judicabit? Quis interpretabitur?* ['Who will decide? Who will interpret?'] Who answers *in concreto*, on behalf of the concrete, autonomously acting human being, the question of what is spiritual, what is worldly and what is the case with the *res mixtae*.[1]

Thomas Hobbes taught that in a fractured world, where tradition, shared values or a common God no longer guaranteed meaning, the lawfulness of authority could only be grounded upon the capacity to protect. Yet the turn to protection as the basis of authority raised a new question: who decides? Who decides what protection means and which claimant to authority can guarantee it? Who decides whether a particular government is in fact capable of protecting its population and bringing peace to its territory? Who has the authority to judge the legitimacy of rulers? Who speaks for peace in a particular time and place?

Those questions were central to the project of establishing and consolidating the authority of the modern state. When Hobbes argued that the lawfulness of authority was grounded upon the capacity to protect, he was playing a part in a much broader struggle between church and state, or spiritual and temporal authority. Central to that struggle was the question of whether the Pope had jurisdiction to declare that a ruler was unlawful and should be deposed or resisted. That was far from being a purely doctrinal or academic problem. Successive popes had not only claimed the authority to depose rulers, but had regularly practiced that authority. European rulers knew only too well that to be declared a

---

[1] Carl Schmitt, *Political Theology II: The Myth of the Closure of Any Political Theology*, Michael Hoelzl and Graham Ward trans. (Cambridge: Polity Press, 2008) (first published 1970), p. 115.

tyrant or a heretic by the Pope could lead to wars being waged by foreign rulers or rebellions being staged by the faithful within a kingdom. For many sovereigns and their advisers, the papal claim to depose kings had become a threat to European peace. Thus the relation between competing forms of jurisdiction, temporal and spiritual, was key to political and legal debate in the early modern period. While many theologians developed detailed arguments explaining why spiritual authority was superior to temporal authority, it was Hobbes who developed a systematic argument in support of the superior jurisdiction of the civil authority.

As the state emerged to become the dominant political form in Europe, the universal jurisdiction of the Pope and the Holy Roman Emperor ceased to pose a real challenge to the authority of temporal rulers. Yet the question of 'who decides' proved persistent. One form in which the question of 'who decides' returned was in international legal doctrines concerning the effect of the recognition of a government or of a new state. According to the declaratory theory of recognition, which was dominant until the late eighteenth century, the 'legal status' of a ruler was understood to be 'derived and perfected from within'.[2] As a result, 'internal legality' determined 'external legality'.[3] If the legitimacy of a government were understood to depend upon external recognition or championing by external powers, the uneasy peace that existed in the aftermath of the European wars of religion could quickly unravel. Even during a period of interregnum or civil war, the state was treated as having the jurisdiction to determine the legitimacy of its rulers, and external actors had no right to interfere in that decision. Yet beginning in the early nineteenth century, in response to revolutions in Europe and the New World, this began to change. The law of nations began to treat legitimacy as a question that had to be determined both internally and externally. External recognition began to be seen as constitutive – as an act that 'renders the sovereignty of a new State perfect and complete'.[4]

In the post-UN era, the role of external actors in determining the legitimacy of governments became linked to international jurisdiction. In that context, the question of who decides began to function on a number of different levels. First, as in earlier debates about recognition, the question of who decides manifested as a question about

[2] C. H. Alexandrowicz, 'The Theory of Recognition *in Fieri*', *British Year Book of International Law* 34 (1958), 176 at 179.
[3] *Ibid.* [4] *Ibid.*

representation and jurisdiction. Is the legitimacy of a government or a ruler an internal matter? Or is governmental legitimacy a matter for the broader international community? Secondly, if the question of whether a ruler is willing and able to protect the people is considered to be a matter for the international community to decide, who has the authority to represent the international community and interpret the meaning of peace and protection in a particular situation? The question of who decides in that sense has been at the heart of debates about the role of the UN in the decolonised world since at least the early 1960s. In his famous attack on the neutrality of Secretary-General Dag Hammarskjöld, then Russian President Khrushchev addressed precisely this question of the power to interpret the meaning of peace and protection in a given situation:

> The responsibility for interpreting and executing all the decisions of the General Assembly and the Security Council at present falls upon one man. But there is an old saying that there are not, and never were, any saints on earth. Let those who believe in saints hold to their opinion; we do not credit such tales. So this one man – at the present time, Mr Hammarskjöld – has to interpret and execute the decisions of the General Assembly and the Security Council, bearing in mind the interests of the monopoly-capitalist countries as well as those of the socialist countries and of the neutral countries. But this is not possible. Everyone has heard how vigorously the imperialist countries defend Mr Hammarskjöld's position. Is it not clear then, in whose interest he interprets and executes those decisions, whose 'saint' he is? Mr. Hammarskjöld has always been prejudiced in his attitude towards the socialist countries; he has always upheld the interests of the United States of America and the other monopoly-capitalist countries. The events in the Congo (Leopoldville), where he played a simply deplorable role, were merely the last drop which filled the cup of our patience to overflowing.[5]

In response, Hammarskjöld sought to argue that the question of who decides is an inappropriately personal one that bears no relation to the broader issue of institutional responsibility and effectiveness:

> I have no reason to defend myself or my colleagues against the accusations and judgements to which you have listened. Let me say only this: that you, all of you, are the judges. No single party can claim that authority. I am sure that you will be guided by truth and justice ... I

---

[5] Nikita Khrushchev, Chairman of the Council of Ministers of the Union of the Soviet Socialist Republics, 'Statement to the UN General Assembly', UN GAOR, 15th Sess., 882nd Plen. Mtg., Agenda Item 9, UN Doc. A/PV.882, 3 October 1960, paras. 22–4.

regret that the intervention to which I found it necessary to reply has again tended to personalize an issue which, as I have said, in my view is not a question of a man but of an institution. The man does not count; the institution does. A weak or non-existent executive would mean that the United Nations would no longer be able to serve as an effective instrument for active protection of the interests of those many Members who need such protection.[6]

As this debate illustrates, the strengthening of international authority over the decolonised world still leaves open the question of *which* body claiming to represent the universal or the international community has the authority to state whether a ruler is lawful or what protection demands in a given time and place. If it is decided that the UN has jurisdiction to determine whether a state is able to maintain order and guarantee protection, which representatives of the UN should make that decision – executive bodies such as the Security Council or the Secretariat, parliamentary bodies such as the General Assembly or judicial bodies such as the International Court of Justice (ICJ)? Alternatively, perhaps it is for the representatives of a higher truth to judge the lawfulness of authority – whether those representatives be human rights bodies, the International Criminal Court or the World Bank. Each claims the jurisdiction to examine the lawfulness of government action in the decolonised world.

Questions about the authority to determine the lawfulness of governments and rulers have been reopened with the emergence of the responsibility to protect concept. The formulation of the responsibility to protect concept in the World Summit Outcome was a matter of intense negotiation in the lead-up to the World Summit of the General Assembly. Many states, particularly from the global South, were very concerned at the potential expansion of international authority that might follow from any official endorsement of the responsibility to protect concept. As a result, states looked to the definition of jurisdictional issues as a means of limiting the situations in which the international community might claim that an international responsibility to protect had arisen. Yet while the provisions of the World Summit Outcome addressing the responsibility to protect concept stress the primary authority of the state as the guarantor of protection,

---

[6] Dag Hammarskjöld, UN Secretary-General, 'Statement to the UN General Assembly', UN GAOR, 15th Sess., 883rd Plen. Mtg., Agenda Item 9, UN Doc. A/PV.883, 3 October 1960, paras. 8–9.

[handwritten annotation: not The int'l Community but the Security-Council]

they also imply that the 'international community' has the jurisdiction to determine whether and when a government has manifestly failed to protect its population. In addition, other provisions of the World Summit Outcome reinforce the jurisdiction of other claimants to authority in the decolonised world, such as the International Criminal Court and the Bretton Woods institutions. This chapter concludes that at stake in the implementation of the responsibility to protect concept is whether it will consolidate a shift of jurisdiction to the international community in general, and to the executive organs of the UN in particular.

[handwritten annotation: But it already has made that shift]

Jurisdiction, control and the modern state

The relationship between jurisdiction ('the power of stating what is lawful'[7]) and control over territory has long been a contested one. As the modern state gradually replaced the Holy Roman Empire to become the dominant form of political organisation in Western Europe, questions about the limits and divisibility of power began to be framed as questions about the relationship between jurisdiction and territory. The emergence of the territorial state during the sixteenth and seventeenth centuries posed a challenge to the universal jurisdiction of both the Pope and the Holy Roman Emperor within Europe. Both the Pope and the Emperor claimed the right to exercise jurisdiction over the world as a matter of right, even if they had no control over particular territories as a matter of empirical fact. The relationship between jurisdiction and territory was not only an issue within Europe. During the sixteenth and seventeenth centuries, debates about the authority of European sovereigns to rule newly discovered territories in the New World also began to be articulated in terms of the relation between jurisdiction and control over territory. Disputes among European powers about which Christian monarchs could claim rights of *dominium* over territory in the New World turned on whether the Pope had the authority and jurisdiction to grant such rights.[8]

---

[7] Peter Stein, *Roman Law in European History* (Cambridge: Cambridge University Press, 1999), p. 60.

[8] See, for example, Francisco de Vitoria, *Political Writings*, Anthony Pagden and Jeremy Lawrance (eds.) (Cambridge: Cambridge University Press, 1991), pp. 84–92; Richard Hakluyt, *A Discourse concerning Western Planting, Written in the Year 1584*, Charles Deane (ed.) (Cambridge: Cambridge University Press, 1877), pp. 129–51. See also Ken MacMillan, *Sovereignty and Possession in the English New World: The Legal Foundations of Empire, 1576–1640* (Cambridge: Cambridge University Press, 2006), pp. 64–74

The triumph of the territorial state as the dominant political form globally has meant that jurisdiction and territory have come to be understood as closely related terms. Richard Ford, for example, argues that modern jurisdiction is always 'defined by area'.[9] While in theory an entity could be defined in terms of genre (for example, as an entity with 'authority over "all oil, wherever it is found"'), that entity 'would not be a jurisdiction but an authority of another kind. A jurisdiction is territorially defined.'[10] Yet if we look at the history of the debate over the right of external actors to determine the legitimacy of control over territory, we can see that the relation between jurisdiction and territory has never been finally determined. That debate stretches across 600 years, from fifteenth-century arguments about the extent of papal or imperial jurisdiction to decide who has authority over territories in Europe or the New World, through to contemporary debates about whether the international community has jurisdiction to intervene in situations where states are ruled by tyrants or by governments that are unable or unwilling to protect the population.

The debate, as with many debates over authority in Europe during that time, was framed using the language and concepts of Roman law.[11] The most important of these Roman law concepts to this debate were those of *ius*, *dominium*, *imperium* and *iurisdictio*. In early Roman law, the concept of *ius* was used to refer to the outcome of a 'method of divine judgement'.[12] Disputants were required to take an oath attesting to the righteousness of their claim, and these claims would then be tested by 'ordeal or other supernatural judgement. The favorable verdict was a *ius*.'[13] A *ius* was thus both 'something objectively right' and something intimately connected with 'private, bilateral relationships' and the 'right

(discussing the English response to papal claims of authority and jurisdiction to distribute lands in the New World).

[9] Richard T. Ford, 'Law's Territory (A History of Jurisdiction)', *Michigan Law Review* 97 (1999), 843 at 852.

[10] *Ibid.*

[11] See *ibid.*, 38–67 (discussing the twelfth-century recovery of Roman law in Western Europe). For two analyses of the importance of Roman law to debates about the limits of imperial authority during the medieval and early modern periods, see David Armitage, *The Ideological Origins of the British Empire* (Cambridge: Cambridge University Press, 2000), pp. 29–36; Anthony Pagden, *Lords of All the World: Ideologies of Empire in Spain, Britain and France c.1500–c.1800* (New Haven: Yale University Press, 1995), pp. 11–28.

[12] Richard Tuck, *Natural Rights Theories: Their Origin and Development* (Cambridge: Cambridge University Press, 1979), p. 8.

[13] *Ibid.*

way in which two disputants should behave towards each other'.[14] A *ius* could also come into existence through agreements, such as agreements between neighbours. The objective and relational quality of *ius* distinguished it from the concept of *dominium*. Classical lawyers distinguished between 'having *dominium* in something and having a *ius* in it'.[15] *Dominium* was not constituted through agreements or relationships. Instead, it was 'simply given by the fact, as it seemed to the Romans, of a man's total control over his physical world'.[16] In the later Empire, the distinction between notions of *ius* and *dominium* would become much less clean-cut. As the Emperor became more powerful and able to intervene in all aspects of life, the idea that a citizen might have 'total control over his physical world' began to seem 'increasingly implausible'.[17] Everything, including *dominium*, was mediated through the Emperor. The Emperor was the citizen 'with whom all other Roman citizens had the most extensive relationships'.[18] *Dominium* began increasingly to be seen as a form of *ius*.

Nonetheless, the distinction between *ius* as an objective right that was ultimately determinable by divine judgment, and *dominium* as a form of property that was determinable by ascertaining who had control over the physical world, would reappear in medieval debates over the reach of papal or imperial authority. Central to those debates was the question of whether either the Pope or the Holy Roman Emperor could properly claim to exercise universal jurisdiction (*ius dicere*) as *dominus mundi* or lord of the world. The idea that the papacy and the Emperor exercised dual forms of universal jurisdiction shaped medieval legal thought.[19] The extent of papal and imperial jurisdiction, and the relation between jurisdiction and control (or *ius* and fact), had important implications both within and beyond Europe.

To take one example, the extent of papal jurisdiction was at the heart of the dispute about the legitimacy of Alexander VI's Bulls of Donation, through which the Spanish Crown claimed *dominium* over the New World. The papal bull *Inter caetera*, issued by Alexander VI in 1493, granted to 'the illustrious sovereigns' King Ferdinand and Queen Isabella, and to their 'heirs and successors, kings of Castile and Leon', 'all islands and mainlands found and to be found, discovered and to be discovered' in the Atlantic world 'towards the west and south' of a line

---

[14] *Ibid.*   [15] *Ibid.*, p. 10.   [16] *Ibid.*   [17] *Ibid.*   [18] *Ibid.*, p. 12.
[19] James Muldoon, *Empire and Order: The Concept of Empire, 800–1800* (Basingstoke: Palgrave Macmillan, 1999), p. 65.

bisecting the Atlantic ocean.[20] The proviso to this 'gift, grant, and assign-
ment' was that 'no right acquired by any Christian prince, who may be in
actual possession of said islands and mainlands' could be 'withdrawn or
taken away'.[21] By implication, *imperium* and *dominium* did not vest with
indigenous peoples.[22] The Spanish crown interpreted *Inter caetera* and
the other Bulls of Donation as grants that authorised Spanish *dominium*
over the lands they 'discovered' in the New World. Ferdinand and
Isabella appeared to believe not only that the Pope had the authority to
dispose of *dominium* over lands in the New World, but that they needed
a papal grant in order to acquire *dominium* over such lands.[23] The Bulls
of Donation were drafted in consultation with Ferdinand and Isabella,
and proof of the value that the Spanish monarchs attached to the bulls
can be seen 'in their anxiety that the things which they desired should be
incorporated in them, and also in the revisions to which ... they subsequently caused them to be subjected'.[24]

The bulls continued to be invoked both by the Spanish crown and by
its imperial rivals in debates over the legal justifications for Spanish
conquest of the New World until the late seventeenth century.[25] To
take just one example, when Sir Francis Drake returned to England
after his circumnavigation of the world in September 1580, with reports
of having claimed land including Nova Albion (today's California or
Oregon) and with commodities from the West Indies and South
America, the Spanish ambassador Mendoza lodged a formal complaint
with Queen Elizabeth.[26] Mendoza claimed 'that these territories
belonged to the King of Spain by virtue of first discovery and the papal
bull of donation'.[27] In return, almost every 'French or English attack on
the claims to Spanish sovereignty overseas' involved 'a rejection of the
validity of both the Bulls and the terms of the Treaty of Tordesillas'.[28]

---

[20] Alexander VI, *The Bull* Inter Caetera (1493), as reprinted in Frances Gardiner Davenport
(ed.), *European Treaties Bearing on the History of the United States and Its Dependencies
to 1648* (Washington DC: Carnegie Institution of Washington, 1917), p. 71 at pp. 75–8.
[21] *Ibid.*, p. 77.
[22] Antony Anghie, *Imperialism, Sovereignty and the Making of International Law*
(Cambridge: Cambridge University Press, 2004), p. 17.
[23] H. Vander Linden, 'Alexander VI and the Demarcation of the Maritime and Colonial
Domains of Spain and Portugal, 1493–1494', *American Historical Review* 22 (1916), 1 at
15–16.
[24] *Ibid.*, p. 16.
[25] MacMillan, *Sovereignty and Possession*, pp. 66–74; Pagden, *Lords of All the World*, p. 48.
[26] MacMillan, *Sovereignty and Possession*, pp. 52, 75.   [27] *Ibid.*, p. 75.
[28] Pagden, *Lords of All the World*, p. 48.

Most challenges to the validity of the Bulls of Donation argued that the Pope did not have jurisdiction to grant rights to territory. Perhaps the most famous of these were the challenges to Spanish conquest of the New World posed by Francisco de Vitoria and his followers. Vitoria argued that 'the [P]ope has no dominion (*dominium*) in the lands of the infidel' and those who think that the Pope 'has temporal authority and jurisdiction over all princes in the world, are wrong'.[29] According to Vitoria, '*the [P]ope has no power, at least in the ordinary course of events, to judge the cases of princes, or the titles of jurisdictions or realms*'.[30] While Vitoria did accept that the Pope had authority 'to use temporal means' where necessary to fulfil a spiritual purpose,[31] he considered that this did not give the Pope authority 'to award rights of *imperium* and *dominium* over *terra incognita*, which was within the jurisdiction of temporal, Roman law'.[32] The spiritual jurisdiction of the Pope thus did not extend to the temporal world. A similar challenge to the legitimacy of the Bulls of Donation was made by the Anglican priest Richard Hakluyt the younger. Hakluyt argued that the Pope had no authority to dispose of or distribute 'kingdomes and empires'.[33] According to Hakluyt, ecclesiastical jurisdiction 'hath nothinge to doe with absolution donation and devidinge of mere temporalities and earthly kingdomes'.[34] The Bulls of Donation therefore posed no limitations upon the rights of the English to trade, settle or plant in the New World, as 'no Pope had any lawfull aucthoritie to give any suche donation at all'.[35]

There were, however, some advisers to the English crown who accepted that the Pope had jurisdiction to make the donation of territory and invest the Spanish king with rights to the New World. In particular, this argument was made by the 'English renaissance polymath' John Dee,[36] who was one of the advisers commissioned by Elizabeth to consider whether, and on what basis, English activities in the New World could be justified. Dee's writings drew on his training in geography and mathematics, as well as his knowledge of law and history.[37] Unlike some of his

---

[29] Vitoria, *Political Writings*, p. 84.   [30] *Ibid.*, p. 87 (emphasis in original).
[31] *Ibid.*, p. 92.   [32] MacMillan, *Sovereignty and Possession*, p. 68.
[33] Hakluyt, *Discourse concerning Western Planting*, p. 130.   [34] *Ibid.*
[35] *Ibid.*, p. 129. Hakluyt's challenge to papal authority is discussed in MacMillan, *Sovereignty and Possession*, p. 67.
[36] Ken MacMillan, 'Introduction: Discourse on History, Geography, and Law' in John Dee, *The Limits of the British Empire*, Ken MacMillan with Jennifer Abeles (eds.) (London: Praeger, 2004), p. 1 at p. 2.
[37] See generally Dee, *The Limits of the British Empire*.

contemporaries, Dee was prepared to concede that Alexander VI had 'authoretie' to 'gift' land in the New World and that such an act was 'of force sufficient by Gods lawe or mans lawe against all other Christian princes'.[38] Dee was willing to accept that the Pope had such authority because he saw 'the jurisdiction assumed by the [P]ope and his bull' as 'legally analogous to that of Elizabeth' and the letters patent she issued to petitioners seeking authorisation to claim *dominium* over territories in the New World.[39] For Dee, Elizabeth, as 'the leader of the Anglican Church and a holder of *imperium*', was able to 'authorize settlement in the New World', in the same way that 'the [P]ope, the leader of the Catholic Church and a holder of *imperium*' was able to donate territory.[40] Just as the Spanish *conquistadores* traced their rights to territory in the New World to the Bulls of Donation, English settlers and trading companies traced their rights to territory in the New World to the letters patent issued by Elizabeth. Both the papal bulls and the letters patent were represented as exercises of jurisdiction, through which the power to authorise rights to territory was expressed in writing. These documents did not simply claim jurisdiction but also *performed* jurisdiction. By this I mean that jurisdiction involves the process by which a worldly claimant to authority is transformed through the successful performance of the power to declare the law. To the extent that the Pope or Elizabeth claimed to have a form of jurisdiction that enabled them to declare rights to title in far-flung territories, they represented themselves as something other than mere tyrants or de facto rulers whose armies or followers were able to gain control of territory by force.

In addition to debates over the extent of the spiritual jurisdiction exercised by the Pope, the extent of the Holy Roman Emperor's jurisdiction was also contested within Europe and beyond. The secular jurisdiction of the Holy Roman Emperor was conceived of as universal. The medieval jurist Bartolus of Sassoferrato made this clear in his defence of the claim that the Emperor was lord of the world despite the fact that 'foreign peoples, the cities of Italy, and the kings of France and England did not obey him'.[41] Bartolus sought to

---

[38] *Ibid.*, p. 91. See also *ibid.*, pp. 92–3 (challenging the Iberian interpretation of the grant as being too liberal because, according to Dee, the bull was intended by the Pope to be proscriptive and to limit Spanish domination of the New World to a particular geographically defined area); MacMillan, *Sovereignty and Possession*, pp. 49–78 (providing a detailed analysis of Dee's arguments).

[39] MacMillan, *Sovereignty and Possession*, pp. 73, 107.   [40] *Ibid.*, p. 73.

[41] Constantin Fasolt, *The Limits of History* (Chicago: University of Chicago Press, 2004), p. 192.

show that the Emperor's universal jurisdiction could survive and co-exist with the new forms of territorial jurisdiction beginning to be exercised by princes and kings. The Emperor was lord of the world, not because he was lord of all the particular things, places and people in the world, but rather because 'he alone had *dominium* over the world considered as a single whole'.[42] Bartolus defended this claim by distinguishing between the universal jurisdiction of the Emperor and the particular jurisdictions of other rulers, such as the kings of England and France. The two could coexist because they were of a different nature. The universal jurisdiction of the Emperor involved jurisdiction 'over the world considered as a single whole' rather than as a collection of 'particular things', while the jurisdiction of kings constituted jurisdiction over particular things (such as England or France).[43] Jurisdiction was not an effect of power, but a form of power. The Emperor had universal jurisdiction over the world as a matter of right, not as a question of fact. However, when ambitious monarchs like Charles V or Ferdinand II succeeded to the title of Emperor, they sought to combine temporal authority with the universal rights to which they felt entitled as rulers of the Roman Empire.[44] It was during such periods when the reach of imperial authority became more worldly and threatening to peace in Europe that theologians and jurists developed elaborate analyses of the proper relation between spiritual and temporal authorities.

For centuries in the Christian West, that relation had been interpreted through the principle of dualism. Dualism was premised upon the idea that spiritual power was independent of temporal power, and that each was superior in its own sphere. Yet that neat division of jurisdictional authority never fully succeeded in resolving the worldly problem of who decides whether a matter is spiritual and thus properly within the scope of papal authority, or temporal and thus within the scope of secular authority. Competing interpretations of the proper relationship between pope, emperor and monarch showed 'how dualism could be tempered'.[45] For example, an expansive reading of dualism that could be used to justify the collapse of 'ecclesiological dualism into a unified power structure favouring Rome' emerged alongside the expansive ambitions of the papal monarchy from 1050 to 1300.[46] Dualism according to

---

[42] *Ibid.*   [43] *Ibid.*   [44] *Ibid.*, p. 93 (discussing Ferdinand II).

[45] J. A. Watt, 'Spiritual and Temporal Powers' in J. H. Burns (ed.), *The Cambridge History of Medieval Political Thought c.350–c.1450* (Cambridge: Cambridge University Press, 1988), p. 367 at p. 369.

[46] Jeffrey R. Collins, *The Allegiance of Thomas Hobbes* (Oxford: Oxford University Press, 2005), p. 16.

that papal interpretation meant that there existed two orders – 'corporal and spiritual, earthly and heavenly, spiritual and temporal'.[47] Because spiritual life was of more value than temporal life, it followed that spiritual authority was superior to temporal authority. The superiority of spiritual authority was translated into juridical terms to explain why it was for the Pope 'to establish the temporal power and to judge it if it fails to do good'.[48] Yet even as it enthusiastically argued for the supremacy of spiritual over temporal jurisdiction, the Papacy never completely abandoned its allegiance to the dualist tradition.

The rulers of emerging states in Europe thus faced 'two universal antagonists outside their own realms', in the form of the Papacy and the Empire.[49] Both claimed authority as a supranational body descended from the Roman Empire, and both alleged that this legacy gave them universal jurisdiction, understood as the power to state what is lawful for the whole world. Those who opposed medieval forms of government sought to counter papal and imperial authority with detailed arguments showing why the claim to be *dominus mundi* or lord of the world was flawed, and why the Pope could not claim jurisdiction to determine the lawfulness of rulers or to grant *dominium*. As the next section shows, these statist arguments were premised on the claim that sovereignty, and thus jurisdiction, depended upon de facto control over territory. Worldly authority, to be legitimate, must be effective.

Completing the Reformation: Hobbes, Bellarmine and the struggle of institutions

As the state emerged to challenge the authority of the Holy Roman Empire, scholars like Thomas Hobbes developed detailed accounts grounding the authority and jurisdiction of the state on its capacity to guarantee protection and realise peace. Yet Hobbes was well aware that to justify the lawfulness of authority on the basis of the capacity to seek peace and guarantee protection would not finally resolve the contest between ecclesiastical and secular jurisdiction. For Hobbes, papal authority would continue to undermine secular rulers if the Pope were left with any power to decide upon issues that would shape the allegiances or obligations of subjects. In *Leviathan*, Hobbes addressed that problem through a detailed refutation of the arguments made in support

---

[47] Watt, 'Spiritual and Temporal Powers', p. 368.   [48] *Ibid.*, p. 369.
[49] Armitage, *The Ideological Origins of the British Empire*, p. 33.

of papal authority by the Italian Jesuit Cardinal Robert Bellarmine. The argument developed by Hobbes can be located within a long tradition of anti-dualist Christian thought.

Civil peace and the limits to universal jurisdiction

One of the earliest significant examples of the literature challenging Christian dualism was the *Defensor Pacis* (*The Defender of the Peace*) by Marsilius of Padua, completed in 1324.[50] Marsilius there sought to explain 'the particular causes by which civil peace or tranquility is preserved, and also those through which its opposite, strife, arises, is prevented and is removed'.[51] His aim was to help other kingdoms avoid the misery that had befallen the Italian realm.[52] In Italy, 'the Roman bishop' had sought 'to make the prince of the Romans subject to him in coercive or temporal jurisdiction, when that prince neither owes it by right . . . nor has the wish to be subject to him in such judgement'.[53] That 'wrong apprehension on the part of certain Roman bishops' had long 'harassed the realm of Italy with its baneful action' and had kept it 'from tranquility or peace'.[54] The wrongful claim of a 'universal coercive jurisdiction over the entire world' by the Pope could 'infect all other realms of Christian faithful in this world' and thus was a threat to civil peace more generally.[55] The scriptures made clear that Christ not only excluded himself 'from secular principate or coercive judicial power', but also 'barred it from his apostles as well'.[56] Yet despite that, Roman bishops 'teach and preach that subjects should rebel against their own princes', thus disobeying the command of God that power should not be resisted.[57] The claim of temporal authority by the Pope 'entirely destroys the jurisdiction of those who hold princely office'.[58] The only way to avoid war, civil discord and hatred was for the Pope and his successors to 'devote themselves to imitating Christ and the apostles in abdicating secular principates and the ownership of temporal goods absolutely'.[59] There must be only one supreme ruler in a city or realm.[60] All priests and bishops must 'be subject to the jurisdiction of princes in those things that human law commands to be observed'.[61] Like all others who enjoy 'civil

---

[50] Marsilius of Padua, *The Defender of the Peace*, Annabel Brett (ed.) trans. (Cambridge: Cambridge University Press, 2005) (first published 1324).
[51] *Ibid.*, p. 557.   [52] *Ibid.*, p. 470.   [53] *Ibid.*, p. 135.   [54] *Ibid.*, p. 135.
[55] *Ibid.*, pp. 133, 136.   [56] *Ibid.*, p. 172.   [57] *Ibid.*, p. 462.   [58] *Ibid.*, p. 460.
[59] *Ibid.*, p. 470.   [60] *Ibid.*, p. 549.   [61] *Ibid.*, p. 218.

honours and conveniences' such as 'peace and the protection of the human legislator', priests and bishops should only be 'exempted from burdens and from jurisdiction' through 'a decision on the part of that same legislator'.[62] Marsilius concluded with the hope that prince and subject – 'the primary elements of any civil order' – could learn from reading his treatise 'what they must do in order to preserve the peace and their own liberty'.[63] The 'princely' element of the realm would understand that it 'alone' has 'the authority to command the subject multitude', while the subjects of the realm would understand that no authority other than the prince has the power to coerce obedience 'in the status of this present world'.[64]

Such ideas were taken up by radical figures during the Reformation such as the Swiss physician Thomas Erastus, whose posthumously published *Theses* supported attempts by the secular Elector Palatine to exercise control over excommunication and argued that the sins of Christians should be punished by civil authorities.[65] His doctrines were sufficiently influential that Erastianism came to refer somewhat misleadingly to any statist doctrine that opposed clerical dualism and supported the superiority of the state over the church in spiritual matters.[66] The Erastian tradition was at the heart of English Tudor politics and the development of the Anglican church. 'No dynasty in Europe exploited the canonical texts of the Erastian tradition more diligently than the Tudors.'[67] Henry VIII had ordered the *Defensor Pacis* to be translated, and English reformists including Thomas Cromwell, William Tyndale and Edward Fox all developed Erastian arguments for the ecclesiastical authority of the Christian prince, often producing 'Erastian polemics on the King's behalf'.[68] By the time Elizabeth came to power, 'the English church was unambiguously dependent on statist ecclesiology and a pronounced hostility to clerical dualism'.[69]

The limits of temporal and spiritual jurisdiction had become a serious practical issue in Elizabethan and Jacobean England, as a result of the papacy's repeated exercise of the contested power to depose and denounce rulers. During the latter part of Queen Elizabeth's reign, Pope Pius V and Cardinal William Allen had 'declared the queen an unlawful usurper, had declared her deposed,

---

[62] *Ibid.*, p. 220.   [63] *Ibid.*, p. 557.   [64] *Ibid.*
[65] Collins, *The Allegiance of Thomas Hobbes*, p. 18.   [66] *Ibid.*, p. 18.   [67] *Ibid.*
[68] *Ibid.*, pp. 18–19.   [69] *Ibid.*, p. 19.

and had called upon her subjects to withhold their obedience from her'.[70] The pope and his defenders had again intervened in English politics when King James I introduced an Oath of Allegiance in the aftermath of the aborted Gunpowder Plot. In a speech to Parliament, James had claimed that the plot was the product of a conspiracy of Roman Catholics,[71] and in response the Parliament passed a series of new laws aimed at securing the king and the realm. Among these was the law requiring 'recusants' to swear an oath of allegiance. The oath required its subscribers to affirm, inter alia, that King James was the lawful king of the realm, that the Pope had no 'power or authority to depose the King, or to dispose of any of his Majesty's kingdoms or dominions, or to authorise any foreign prince to invade or annoy him or his countries, or to discharge any of his subjects of their allegiance or obedience to his Majesty' and that the oath-taker would bear true allegiance to the king regardless of any 'declaration or sentence of excommunication or depriva-tion'.[72] In addition, the oath-taker was required to affirm that: 'I do from my heart abhor, detest, and abjure as impious and heretical, this damnable doctrine and position, that princes which be excommunicated or deprived by the Pope may be deposed or murdered by their subjects or any other whatsoever.'[73]

James later claimed that he had tried to make the oath acceptable to loyal Catholics by removing the suggestion that the Pope lacked the power to excommunicate kings from the church. Nonetheless the oath did deny the Papacy a right it had 'long claimed and recently sought to put into practice', and required its subscribers to disavow a current doctrine of the Church at the behest of the English King and Parliament.[74] Pope Paul V wrote a letter to English Catholics on 22 September 1606, forbidding them to 'come unto the churches of the Heretikes' or to 'binde your selves by the Oath'.[75] The English Archpriest George Blackwell was censured by Cardinal Bellarmine and later dismissed for taking the oath and failing to distribute the Pope's letter. In his letter to Blackwell, Bellarmine argued that the effect of the

---

[70] W. B. Patterson, *King James VI and I and the Reunion of Christendom* (Cambridge: Cambridge University Press, 1997), p. 80.

[71] King James VI and I, 'A Speech in the Parliament House, as Neere the Very Words as Could be Gathered at the Instant' in Johann P. Sommerville (ed.), *Political Writings* (Cambridge: Cambridge University Press, 1994), p. 147 at p. 152.

[72] Patterson, *King James VI and I and the Reunion of Christendom*, pp. 79–80.

[73] *Ibid.*, p. 80.   [74] *Ibid.*, p. 81.   [75] *Ibid.*

oath was to transfer the authority of the head of the Church in England from 'the successour of S. Peter, to the successour of King Henry the eight' and dismissed the 'pretended' danger to the King's life as a 'vaine pretexte'.[76] 'For it was never heard of from the Churches infancie untill this day, that ever any Pope did command, that any Prince, though an Heretike, though an Ethnike, though a persecutor, should be murdered; or did approve of the fact, when it was done by any other.'[77] The intervention of Bellarmine in the debate was particularly significant. Long before the controversy over the Oath of Allegiance, Bellarmine had developed a reputation as a 'great defender of a unified Christendom'.[78] His earlier writings, particularly his *Disputationes de Controversiis Christianae Fidei Adversus Huius Temporis Haereticos* (1581–92) defending the Catholic Church and the powers of the Papacy against Protestant challenges, had made him a controversial figure in England.[79] Bellarmine argued that although it was possible to distinguish between spiritual and temporal jurisdiction, spiritual jurisdiction was nonetheless superior to the temporal. The Pope had jurisdiction over temporal issues that impinged upon spiritual matters. Thus, for example, the Pope could declare laws invalid if they endangered the one faith or depose rulers who were heretics.[80]

James wrote two responses to the Pope and his theologians. The first, the *Triplici nodo, triplex cuneus: or an apologie for the oath of allegiance*, dated 1607, described the oath as a means of separating good subjects 'who although they were otherwise Popishly affected, yet retained in their hearts the print of their naturall duetie to their Soueraigne' from 'unfaithfull Traitors' who 'thought diuersitie of religion a safe pretext for all kinde of treasons, and rebellions against their Soueraigne'.[81] According to James, the oath merely sought to ensure 'temporall obedience to a temporall Magistrate' and 'did nothing repugne to matters of

---

[76] King James VI and I, '*Triplici Nodo, Triplex Cuneus*: or an Apologie for the Oath of Allegiance' in Johann P. Sommerville (ed.), *Political Writings* (Cambridge: Cambridge University Press, 1994), pp. 99–100.

[77] *Ibid.*, p. 100.

[78] Paul J. Weithman, 'Religion and Political Philosophy' in Edward Craig (ed.), *Routledge Encyclopedia of Philosophy* (London and New York: Routledge, 1998), vol. 8, pp. 224, 226.

[79] Patricia Springborg, 'Thomas Hobbes and Cardinal Bellarmine: Leviathan and "The Ghost of the Roman Empire"', *History of Political Thought* XVI (1995), 503 at 515–16.

[80] Weithman, 'Religion and Political Philosophy', p. 227.

[81] King James VI and I, 'Apologie for the Oath of Allegiance' in *Political Writings*, p. 86.

faith or salutation of soules'.[82] It thus did not challenge the Pope's supremacy in spiritual matters. James specifically addressed Bellarmine's claim that no Pope had ever commanded a prince to be killed, commenting that the Cardinal had omitted 'the rest of the points mentioned in that Oath, for deposing, degrading, stirring vp of armies, or rebelling against them'.[83] 'How many Emperours did the Pope raise warre against in their owne bowels?'[84] Given the praise and approbation the Pope gave to the murder of King Henry III of France, and the many attempts made against the life of Queen Elizabeth enjoined to traitors by their confessors, how could Bellarmine deny the danger posed by such practices?[85] In his later response, the *Premonition* published in 1609, James argued that the papal claim of the right to depose kings 'conveyed a threat to European peace and stability'.[86]

The problem of divided obligations

To say that the world could be divided into two jurisdictions clearly did not solve the institutional problem of who decides what counts as a spiritual or a temporal matter. When popes claimed and practised the right to judge the conduct of secular rulers or to depose rulers who left the true church, they put in 'doubt the independence and supremacy of the temporal power in its own sphere' and effectively asserted 'a unity of the powers founded on the supremacy of the spiritual'.[87] Similarly, when James and other rulers sought to rule upon the legitimacy of doctrines such as that concerning the right to depose kings, they asserted the supremacy of the temporal over the spiritual. The question that remained open was which institution had jurisdiction to decide which matters were spiritual and which were temporal.

In *Leviathan*, Hobbes offered a detailed answer to that question in a chapter providing a refutation of Bellarmine's reading of the relation between church and state. For Hobbes, the conflict between ecclesiastical and secular authority was a threat to peace because it resulted in potentially conflicting demands upon the allegiance of subjects. Hobbes considered that in order for unity and peace to be maintained, there could only be one temporal authority:

[82] *Ibid.*, p. 95.
[83] *Ibid.*, p. 111.   [84] *Ibid.*   [85] *Ibid.*, pp. 111–12.
[86] Patterson, *King James VI and I and the Reunion of Christendom*, p. 93.
[87] Watt, 'Spiritual and Temporal Powers', p. 367.

that governor must be one; or else there must needs follow faction and civil war in the commonwealth, between the *Church* and *State*; between *spiritualists* and *temporalists*; between the *sword of justice*, and the *shield of faith*: and (which is more) in every Christian man's own breast, between the *Christian* and the *man*.[88]

For Hobbes, the most frequent cause 'of sedition, and civil war, in Christian commonwealths' followed from the 'difficulty, not yet sufficiently resolved, of obeying at once, both God and man', particularly when 'their commandments are one contrary to the other'.[89] Competing authorities produced a sense of divided obligations or conflicting demands for obedience, so that 'no man be able to know which of his masters he must obey'.[90] The problem did not arise from the difficulty of choosing between the commandments of God and the commandments of man – it was clear that 'when a man receiveth two contrary commandments and knows that one of them is God's, he ought to obey that and not the other, though it be the command even of his lawful sovereign'.[91] Rather, the problem lay in knowing whether the command really came from God 'or whether he that commandeth, do but abuse God's name for some private ends of his own'.[92] The solution was to constitute a single authority, with jurisdiction over both temporal and spiritual matters, able to represent a unified community, resolve the problem of divided loyalties and so keep the peace.

Hobbes was happy to acknowledge that if an authority existed that could represent the world as a whole, that authority would be sovereign. More specifically, if there were a figure capable of representing the universal Church, all Christendom would be one commonwealth and the sovereign of that commonwealth would be 'this representant, both in things spiritual and temporal'.[93] However, that was clearly not the case. There was no 'general or universal Church' until it had a 'representant, which it hath not on earth'.[94] The Pope did not represent the world as a whole because he lacked the worldly authority to command, judge or punish.

[88] Thomas Hobbes, *Leviathan*, J. C. A. Gaskin (ed.) (Oxford: Oxford University Press, 2006) (first published 1651), p. 312.
[89] *Ibid.*, p. 390.
[90] Thomas Hobbes, *Behemoth or the Long Parliament* (Chicago: University of Chicago Press, 1990) (first published 1682), p. 8.
[91] Hobbes, *Leviathan*, p. 390.   [92] *Ibid.*   [93] *Ibid.*, p. 385.   [94] *Ibid.*

The monopoly of the state over decision-making

According to Hobbes, it therefore fell to secular rulers who could in fact exercise authority over particular territories to act as the guarantors of peace. In order to act effectively as guarantors of peace, secular rulers must not only have power over matters that were regarded as temporal, but must also be the supreme interpreters of the word of God within the territories under their control. The power to state the law must be unified rather than split between spiritual and temporal authorities, and that unified jurisdiction must vest in the state rather than the church. According to Hobbes, neither the Pope nor other bishops have 'any jurisdiction at all'.[95]

> For jurisdiction is the power of hearing and determining causes between man and man; and can only belong to none, but him that hath the power to prescribe the rules of right and wrong; that is, to make laws; and with the sword of justice to compel men to obey his decisions, pronounced either by himself, or by the judges he ordaineth thereunto; which none can lawfully do but the civil sovereign.[96]

Hobbes found scriptural basis for this argument, for 'St Peter had not only no jurisdiction given him in this world, but a charge to teach all the other apostles, that they also should have none'.[97] Christ made clear that he had not come 'to judge of causes between man and man: for that is a power which he refused to take upon himself, saying, *Who made me a judge, or a divider, amongst you?* and in another place, *My kingdom is not of this world*'.[98] History showed that 'the large jurisdiction of the Pope was given him by those that had it, that is, by the Emperors of Rome', and similarly 'all other bishops have their jurisdiction from the sovereigns of the place wherein they exercise the same'.[99] Thus to the extent that the Pope or his bishops exercised jurisdiction, it derived from the authority of temporal rulers.

Hobbes therefore rejected Bellarmine's argument that 'temporal authority' belonged to the Pope as 'of right'. In particular, Hobbes criticised Bellarmine's argument that the Pope 'hath a right to change kingdoms, giving them to one, and taking them from another, when he shall think it conduces to the salvation of souls'.[100] Such arguments divided the obligations of subjects. When the Pope claimed supremacy over the temporal sovereign 'he teacheth men to disobey the civil

---

[95] *Ibid.*, p. 379.   [96] *Ibid.*   [97] *Ibid.*, p. 372.   [98] *Ibid.*, p. 380.   [99] *Ibid.*, p. 381.
[100] *Ibid.*, pp. 382–3.

sovereign'.[101] This went against the primary commandment to make peace. Jurisdiction and the freedom to legislate at will were not a matter of right, but a consequence of the fact of control. Thus the civil sovereign must have the final power to decide what was lawful.

> From this consolidation of the right politic, and ecclesiastic in Christian sovereigns, it is evident, they have all manner of power over their subjects, that can be given to man, for the government of men's external actions, both in policy, and religion; and may make such laws, as themselves shall judge fittest, for the government of their own subjects, both as they are the commonwealth, and as they are the Church: for both State, and Church are the same men.[102]

The approach taken by Hobbes to the relation between spiritual and temporal authority provided a means of resolving the key question of authority more generally: '*whether Christian kings, and the sovereign assemblies in Christian commonwealths, be absolute in their own territories, immediately under God; or subject to one Vicar of Christ, constituted over the universal church; to be judged, condemned, deposed, and put to death, as he shall think expedient, or necessary for the common good*'.[103] Hobbes' answer was that the Pope had no authority to judge, condemn, depose or put to death Christian kings or assemblies, because only the sovereign had the authority to interpret the Scripture. Hobbes based his argument in support of this expansive assertion of secular jurisdiction on the story of Moses. According to Hobbes, the authority of Moses did not come from inheritance or from a direct commandment given by God to the people, since God spoke to the people through the mediation of Moses. Instead, the authority of Moses 'as the authority of all other princes, must be grounded on the consent of the people, and their promise to obey him' ('*And they said unto Moses: speak thou with us, and we will hear*').[104] As a result of that authorisation, only Moses could speak directly with God and tell the people 'what it was that God required at their hands'.[105] From this Hobbes concluded that 'whosoever in a Christian commonwealth holdeth the place of Moses, is the sole messenger of God, and interpreter of the commandments' and therefore 'no man ought in the interpretation of the Scripture to proceed further than the bounds which are set by their several sovereigns'.[106] It is not for any other authority to judge whether the laws or conduct of the sovereign comply with the word of God: 'to interpret them; that is, to pry into what

---

[101] *Ibid.*, p. 374. [102] *Ibid.*, p. 366. [103] *Ibid.*, p. 260. Emphasis in original.
[104] *Ibid.*, p. 314. Emphasis in original. [105] *Ibid.*, p. 315. [106] *Ibid.*, p. 316.

God saith to him whom he appointeth to govern under him, and make themselves judges whether he govern as God commandeth him, or not, is to transgress the bounds God hath set us, and to gaze upon God irreverently'.[107] For this reason, the Pope had no right to depose or condemn a sovereign.

For Hobbes, the only way to avoid civil war and rebellion in a divided world of territorially defined states was to deny external actors the jurisdiction to declare the law or to pronounce judgments upon the conduct of rulers. External authorities had no basis upon which to claim for themselves the power to pronounce the word of God and judge the behaviour of rulers accordingly.

> For when Christian men, take not their Christian sovereign, for God's prophet; they must either take their own dreams, for the prophecy they mean to be governed by, and the tumour of their own hearts for the Spirit of God; or they must suffer themselves to be led by some strange prince; or by some of their fellow-subjects, that can bewitch them, by slander of the government, into rebellion ... and by this means destroying all laws, both divine, and human, reduce all order, government, and society, to the first chaos of violence, and civil war.[108]

As a result, Hobbes argued that every apparent competition of obligations is false. The question of obligation can always be determined by answering 'who decides' – and the answer to 'who decides' is always the civil sovereign. Any apparent conflict between the church and the state could be resolved in favour of the state. So, for example, the civil authority had power to determine what doctrines should be taught within the state and which doctrines threatened the peace. Because pastors and ministers derived their authority from the sovereign and not the church, they owed their primary obedience and loyalty to the sovereign.

> Seeing then in every Christian commonwealth, the civil sovereign is the supreme pastor, to whose charge the whole flock of his subjects is committed, and consequently that it is by his authority, that all other pastors are made, and have power to teach, and perform all other pastoral offices; it followeth also, that it is from the civil sovereign, that all other pastors derive their right of teaching, preaching, and other functions pertaining to that office; and that they are but his ministers; in the same manner as the magistrates of towns, judges in courts of justice, and commanders of armies, are all but ministers of him that is the magistrate of the whole commonwealth, judge of all causes, and commander of the

---

[107] *Ibid.*   [108] *Ibid.*, p. 290.

> whole militia, which is always the civil sovereign. And the reason hereof,
> is not because they that teach, but because they that are to learn, are his
> subjects.[109]

Hobbes thus agreed with many Catholic theologians that human beings could only be subject to one ultimate authority, but for Hobbes the superior authority was not the church but the state. There was no one universal church but rather many Christians living in the dominions of princes and states, each subject to the commonwealth of which they were a member.

> And therefore a Church, such a one as is capable to command, to judge,
> absolve, condemn, or do any other act, is the same thing with a civil
> commonwealth, consisting of Christian men; and is called a *civil state*, for
> that the subjects of it are *men*; and a *Church*, for that the subjects thereof
> are *Christians*. *Temporal* and *spiritual* government, are but two words
> brought into the world, to make men see double, and mistake their *lawful
> sovereign*.[110]

Carl Schmitt argued that in developing these extreme statist arguments, Hobbes had '*brought the Reformation to a conclusion* by recognising the state as a clear alternative to the Roman Catholic church's monopoly on decision-making'.[111] According to Schmitt, the apparent conflict between ecclesiastical authority and secular authority should be understood not as a conflict between abstract ideas like theology and politics, but between concrete institutions. Unless the hierarchy between such institutions was clearly defined and policed, with one superior to the other, political conflicts between the two forms of authority would continue to arise.

> A conflict is always a struggle between organisations and institutions in
> the sense of concrete orders. It is a struggle of *institutions* over *stances*.
> Substances must first of all have found their *form*; they must have been
> brought into a *formation* before they can actually encounter each other as
> contesting subjects in a conflict, that is, as *parties belligérantes*.[112]

For Schmitt, it was Hobbes who posed the 'big question' of which concrete institution decides what is political and what is not, what lies within the absolute authority of the state and what lies outside. By answering that the state has the absolute authority to make such decisions, Hobbes offered a mirror of Catholicism. It was perhaps for that

---

[109] *Ibid.*, p. 361.   [110] *Ibid.*, p. 311.   [111] Schmitt, *Political Theology II*, pp. 125–6.
[112] *Ibid.*, p. 114.

reason that the Catholic church and theologians such as Bellarmine were the target of detailed polemics by Hobbes.[113]

Yet although Schmitt argued that Hobbes had completed the Reformation, Hobbes himself was aware of the possibility that the contest between the secular and the spiritual, or in today's language the particular and the universal, might be ongoing. In the concluding sentences of *Leviathan*, Hobbes wrote:

> But who knows that this spirit of Rome, now gone out, and walking by missions through the dry places of China, Japan, and the Indies, that yield him little fruit, may not return, or rather an assembly of spirits worse than he, enter, and inhabit this clean swept house, and make the end thereof worse than the beginning? For it is not the Roman clergy only, that pretends the kingdom of God to be of this world, and thereby to have power therein, distinct from that of the civil state.[114]

Recognition, revolution and the family of nations

With the triumph of the modern state and the demise of the Holy Roman Empire, debates over the divisibility of power ceased to be framed in terms of the competition between spiritual and temporal jurisdiction. However, this is not to say that the rise of the state meant that issues of conflicts of jurisdiction and debates about the capacity of external actors to denounce rulers no longer arose. It was certainly no longer plausible to argue that the Holy Roman Emperor had universal jurisdiction as lord of the world, while princes had rights to particular jurisdiction, and that both forms of jurisdiction could apply over the same territory. However, the ideas that authority might be divided, or that people, places and things might be subject to plural laws, did not disappear. Instead, they changed form.

In particular, these ideas persisted in two debates that have since informed the development of the responsibility to protect concept. The first debate concerned the role of external actors in the recognition of a government, or even of a new state, and whether any external recognition should be understood as declaratory or constitutive. According to the declaratory theory, which was dominant until at least the late eighteenth century, the 'legal status' of a ruler was understood to be 'derived and perfected from

---

[113] Springborg, 'Thomas Hobbes and Cardinal Bellarmine', 510.
[114] Hobbes, *Leviathan*, p. 465.

within'.[115] External legality followed from internal legality.[116] Within Europe, the law of nature and of nations had little to say about the basis of state legitimacy. The question of whether a duly appointed or elected ruler properly had authority over territory was not treated as a question for interstate relations. If the people of a state thought a person 'worthy of election to the throne of their country and useful to their welfare', that election was not 'capable of being validly challenged by other States'.[117] To give foreign rulers or powers 'the *right to recognition* ... would mean intervention and result in submission which would stultify the fundamental right of States to equality guaranteed by the law of nature and nations'.[118] More importantly, to give external powers the right to judge the legitimacy of a government would reintroduce the problem of conflicting obligations and the possibility of civil war that the creation of state authority had been designed to resolve. Thus the de facto existence of control over territory was considered as sufficient to establish the lawfulness of authority.

From the early nineteenth century onwards, however, the law of nations began to treat the status of authority as a question that could not definitively be determined internally. International lawyers such as Henry Wheaton were confronted with 'frequent changes in membership of the Family of Nations' as a result of revolutions in Europe and the New World,[119] and questions about the normative criteria of statehood began to appear in urgent need of resolution. Wheaton and his contemporaries began to argue that while 'internal sovereignty' was a question of 'factual formation', 'external sovereignty' of a state 'was not *derived* from within', but instead required 'action from without which must be taken by the existing Member States of the Family of Nations'.[120] States began to treat external recognition as the act that perfected sovereignty.[121] In that sense, de facto control over territory was no longer sufficient to ground a claim to statehood.

Questions about whether fact or right should determine membership of the family of nations were also raised by the experience of empire. For example, the expansion and nature of the British Empire played a major

---

[115] Alexandrowicz, 'The Theory of Recognition *in Fieri*', 179. [116] *Ibid.*
[117] *Ibid.*, p. 177. [118] *Ibid.* [119] *Ibid.*, p. 196.
[120] *Ibid.*, p. 195; see also Jennifer L. Beard, *The Political Economy of Desire: International Law, Development and the Nation State* (Oxon: Routledge-Cavendish, 2006), pp. 124–49 (offering a critical reading of these practices of recognition).
[121] Alexandrowicz, 'The Theory of Recognition *in Fieri*', 195.

role in shaping British notions about membership of the family of nations during the nineteenth century. Although European states had long entered into commercial relations and treaties with Ottomans, British international lawyers were at the forefront of the nineteenth-century revisionist history that treated the Ottoman Empire as incapable of being included in the membership of the family of nations.[122] By the end of the nineteenth century, the problem European international lawyers more generally had set themselves was how to create order 'among entities characterized as belonging to entirely different cultural systems'.[123] The centuries-long history of European states entering into trade and diplomatic relations, treaties and alliances with rulers outside Europe was ignored or reinterpreted. That history would only be revisited again in the era of decolonisation, in the context of judicial findings that the eighteenth-century law of nations allowed for the recognition of the legal personality of an independent Asian state,[124] and in scholarship pointing to numerous treaties entered into by the Dutch, Portuguese, British and French prior to the nineteenth century recognising extra-European rulers as sovereign.[125]

Debates about who had authority to determine the legitimacy of rulers were also shaped by the jurisdictional contests that emerged alongside various claims to govern 'according to truth'.[126] In the seventeenth century, the idea that matters of religious truth lay beyond the jurisdiction of the state strengthened those voluntary civil organisations that claimed to represent the moral authority of conscience,[127] and fuelled both internal rebellion and external invasion. From the nineteenth century onwards, the idea that the spheres of private life and civil society were subject to truths or laws that lay beyond the jurisdiction of the state

[122] Jennifer Pitts, 'Boundaries of Victorian International Law' in Duncan Bell (ed.), *Victorian Visions of Global Order: Empire and International Relations in Nineteenth-Century Political Thought* (Cambridge: Cambridge University Press, 2007).
[123] Anghie, *Imperialism, Sovereignty and the Making of International Law*, p. 37.
[124] *Right to Passage over Indian Territory (India v. Portugal) (Merits)* [1960] ICJ Rep. 35 at 87.
[125] C. H. Alexandrowicz, 'Doctrinal Aspects of the Universality of the Law of Nations', *British Year Book of International Law* 37 (1961), 506; R. P. Anand, *New States and International Law* (Delhi: Vikas Publishing House, 1972).
[126] Michel Foucault, *The Birth of Biopolitics: Lectures at the Collège de France 1978–1979* Michel Senellart (ed.) and Graham Burchell trans. (New York: Palgrave Macmillan, 2008), p. 313.
[127] Reinhart Koselleck, *Critique and Crisis: Enlightenment and the Pathogenesis of Modern Society* (Cambridge: The MIT Press, 1988), p. 183.

also began to empower those who spoke for the higher truths that governed the economic realm – a realm governed by natural laws said to be beyond the sovereign's comprehension or jurisdiction.

Thus although by the end of the nineteenth century the state would appear to have emerged as the dominant political form in Europe, the state's claim to authority was not unchallenged. At periods of revolution and change, European international lawyers had tended to stress the constitutive character of the task facing international law. The two significant limitations on the authority of the state – the idea that an external authority might exist that could determine the legitimacy of particular claimants to rule, and the idea that state power was limited by the obligation to respect individual rights or economic liberty – converged with the creation of international institutions in the twentieth century.

International jurisdiction and decolonisation: from form to function

Jurisdiction under the UN Charter

As Chapter 1 noted, international law has long treated effective control over territory as an important criterion of statehood.[128] Yet the creation of the UN in 1945 ushered in the emergence of an international regime in which the principles of self-determination, sovereign equality and the prohibition against the use of force were also treated as central to determining the lawfulness of particular claimants to authority.[129] The preamble of the UN Charter also expressed a determination 'to reaffirm faith in fundamental human rights' and 'the dignity and worth of the human person'. That faith would inform the body of international human rights law and international humanitarian law that developed over the course of the twentieth century as an additional external measure of the legitimacy of governments. Under the UN Charter, the lawfulness of authority over a given territory was thus treated as a matter both of fact and of right.

---

[128] James Crawford, *The Creation of States in International Law*, 2nd edn (Oxford: Oxford University Press, 2006), pp. 37–89.
[129] *Ibid.*, pp. 96–173.

That understanding of state authority informed the way in which the UN Charter attempted to formulate the relationship between domestic and international jurisdiction. As the authority of sovereign states was understood to be an expression both of effective control over territory and of fundamental principles such as the right to self-determination, external intervention in the internal affairs of states was prima facie illegitimate. Yet, because the legitimacy of state authority had become a matter for international law, as overseen by an organisation with supra-national authority, intervention in the internal affairs of states must also, in some circumstances, be legitimate. As the earlier debates about the role of external actors in recognising elected monarchs or revolutionary states made clear, the treatment of authority as a matter for international law opened up new possibilities for destabilising external intervention and new threats to peace. It was the task of the UN Charter to articulate the jurisdictional grounds upon which the new organisation might exercise its authority to police and perfect the state, while at the same time establishing a commitment to fundamental principles of sovereign equality and self-determination.

The UN Charter appears to settle these jurisdictional questions by authorising international intervention only in defined situations. The preamble to the Charter provides that 'armed force shall not be used, save in the common interest'[130] and all members agree to 'refrain in their international relations from the threat or use of force' in any manner 'inconsistent with the Purposes of the United Nations'.[131] The Charter vests the international police function in the Security Council – the organ given the 'primary responsibility for the maintenance of international peace and security'.[132] Like the other organs of the UN, the Security Council is effectively given the power to determine the extent of its jurisdiction, including its jurisdiction to authorise force when there is a 'threat to the peace, breach of the peace, or act of aggression'.[133] To the extent that there are limitations on Security Council jurisdiction, they

---

[130] Ibid.   [131] Charter of the United Nations, art. 2(4).
[132] Charter of the United Nations, art. 24(1). See also Hans Kelsen, Collective Security under International Law (Newport: Naval War College, International Law Studies, Series No. 49, 1957), pp. 4, 114, 142 (fn. 20) (characterising the collective security system established under the Charter of the United Nations in terms of international police action); Martti Koskenniemi, 'The Police in the Temple: Order, Justice and the UN: A Dialectical View', European Journal of International Law 6 (1995), 325 at 344 (analysing the Security Council as 'the technician of peace, the police').
[133] See Certain Expenses of the United Nations (Article 17, Paragraph 2, of the Charter) (Advisory Opinion) [1962] ICJ Rep. 151 at 168.

have been seen to flow from Articles 24 and 39 of the Charter, which establish the scope of the police function of the Security Council and its role within the broader Charter system.[134] The Council determines whether a particular event triggers its jurisdiction under Chapter VII, and decides what measures should be taken to restore peace and security.[135] Any decision by the Security Council to authorise the use of force against a state requires the discipline of a multilateral decision-making process. This commitment to multilateralism has been seen as a significant bulwark against a resurgence of imperialism.[136] It means that a powerful state does not have the right to undertake police action against another state without Security Council authorisation. For lawyers, the legal regime governing peace and security is premised upon a commitment to the core principles of sovereign equality, self-determination and territorial integrity. These principles have been seen as desirable both in achieving realist ends (preserving the status quo and the international order from the threat of world wars and mass destruction) and for more idealistic reasons (a commitment to international justice and the defence of newly decolonised states from hegemonic powers with imperial appetites).

The Charter also envisages a more expansive jurisdiction to police and perfect the conduct of Member States in the areas of human rights, economic development and social policy. The purposes of the UN include developing 'friendly relations among nations based on respect for the principle of equal rights and self-determination of peoples', taking 'appropriate measures to strengthen universal peace' and achieving 'international co-operation in solving international problems of an economic, social, cultural, or humanitarian character, and in promoting and encouraging respect for human rights and for fundamental freedoms for all'.[137] The UN Charter not only established a 'hard' regime governing public law questions relating to territory and the use of force, but also a 'soft' regime concerned with those economic

---

[134] *Charter of the United Nations*, art. 24 (providing that 'In discharging these duties the Security Council shall act in accordance with the Purposes and Principles of the United Nations'); *ibid.*, art. 39 (granting to the Security Council the authority to 'determine the existence of any threat to the peace, breach of the peace, or act of aggression' and to 'decide what measures shall be taken . . . to maintain or restore international peace and security').

[135] *Ibid.*, art. 39.

[136] See generally Ralph Zacklin, *The United Nations Secretariat and the Use of Force in a Unipolar World: Power v Principle* (Cambridge: Cambridge University Press, 2010).

[137] *Charter of the United Nations*, art. 1.

and social issues.[138] The soft regime was institutionally based in the parliamentary organ of the General Assembly. The more expansive jurisdiction of the General Assembly was balanced against the lack of enforcement mechanisms available to it. Resolutions could be passed dealing with a wide range of issues of social and economic importance, but no real mechanisms existed for obliging states to comply with these resolutions.[139] In addition, the statement in Article 2(7) of the UN Charter that nothing contained in the Charter, other than the enforcement measures envisaged under Chapter VII, 'shall authorize the United Nations to intervene in matters which are essentially within the domestic jurisdiction of any state' was designed to limit soft forms of UN intervention.[140]

Functionalist approaches to UN jurisdiction

That jurisdictional division of labour became the subject of contest almost as soon as it was enshrined in the UN Charter. Already by the 1950s, the distinction between the work of the Security Council and that of the General Assembly began to break down. The General Assembly started to concern itself with security matters, beginning with the Uniting for Peace resolution passed in 1950 in response to the Soviet veto of Security Council resolutions endorsing UN intervention in the Korean War.[141] The Uniting for Peace resolution declared that:

> if the Security Council, because of lack of unanimity of the permanent members, fails to exercise its primary responsibility for the maintenance of international peace and security in any case where there appears to be a threat to the peace, breach of the peace, or act of aggression, the General Assembly shall consider the matter immediately with a view to making appropriate recommendations to Members for collective measures,

---

[138] Koskenniemi, 'The Police in the Temple', 336.   [139] *Ibid.*, pp. 338–9.

[140] Article 2(7) of the Charter of the United Nations provides that: 'Nothing contained in the present Charter shall authorize the United Nations to intervene in matters which are essentially within the domestic jurisdiction of any [S]tate or shall require the Members to submit such matters to settlement under the present Charter; but this principle shall not prejudice the application of enforcement measures under Chapter VII.'

[141] Uniting for Peace, GA Res. 377(V), UN GAOR, 1st Comm., 5th Sess., 302nd Plen. Mtg., UN Doc. A/RES/377(V), 3 November 1950. For a discussion of the context in which the Uniting for Peace Resolution was passed, see William Stueck, 'The United Nations, the Security Council, and the Korean War' in Vaughan Lowe *et al.* (eds.), *The United Nations Security Council and War: The Evolution of Thought and Practice since 1945* (Oxford: Oxford University Press, 2008), p. 265.

including in the case of a breach of the peace or act of aggression the use of armed force when necessary, to maintain or restore international peace and security.[142]

As the General Assembly began to be dominated by newly decolonised states, it also began to pass resolutions, such as those concerned with the new international economic order, questioning the liberal distinction between public and private, order and justice.[143] While the big jurisdictional questions about authority and intervention have generally been debated in relation to the use of force, international governance also quietly expanded from the 1960s onwards through the consensual involvement of the aid, human rights, development and humanitarian communities in the administration and management of economic and social life within African, Middle Eastern, Asian, Latin American and Eastern European states.[144]

The Security Council, in turn, began to concern itself with broader public good questions – both within and between states. The willingness of the Security Council to expand its jurisdiction with a broad reading of 'threats to the peace' was first evidenced by the statement issued from its 1992 Summit Meeting. The members of the Security Council there declared that the 'absence of war and military conflicts amongst States does not in itself ensure international peace and security' and that 'non-military sources of instability in the economic, social, humanitarian and ecological fields have become threats to peace and security'.[145] The range and nature of resolutions passed by the Security Council in the decade following the end of the Cold War reinforced the sense that the Council was willing to treat the failure to guarantee democracy or human rights, or to protect against humanitarian abuses, as a threat to peace and security. While these resolutions were hotly debated, they were generally thought to have 'stretched the literal text of Chapter VII' rather than to have violated the Charter prohibition on recourse to force.[146] These

---

[142] *Ibid.*
[143] See, for example, Charter of Economic Rights and Duties of States, GA Res. 3281 (XXIX), UN GAOR, 29th Sess., 2315th Plen. Mtg., UN Doc. A/RES/29/3281 (XXIX), 12 December 1974.
[144] Anne Orford, 'The Gift of Formalism', *European Journal of International Law* 15 (2004), 179.
[145] President of the Security Council, 'Note by the President of the Security Council', UN SCOR, 47th Sess., UN Doc. S/23500, 31 January 1992, p. 3.
[146] Thomas M. Franck, *Recourse to Force: State Action against Threats and Armed Attacks* (Cambridge: Cambridge University Press, 2002), p. 137.

decisions were not seen to threaten the key principles of sovereign equality, territorial integrity and self–determination. The notion that international police action was exceptional still governed.

Perhaps the most dramatic shift in international jurisdiction during the era of decolonisation occurred as a result of the development of international executive action by the Secretary-General. In his introduction to the 16th Annual Report to the General Assembly, Dag Hammarskjöld commented that while the principles and purposes of the UN had been set out in detail in the Charter, executive functions had received little attention.

> While great attention is given to the principles and purposes, and considerable space is devoted to an elaboration of what may be called the parliamentary aspects of the Organization, little is said about executive arrangements ... In fact, therefore, the executive functions and their form have been left largely to practice ... The forms used for executive action by the Security Council – or, when the Council has not been able to reach decisions, in some cases, by the General Assembly – are varied and are to be explained by an effort to adjust the measures to the needs of each single situation. However, some main types are recurrent. Sub-committees have been set up for fact-finding or negotiation on the spot. Missions have been placed in areas of conflict for the purpose of observation and local negotiation. Observer groups of a temporary nature have been set out. And, finally, police forces under the aegis of the United Nations have been organized for the assistance of the Governments concerned with a view to upholding the principles of the Charter. As these, or many of these, arrangements require centralized administrative measures which cannot be performed by the Council or the General Assembly, Members have to a large extent used the possibility to request the Secretary-General to perform special functions by instructing him to take the necessary executive steps for implementation of the action decided upon.[147]

As Chapter 2 showed, Hammarskjöld systematically expanded the forms of executive action undertaken to maintain international peace and security and to uphold the principles of the Charter. The practices of executive action that developed during the tenure of Hammarskjöld led to an expansion of international jurisdiction in situations of civil war or emergency. Thus although it appears clear from the drafting history that the UN Charter was not 'intended to authorize a role for the United

---

[147] UN Secretary-General, 'Introduction to the Annual Report of the Secretary-General on the Work of the Organization', UN GAOR, 16th Sess., Supp. No. 1A, UN Doc. A/4800/Add.1, 1961, p. 5.

Nations in civil wars' and that in fact Articles 2(4) and 2(7) would 'appear to forbid such intervention',[148] the UN intervention in the Congo discussed in Chapter 2 was the first of many such UN interventions in internal conflicts, including in the former Yugoslavia, Somalia, Haiti and Sierra Leone.[149] The functional approach taken to the jurisdiction of the Secretary-General has meant that, in the words of one former senior UN official: 'it has become pointless to try to locate the precise source of authority of each of the Secretary-General's political actions. The fact is that the Secretary-General can in the political field do what he can get away with, i.e. in a given situation what the competent representative organs will encourage or at least tolerate, and preferably what is acceptable to any specially concerned states or other entities.'[150]

The fact that the Charter does not explicitly authorise practices of international executive rule such as fact-finding, peacekeeping or territorial administration has never been treated as a constraint on UN involvement in these activities – 'the UN and its members have never interpreted the Charter so narrowly, searching for a specific authorization for each new activity'.[151] Similarly, the fact that the UN Charter specifically requires that UN members relate to each other on the basis of respect for the formal principle of sovereign equality rather than trusteeship has not been treated as precluding the administration of Member States by UN officials.[152] Instead, the approach has been to ask whether such practices are necessary to the performance of the function of maintaining international peace and security entrusted to the UN and not explicitly prohibited in the Charter.[153] Early in the history of the organisation, the ICJ endorsed such an approach, holding that the UN 'must be deemed to have those powers, which, though not expressly provided in the Charter, are conferred on it by necessary implication as being essential to the performance of its

---

[148] Thomas M. Franck, *Recourse to Force*, p. 41.   [149] *Ibid.*

[150] Paul C. Szasz, 'The Role of the UN Secretary-General: Some Legal Aspects', *New York University Journal of International Law and Politics* 24 (1991), 161 at 191.

[151] Steven R. Ratner, *The New UN Peacekeeping: Building Peace in Lands of Conflict after the Cold War* (New York: St Martin's Press, 1995), p. 30.

[152] Charter of the United Nations, art. 78. That provision was included in the Charter at the urging of Syria and Lebanon, both founding members of the UN. Those states were particularly concerned to ensure that the UN trusteeship system could not be used by France as a basis for exercising trust powers over independent states that had been former French colonies. See further Bruno Simma (ed.), *The Charter of the United Nations: A Commentary*, 2nd edn. (Oxford: Oxford University Press, 2002), p. 1117.

[153] *Ibid.*

duties'.[154] In a later decision dealing with the UN operations in the Suez and Congo, the ICJ held that when the UN 'takes action which warrants the assertion that it was appropriate for the fulfilment of one of the stated purposes of the United Nations, the presumption is that such action is not *ultra vires* the Organization'.[155] The drafters of the UN Charter rejected proposals 'to place the ultimate authority to interpret the Charter in the International Court of Justice', and as a result each UN organ 'must, in the first place at least, determine its own jurisdiction'.[156] As UN organs expanded the range of actions that they considered necessary for maintaining peace and security, the conception of 'international peace and security' itself gradually expanded.

According to this functionalist account of authority, the exercise of executive power by the UN does not affect the status of a territory under administration. From as early as 1956, it had been argued that international executive rule did not have any effect on the status of territories being administered. In a 1956 survey of the contemporary practice of the United Kingdom, Eli Lauterpacht argued that it was necessary to 'distinguish between the two principal meanings attributed to the word "sovereignty"'.[157] First, sovereignty could mean 'the right of ownership' or 'the legal sovereignty'.[158] Secondly it could mean 'the jurisdiction and control which a State may exercise over territory, regardless of the question of where ultimate title to the territory may lie'.[159] Although sovereignty as title and sovereignty as control were usually vested in the same entity, Lauterpacht could see no legal reason why that should be so.[160] The important question was who could exercise the latter form of sovereignty:

> The question of who has the residual legal title to [a territory] is of negligible importance in comparison with the question of who is entitled to exercise jurisdiction and control over it, to grant licences to prospectors seeking to ascertain the existence of its mineral wealth, or to regulate the exploitation of its natural resources.[161]

---

[154] *Reparation for Injuries Suffered in the Service of the United Nations (Advisory Opinion)* [1949] ICJ Rep. 174 at 182.

[155] *Certain Expenses of the United Nations* [1962] ICJ Rep. 151 at 168.   [156] *Ibid.*

[157] E. Lauterpacht, 'The Contemporary Practice of the United Kingdom in the Field of International Law – Survey and Comment', *International and Comparative Law Quarterly* 5 (1956), 405 at 410.

[158] *Ibid.*   [159] *Ibid.*   [160] *Ibid.*   [161] *Ibid.*

The consensus in international law since the 1950s has been that if the UN or another organisation takes control over a territory for protection purposes, this has no effect upon the sovereignty or status of that territory. By the twenty-first century, it had become axiomatic that UN administration does not affect the juridical status of administered territories. Instead, legal scholars agree that the effect of international executive rule on existing states and state territories in the decolonised world has been to affirm the existing status of the territories under administration, while diminishing sovereignty as control.[162] Such scholarship is dismissive of the 'now dated sovereignty question'.[163] International rule does not transfer 'sovereignty-as-title' to international entities, and thus does not alter the 'juridical status' of territories subject to international administration.[164] Legal authority over territories under administration has been 'disaggregated' and the focus should instead be upon 'the *functions* served by international governance'.[165]

Representatives of a secular church

The expansion of international authority to administer the decolonised world and to judge the conduct of rulers in the name of maintaining international peace has been accompanied by an affirmation of dualism. For example, early in his time as Secretary-General, Hammarskjöld outlined his vision of 'the proper place of the United Nations in our world'.[166] According to Hammarskjöld, the task facing the 'friends and believers in the United Nations' could be understood in the terms suggested by Dostoevsky in *The Brothers Karamazov*, 'where he has one of his heroes say that the future may be one of a struggle between the State trying to make itself Church and the Church trying to

---

[162] See, for example, Ralph Wilde, *International Territorial Administration How Trusteeship and the Civilizing Mission Never Went Away* (Oxford: Oxford University Press, 2008), p. 145; Gregory H. Fox, *Humanitarian Occupation* (Cambridge: Cambridge University Press, 2008), pp. 32–3. For a review of recent scholarship that develops a functionalist analysis of international territorial administration, see Anne Orford, 'International Territorial Administration and the Management of Decolonisation', *International and Comparative Law Quarterly* 59 (2010), 227.
[163] Fox, *Humanitarian Occupation*, p. 32.
[164] Wilde, *International Territorial Administration*, pp. 105, 108–9, 189.
[165] Fox, *Humanitarian Occupation*, pp. 32–3.
[166] Dag Hammarskjöld, 'The New "Santa Maria"' in Wilder Foote (ed.), *The Servant of Peace: A Selection of the Speeches and Statements of Dag Hammarskjöld* (London: The Bodley Head, 1962), p. 40.

make itself State'.[167] Both must be resisted. In particular, it is not possible 'to establish "one world" by force of arms'.[168]

> No state, no group of states, can grip the world and shape it, neither by force, nor by any formula of words in a charter or a treaty. There are no absolute answers to the agonies and searchings of our time.[169]

While this was true for states, it was also true for the UN. While the UN 'represents ideals at least professed by all nations', it is not and should not become 'a super-state trying to impose on people any "right" way of life or any way of life different from one freely chosen by the people'.[170] The UN is instead 'the repository and voice of a common heritage of ideals' and in that role it seeks to influence the conduct of states 'towards a wider realization of those ideals'.[171] The Secretariat and the Secretary-General can thus be understood 'as representatives of a secular "church" of ideals and principles in international affairs of which the United Nations is the expression'.[172]

As representatives of a secular church, the UN executive had a particular role to play in the maintenance of international peace and security. It was not for the Secretary-General to represent 'a "third line" in the international debate'.[173] Rather, the role of the Secretary-General and the Secretariat was to stand above international politics, form an objective picture of the competing aims and interests of Members, anticipate conflicts that might arise between Members and make suggestions to governments aimed at preventing such conflicts before they gave rise to public controversy. When matters of peace and security came before the UN, the Secretary-General was required to draw conclusions that were 'completely detached from any national interest or policy and based solely on the principles and ideals to which the governments have adhered as Members of the United Nations', and then express those conclusions 'with full frankness' to governments.[174] Hammarskjöld thus saw conflict prevention and resolution, rather than the enforcement of the collective will of the organisation, as the contribution that the UN could make to peace and security.[175]

Yet when it came to the decolonised world, the distinction between preventing conflict and enforcing the collective will broke down. Hammarskjöld considered that preventing conflict between the Cold

---

[167] *Ibid.*, p. 45.   [168] *Ibid.*, p. 44.   [169] *Ibid.*, p. 45.   [170] *Ibid.*   [171] *Ibid.*
[172] *Ibid.*, p. 47.   [173] *Ibid.*, p. 46.   [174] *Ibid.*
[175] Alex J. Bellamy, 'Conflict Prevention and the Responsibility to Protect', *Global Governance* 14 (2008), 135 at 136.

War blocs sometimes required imposing the will of the international community. His approach to preventive diplomacy was directed to filling 'power vacuums' in the 'peripheral' or 'underdeveloped areas'.[176] When, as in the Congo, a government challenged the UN's perception that there was a 'vacuum' to be filled, or its interpretation of what actions were necessary to secure peace and security, Hammarskjöld made clear that in his view the jurisdiction of the UN was superior to that of states.

> Whatever development the executive activities of the Organization may show in the field, there should never be any suspicion that the world community would wish or, indeed, could ever wish to maintain for itself, through the United Nations, a position of power or control in a Member country. Were political groups in a country really to believe in such a risk, the explanation would seem to be that, as has indeed happened in the case of Governments of Member countries with long established independence, they may find it difficult to accept the judgement of the majority of the nations of the world as to what in a specific situation is necessary in order to safeguard international peace and security, when such a judgement appears to be in conflict with the immediate aims of the group. With growing respect for the decisions of the Organization and growing understanding of its principles, the risks for such misinterpretations should be eliminated.[177]

Hammarskjöld represented international politics as a dualist system, in which the world could be neatly divided between states on the one hand and the 'secular church' of the UN on the other. Each had its own sphere of jurisdiction – states were responsible for issues of national interest, while the UN was responsible for issues of international peace and security. Yet when it came to the decolonised world, Hammarskjöld's interpretation of dualism assumed that it was for the representatives of the world as a whole to decide whether a matter raised issues of national security or international peace. Hammarskjöld recognised that sceptics might think that the international executive could not decide such questions neutrally and might argue that 'nobody can serve two masters'.[178] However, Hammarskjöld dismissed the apparent problem of 'whether international service is possible without split loyalties in a divided world'

---

[176] Oscar Schachter, 'Dag Hammarskjöld and the Relation of Law to Politics', *American Journal of International Law* 56 (1962), 1 at 7.

[177] UN Secretary-General, *Introduction to the 1961 Annual Report*, p. 8.

[178] Dag Hammarskjöld, 'International Service' in Wilder Foote (ed.), *The Servant of Peace: A Selection of the Speeches and Statements of Dag Hammarskjöld* (London: The Bodley Head, 1962), p. 80.

as in fact 'unreal'.[179] Ideological conflicts, violent clashes of interests and technological and economic developments had brought people 'together as members of one human family, unified beyond race or creed on a shrinking globe, in face of dangers of our own making'.[180] In such a situation, 'inherited standards' were no longer sufficient to deal with ethical problems.[181] The ideals and interests 'to which we are bounden' are no longer national but are those that 'we can fully endorse after having opened our minds, with great honesty, to the many voices of the world'.[182] International service calls upon each person 'to represent . . . what survives or emerges as one's own after such a test'.[183] There could not by definition be any conflict between domestic and international jurisdiction in such situations. If a matter posed a threat to international peace and security, it was for the world community, acting through the UN, to take the measures that were necessary to maintain order and protect life.

The proliferation of claimants to international authority

At the time Hammarskjöld was writing, there were no other strong claimants to international jurisdiction. As a result, from the UN perspective it must have seemed safe to take a somewhat nonchalant approach to the formal constraints on international jurisdiction found in the UN Charter. It could be assumed that the expansion of international jurisdiction on functional grounds equated to the expansion of UN jurisdiction. Yet the intervening decades have seen a proliferation of actors with claims to act as the guarantors of a truth that lies beyond the state. Jurisdictional contests now play out not only between the UN and Members and between UN organs, but also between the UN and the many actors who claim to represent international or universal jurisdiction. In the economic sphere, Hammarskjöld was aware that a jurisdictional rivalry was already emerging in relation to issues of trade and development in the decolonised world. He felt strongly that such matters should not be handled through 'rich men's clubs' such as the General Agreement on Tariffs and Trade and the Organization for Economic Cooperation and Development, and considered that economic and social matters 'were within the rightful jurisdiction of the more democratic and broadly based United Nations'.[184] In the

---

[179] *Ibid.*, p. 81.   [180] *Ibid.*, p. 80.   [181] *Ibid.*   [182] *Ibid.*, pp. 80–1.   [183] *Ibid.*, p. 81.
[184] Brian Urquhart, *Hammarskjöld*, (New York: W.W. Norton, 1972), p. 370.

intervening decades, the Bretton Woods institutions have successfully asserted jurisdiction over many aspects of domestic policy-making that were once considered to be securely within the realm of sovereign authority, and have completely displaced the UN's authority over economic and social issues. Similarly, humanitarian and human rights organisations have emerged as functional challengers to the authority of the UN as the protector of life in the decolonised world, while the International Criminal Court and its prosecutor are now the most visible practitioners of government in the name of defending righteousness and defeating evil. The proliferation of institutions dealing with specific problems such as economics, human rights, security and the environment has thus introduced 'functional differentiation' into international jurisdiction.[185] The UN now competes for authority not only with the governments of states divided along territorial lines, but also with other international organisations divided along functional lines.

Perhaps the strongest challenge to the role of the UN as the supreme judge of the lawfulness of authority in the decolonised world occurred when powerful states began to claim the responsibility to act as guardians of common ideals and humanitarian values. That challenge took a particularly serious form when the enthusiastic embrace of multilateral intervention extended to support for military action undertaken by regional organisations without Security Council authorisation. The most notable of these was the 1999 intervention in Kosovo by the North Atlantic Treaty Organization (NATO), but similar interventions were also undertaken by the Economic Community of West African States in Liberia and Sierra Leone. The conflict of jurisdictions caused by the gradual expansion of international executive action reached a crisis point with these interventions undertaken by coalitions of states. The terms on which these actions were justified seemed to pose a serious threat to the fabric of the post–UN international order. For example, many commentators interpreted the NATO intervention in Kosovo as illegal but legitimate.[186] The action was considered to be illegal because NATO acted in violation of the UN Charter by using force without

[185] Martti Koskenniemi, 'The Fate of Public International Law: Between Technique and Politics', *Modern Law Review* 70 (2007), 1 at 5.

[186] Bruno Simma, 'NATO, the UN and the Use of Force: Legal Aspects', *European Journal of International Law* 10 (1999), 1; Antonio Cassese, '*Ex iniuria ius oritur*: Are We Moving towards International Legitimation of Forcible Humanitarian Countermeasures in the World Community?', *European Journal of International Law* 10 (1999), 23.

Security Council authorisation, but legitimate because NATO took such action as an urgent measure to avert a humanitarian catastrophe and defend the values of the international community. For German Foreign Minister Kinkel, the NATO action was undertaken to respond to the 'state of humanitarian necessity in which the international community found itself' and conformed to the logic of the resolutions on Kosovo that the Security Council had passed.[187] The intervention in Kosovo was part of a broader process of reinventing NATO, in which the North Atlantic Assembly called upon member governments 'to stand ready to act should the UN Security Council be prevented from discharging its purpose of maintaining international peace and security'.[188] US President Clinton illustrated particularly clearly what this formulation could mean for the distribution of authority in the world when he made a speech to the General Assembly on 21 September 1999:

> NATO's actions followed a clear consensus, expressed in several Security Council resolutions that the atrocities committed by Serb forces were unacceptable. Had we chosen to do nothing in the face of this brutality, I do not believe we would have strengthened the United Nations. Instead, we would have risked discrediting everything it stands for. By acting as we did, we helped to vindicate the principles and purposes of the UN Charter, to give the UN the opportunity it now has to play the central role in shaping Kosovo's future.[189]

Clinton's position was a logical extension of the functionalist justification for the expansion of UN jurisdiction that had accompanied international executive action since the 1960s. If the functions of sovereignty had been disaggregated and the international community had become the agent of a system for managing populations and solving world problems effectively, why could other actors not exercise the same functions, particularly if they could do so more efficiently or represent universal values more faithfully? In Somalia, Srebrenica, Rwanda, Zaire and Kosovo, the UN had been attacked for failing to make decisions efficiently, failing to protect populations at risk effectively and failing to conduct itself in conformity with fundamental human rights values. What then was wrong with coalitions of the willing or powerful states taking its place as the executive agent of the world community? For states subject to

---

[187] Simma, 'NATO, the UN and the Use of Force', 12.   [188] *Ibid.*, 16.
[189] Bill Clinton, 'Remarks to the 54th Session of the United Nations General Assembly, 21 September 1999' cited in Samantha Power, *Chasing the Flame: Sergio Vieira de Mello and the Fight to Save the World* (New York: Penguin Press, 2008), p. 284.

intervention, this was indeed the nightmarish end-point of the move away from textually defined limits to external intervention in the domestic jurisdiction of states, and the abandonment of the commitment to principles of sovereign equality and self-determination. That development was equally threatening to UN authority. In the wake of the NATO action in Kosovo, Kofi Annan declared that 'peacekeeping is not, and must not become, an arena of rivalry between the United Nations and NATO . . . We work best when we respect each other's competence and avoid getting in each other's way.'[190]

Jurisdiction, recognition and the responsibility to protect

The responsibility to protect concept emerged as a response to the NATO action and concern about its implications for the international order. In its various formulations, the responsibility to protect concept can be seen as an attempt to redefine and delimit domestic and international jurisdiction, and to reassert the primacy of the UN in the face of proliferating functionalist claimants to international authority.

The early formulations of the situations that triggered the international responsibility to protect were very broad. For example, the ICISS report suggested that the international community has a responsibility to protect the '[m]illions of human beings' who 'remain at the mercy of civil wars, insurgencies, state repression and state collapse'.[191] Both 'the state whose people are directly affected' and 'the broader community of states' have a responsibility to provide 'life-supporting protection and assistance to populations at risk'.[192] The responsibility to protect resides first with the state, but a 'residual responsibility also lies with the broader community of states'.[193] That responsibility of the broader community is 'activated when a particular state is clearly either unwilling or unable to fulfill its responsibility to protect or is itself the actual perpetrator of crimes or atrocities; or where people living outside a particular state are directly threatened by actions taking place there'.[194]

ICISS considered that military intervention 'for human protection purposes' was justified in two situations – where there is a threat of

[190] UN, 'Secretary-General Says Future of Peacekeeping will Depend, in Large Part, on Mobilizing New Forms of Leverage to Bring Parties toward Settlement', UN Press Release SG/SM/6901, 23 February 1999.

[191] ICISS, *The Responsibility to Protect* (Ottowa: International Development Research Centre, 2001), p. 11.

[192] *Ibid.*   [193] *Ibid.*, p. 17.   [194] *Ibid.*

'large scale loss of life, actual or apprehended, with genocidal intent or not, which is the product either of deliberate state action, or state neglect or inability to act, or a failed state situation' or alternatively in situations of 'large scale "ethnic cleansing", actual or apprehended, whether carried out by killing, forced expulsion, acts of terror or rape'.[195] Military intervention in such situations should be authorised by the UN Security Council. If the Security Council fails to discharge its responsibility 'in a conscience-shocking situation crying out for action', it remained an open question for ICISS 'where lies the most harm: in the damage to international order if the Security Council is bypassed or in the damage to that order if human beings are slaughtered while the Security Council stands by'.[196] The idea of the UN as a 'universal organization dedicated to protecting peace and promoting welfare' had survived all the trials of the twentieth century.[197] The UN was the appropriate organisation to conduct military intervention for human protection purposes, because it 'has the moral legitimacy, political credibility and administrative impartiality to mediate, moderate and reconcile the competing pulls and tensions that still plague international relations'.[198] However, if the Security Council would not authorise military intervention 'against regimes that flout the most elementary norms of legitimate governmental behaviour', it could not expect concerned states to 'rule out other means and forms of action to meet the gravity and urgency of these situations'.[199] If such interventions were to be carried out successfully, they 'may have enduringly serious consequences for the stature and credibility of the UN itself'.[200]

Many states were concerned at the potential expansion of international authority that could flow from formal endorsement of the responsibility to protect concept by the General Assembly. In the lead up to the World Summit, there was a strong push to limit the triggers to international jurisdiction in relation to the responsibility to protect. When the General Assembly endorsed the concept, it described the international responsibility to protect as a responsibility 'to help to protect populations from genocide, war crimes, ethnic cleansing and crimes against humanity'.[201] The proposal to link the responsibility to protect populations with

---

[195] *Ibid.*, p. 32 (emphasis omitted).   [196] *Ibid.*, p. 55.   [197] *Ibid.*, p. 52.   [198] *Ibid.*
[199] *Ibid.*, p. 55.   [200] *Ibid.*, p. 55.
[201] 2005 World Summit Outcome, GA Res. 60/1, UN GAOR, 60th Sess., 8th Plen. Mtg., Agenda Items 46 and 120, Supp. No. 49, UN Doc. A/RES/60/1, 24 October 2005 (adopted 16 September 2005), para. 139.

the four crimes of genocide, war crimes, ethnic cleansing and crimes against humanity was put forward by Pakistan's Ambassador to the United Nations, H. E. Akram Mounir, in the lead-up to the World Summit.[202] Pakistan, like 'most countries of the South at the level of the Non-aligned Movement', was strongly opposed to the concept of the responsibility to protect.[203] The introduction of the amendment linking the responsibility to protect to specific crimes was designed to address the fears of those who viewed the principle 'as an instrument that could be used by the powerful countries against the weaker ones'.[204]

The articulation of the responsibility to protect concept in the World Summit Outcome is careful to leave little scope for actors or organisations other than the state or the UN to claim the authority to protect. The World Summit Outcome begins by reaffirming the primary role of the state.

> Each individual State has the responsibility to protect its populations from genocide, war crimes, ethnic cleansing and crimes against humanity. This responsibility entails the prevention of such crimes, including their incitement, through appropriate and necessary means. We accept that responsibility and will act in accordance with it.[205]

The traditional principle that each state has jurisdiction over its territory is thus reinforced in the World Summit Outcome. The obligation upon states to protect their populations is clear. Secretary-General Ban Ki-Moon has since emphasised that in the World Summit Outcome: 'Governments unanimously affirmed the primary and continuing legal obligations of states to protect their populations.' He has described the obligation of each state to protect its population as the 'bedrock' principle of the responsibility to protect.[206] The World Summit Outcome thus reaffirms that the world is divided into spatially defined units, within which politics takes place. The responsibility to protect concept takes as a given that physical space exists as a series of defined and bounded

---

[202] Jean Ping, Chairperson, African Union Commission, 'Keynote Address at the Round-Table High-Level Meeting of Experts on "The Responsibility to Protect in Africa"', 23 October 2008, www.responsibilitytoprotect.org/index.php/component/content/article/ 129-africa/1910-african-unions-commission-on-r2pkeynote-speech-by-chairperson-jean-ping.

[203] Ibid.   [204] Ibid.   [205] 2005 World Summit Outcome, para. 138.

[206] See UN, 'Secretary-General Defends, Clarifies "Responsibility to Protect" at Berlin Event on "Responsibility to Protect: International Cooperation for a Changed World"', UN Press Release SG/SM/11701, 15 July 2008, www.un.org/News/Press/ docs/2008/sgsm11701.doc.htm.

territories. Each territory can be 'associated or identified with a sovereign'.[207] The entity with primary control over, and responsibility for, the inhabitants of those territories is the sovereign state. If people are not protected or are at risk, this is a manifestation of the failure of the state to meet its responsibility to protect its population.

The World Summit Outcome also reinforces the authority of the UN. Almost every reference in the Outcome to actions undertaken by the international community refers to the UN. Paragraph 138 states that: 'The international community should, as appropriate, encourage and help States' to exercise the responsibility to protect, and should 'support the United Nations in establishing an early warning capability'. Paragraph 139 provides that: 'The international community, through the United Nations, also has the responsibility to use appropriate diplomatic, humanitarian and other peaceful means, in accordance with Chapters VI and VIII of the Charter, to help to protect populations from genocide, war crimes, ethnic cleansing and crimes against humanity.' States also agreed 'to take collective action, in a timely and decisive manner, through the Security Council, in accordance with the Charter, including Chapter VII, on a case-by-case basis and in cooperation with relevant regional organizations as appropriate, should peaceful means be inadequate and national authorities are manifestly failing to protect their populations from genocide, war crimes, ethnic cleansing and crimes against humanity'. Finally, in Article 140 states stressed the need for the General Assembly to undertake further consideration of the responsibility to protect, and stated their support for the mission of the Special Adviser of the Secretary-General on the Prevention of Genocide. The Secretary-General's Report on 'Implementing the Responsibility to Protect' also insists upon the authority of the UN as the representative of the international community in matters involving the protection of populations. That report stresses that 'the best way to discourage States or groups of States from misusing the responsibility to protect for inappropriate purposes would be to develop fully the United Nations strategy, standards, processes, tools and practices for the responsibility to protect'.[208]

---

[207] Shaunnagh Dorsett, 'Mapping Territories' in Shaun McVeigh (ed.), *Jurisprudence of Jurisdiction* (Oxon: Routledge-Cavendish, 2007), pp. 137–8.

[208] UN Secretary-General, 'Implementing the Responsibility to Protect: Report of the Secretary-General', UN GAOR, 63rd Sess., Agenda Items 44 and 107, UN Doc. A/63/677, 12 January 2009, p. 1.

The responsibility to protect concept thus asserts the authority of states and the UN in the areas of peace and protection. Yet the World Summit Outcome and later elaborations of the responsibility to protect concept have been unable completely to resolve the conflicts of jurisdiction that give rise to the concept. The first jurisdictional question that is left unresolved by the World Summit Outcome concerns the old problem of who decides when a government is manifestly failing to protect its population and on what basis. The World Summit Outcome envisages two forms of authority – that of the state and that of the international community. Both the state and the international community are represented as having an ongoing responsibility to protect populations from specified crimes. The World Summit Outcome thus envisages the existence of complementary jurisdictions. The state has primary authority for protection of its population, and the international community has both a specific authority to take over the role of protector if the state fails in its obligations and an ongoing authority to help protect populations through diplomatic, humanitarian and other peaceful means, and through capacity-building 'before crises and conflicts break out'.[209] Yet the World Summit Outcome does not elaborate how the encounter between these jurisdictions is to be negotiated, or according to what protocols or procedures the movement between jurisdictions will be conducted.[210] In particular, it is not clear how, and by whom, the determination will be made that a particular event or action constitutes a risk of genocide, war crimes, ethnic cleansing or crimes against humanity. What kind of information or evidence would be necessary before the international police could be called into action? The statement that an international responsibility to protect arises when a state is manifestly failing to protect its population appears in some ways to be a factual one. Much institutional attention since the World Summit Outcome has been paid to increasing the international community's access to facts and information about the performance of governments and the effective utilisation of such information. The Secretary-General's implementation report focuses upon the need for enhanced 'early warning' systems, encourages states to engage in 'risk assessment exercises' and stresses

---

[209] *Ibid.*

[210] On the need for protocols governing the encounter between jurisdictions, see Christine Black, Shaun McVeigh and Richard Johnstone, 'Of the South', *Griffith Law Review* 16 (2007), 299. For an analysis of the European tradition of international law as a possible source of such protocols, see Anne Orford, 'Ritual, Mediation and the International Laws of the South', *Griffith Law Review* 16 (2007), 353.

the need for an 'integrated framework' that can utilise 'the information gathered and insights gained by existing United Nations entities'.[211] In turn, scholars have recommended that there be a greater degree of centralisation in the development of measures for conflict prevention, through the development of early warning mechanisms and the strengthening of the executive functions of the Secretary-General.[212] Yet determining whether and on what basis a state needs help to protect its population or is manifestly failing to do so also involves normative questions. The decision that a state needs help to protect its population does not simply involve the assessment of facts, but requires an account of the social conditions under which protection can best be guaranteed and whether there are other community values that are more important than guaranteeing security in a given situation.[213] Making decisions about whether and how a government can best protect its population goes to the heart of politics.

The second jurisdictional question that appears to have been left unresolved by the World Summit Outcome is where precisely the international responsibility to protect lies at the UN. Since the 1960s, the claim to be exercising a responsibility to protect at the UN has tended to expand the authority of the Security Council and the Secretary-General. The process of reaching agreement on the scope of the responsibility to protect has seen jurisdiction over questions of protection move to the General Assembly. It was the General Assembly that voted to include the responsibility to protect concept in the World Summit Outcome, and it was to the General Assembly that the Secretary-General presented his report on 'Implementing the Responsibility to Protect' in 2009. The need to gain consensus on the scope of the responsibility to protect concept at the General Assembly has been responsible for the focus away from licensing military intervention for protection purposes and towards an expansion of assistance and capacity-building measures. Yet that apparent shift towards subjecting questions of recognition and lawfulness to the jurisdiction of a more parliamentary organ is constrained by the institutional focus upon strengthening existing practices of executive

---

[211] UN Secretary-General, 'Implementing the Responsibility to Protect', p. 31.
[212] Bellamy, 'Conflict Prevention and the Responsibility to Protect', 148.
[213] For a strong critique of an approach to international security that assumes 'we know (or can reliably ascertain) those social conditions in which security flourishes', that everybody would agree on what those conditions are and that everyone would agree that achieving security is always more important than anything else, see Koskenniemi, 'The Police in the Temple', 19.

rule, such as fact-finding, preventive diplomacy, human rights monitoring and administration.

The third jurisdictional question that remains unresolved by the responsibility to protect concept is what should happen when different functional claimants to international authority seek to impose different requirements upon the governments of decolonised states. The World Summit Outcome recognises many of the other actors and regimes that compete with the UN to judge the lawfulness of government action. For example, much of the World Summit Outcome is devoted to setting out detailed statements about the need for economic liberalisation. States reaffirm their commitment to implementing the rule of law as a means of mobilising domestic resources and attracting foreign capital, agree to promote trade as an engine for development,[214] undertake to encourage foreign investment in developing countries through creating a domestic environment conducive to attracting investment,[215] and agree to support developing countries to put in place sound macroeconomic policies to drive economic growth.[216]

The World Summit Outcome also gives a major role to international criminal law in the jurisdictional formulation of the responsibility to protect. The fact that the jurisdiction of the international community is linked to the subject-matter jurisdiction of international criminal law furthers strengthens the authority of civil society groups and experts in the area of international criminality. The subject-matter jurisdiction of international criminal law has traditionally been understood to represent 'principles on the basis of which states can exercise criminal jurisdiction' outside their own territories 'in conformity with international law'.[217] It has been used to explain when a foreign state and, later, the international community, might exercise criminal jurisdiction – that is, the power to judge and to punish. There have been other moves to extend the reach of international criminal law beyond the sphere of criminal jurisdiction and punishment. In particular, in its 2007 judgment in the *Case concerning the Application of the Convention on the Prevention and Punishment of the Crime of Genocide*, the ICJ found that Contracting Parties to the Genocide Convention have a 'normative and compelling' obligation to 'take

---

[214] 2005 World Summit Outcome, para. 21.   [215] *Ibid.*, para. 25.   [216] *Ibid.*, para. 24.
[217] Luc Reydams, *Universal Jurisdiction: International and Municipal Legal Perspectives* (Oxford: Oxford University Press, 2003), p. 21.

such action as they can to prevent genocide from occurring'.[218] This interpretation of the obligation to take action to prevent genocide from occurring envisages something beyond the exercise of criminal jurisdiction and punishment – something more akin to an international responsibility to protect populations wherever they are situated. According to the Court, the obligation to prevent is not 'limited by territory' and applies 'to a state wherever it may be acting or may be able to act in ways appropriate to meeting the obligations in question'.[219] In addition, the Constitutive Act of the African Union treats the risk of international crimes as jurisdictional triggers for regional intervention.[220]

However, it is with the emergence of the responsibility to protect concept that we see an institutionalisation of this expanded role for international criminal law categories in international governance. The risk of international crimes taking place is now posited as the trigger to a broad range of governance and police functions. The jurisdiction of the international community will be triggered by the risk that certain specified crimes may be committed. In order to establish that a state is 'manifestly failing to protect', those who argue that the UN has a responsibility to intervene must make the conflict in question intelligible in terms of the categories of genocide or other mass atrocities. For example, the effect of identifying Darfur as an instance of genocide to which the responsibility to protect should apply was to place 'the crisis within a Manichean framework that was defined by the Holocaust and Rwanda'.[221] Within this framework, it could never be appropriate to negotiate with leaders in Darfur, either with a view to reaching a new peace agreement or in order to ensure access for humanitarian aid. 'Among the most prolific champions of the Darfur cause, any political dealings with Khartoum other than direct threats was considered an

---

[218] *Application of the Convention on the Prevention and Punishment of the Crime of Genocide (Bosnia and Herzegovina v. Serbia and Montenegro) (Judgment)*, ICJ, General List No. 91, 26 February 2007, para. 427.

[219] *Ibid.*, para. 183.

[220] Constitutive Act of the African Union, adopted on 11 July 2000 (entered into force 26 May 2001), art. 4(h) (setting out as one of the principles of the Union '[t]he right of the Union to intervene in a Member State pursuant to a decision of the Assembly in respect of grave circumstances, namely war crimes, genocide and crimes against humanity').

[221] Alex de Waal, 'An Emancipatory Imperium? Power and Principle in the Humanitarian International' in Didier Fassin and Mariella Pandolfi (eds.), *Contemporary States of Emergency: The Politics of Military and Humanitarian Interventions* (New York: Zone Books, 2010), p. 295.

unacceptable compromise with evil'.[222] These situations are lifted outside of worldly politics and into a morally unambiguous realm of good
and evil.

Institutions that represent international criminal law or international
economic liberalisation exercise a form of jurisdiction that is based upon
a claim to represent the truth. Institutions such as the International
Monetary Fund and the International Criminal Court shape the actions
that states may take in the name of protecting the welfare of their
populations. Both sets of institutions take up the responsibilities once
claimed by the Pope of policing the obligations of princes and authenti-
cating obedient subjects. The authority of these representatives of the
international community, like the church before them, derives from their
direct representation of truth, unmediated by the will of states or governments.[223] Their capacity to govern depends not upon control over
territory, but upon the success of their officials (experts in human rights,
development economics, conflict studies or genocide prevention) in
spreading the beliefs underlying Western legality throughout the
world.[224]

Law, politics and the conflict of competences

According to Schmitt, if the struggle between secular and spiritual
authorities could not be resolved definitively, all that remained was the
question of who will decide and who will interpret.

> If both parties in the conflict are unable to negotiate their right of co-
> determination in terms of a concordat, the conflict of competences must
> end in the same way as the confessional civil wars of the sixteenth and
> seventeenth century: *either* in a precise answer to the big question *quis
> judicabit?* ['who will decide'?] *or* in an equally precise *itio in partes*
> ['return to the region'] – that is, in a spatially clear territorial or regional
> demarcation.[225]

The responsibility to protect concept does not offer either a negotiated resolution of the ongoing conflict of competences or a clear
demarcation between the many territorial and functional claimants

[222] *Ibid.*, p. 308.
[223] See generally Carl Schmitt, *Roman Catholicism and Political Form*, G. L. Ulmen trans.
(Westport: Greenwood Press, 1996), p. 30.
[224] Alain Supiot, *Homo Juridicus: On the Anthropological Function of the Law*, Saskia
Brown trans. (London: Verso, 2007), pp. xvi–xvii.
[225] Schmitt, *Political Theology II*, p. 114.

to authority over the decolonised world. Although the responsibility to protect concept seeks to define the jurisdiction of state and international actors more carefully, it does not succeed in finally resolving the questions of jurisdiction that arise in relation to issues of peace and protection. Instead, the World Summit Outcome recognises the multiple authorities that claim jurisdiction to judge the legitimacy of governments. The decolonised world remains a place where many actors have a stake in deciding upon the meaning of 'peace' and 'protection'. The different rationalities represented by the state on the one hand and by international institutions on the other – those of statecraft, human rights, international criminal law and economics, amongst others – may at times support each other, but may also at times conflict and clash. How to deal with a situation involving competing loyalties or the clash of rationalities is in the end a fundamentally political question. It is a question that has not been resolved by the responsibility to protect concept.

The turn to protection is an attempt to justify authority on de facto grounds, as if determining whether or not a government has the will and capacity to protect its population is a question of fact. The responsibility to protect concept acts as if the exercise of international authority to protect populations deemed to be at risk is a purely functional matter, and that international executive action can be undertaken without any implications for the status of protected territories. In that sense, the responsibility to protect concept inherits the approach to recognising and claiming authority over the decolonised world that was initiated by Hammarskjöld.[226] For Hammarskjöld, the formal question of which domestic or international actors should be recognised as the lawful authority in a territory could be avoided. International civil servants did not claim any permanent authority over the territories that they administered, and so did not need to give any account of the grounds, ends or limits of the power they exercised. Those administrators could in turn avoid making any judgments about the legitimacy of the competing local claimants to authority with whom they were confronted. The commitment to principles of independence, impartiality and neutrality meant that international rulers could remain uninvolved in such 'internal' matters. Yet, as Chapter 2 argued, in practice international interveners inevitably asserted their own authority to govern and recognised

---

[226] See the detailed discussion in Chapter 2 above.

certain local actors as exercising control over territory as a matter of fact, if not of right.

The functionalist accounts of international administration developed by international lawyers to explain the practice of international executive rule have also claimed that the exercise of control over territory does not affect the status of that territory. Under international law, the state is now said to have 'positive obligations to secure the welfare of its citizens and to maintain law and order by virtue of its governance mandate'.[227] The state is 'only one contender among others' to fulfil those 'functions'.[228] If it fails to do so, those functions are readily transferable to the international community.[229] While international law used to be directed towards dispute settlement and negotiation between states, modern international law exists to achieve 'other systemic objectives' and 'to vindicate community interests'.[230] This account of international law as a system raises significant constitutional questions, such as who has authority to determine whether a state is acting 'to secure the welfare of its citizens', from whom the state receives its 'governance mandate' and how 'community interests' are defined. Judging whether a ruler has the capacity to realise peace and offer protection, and when that guarantee of peace is less important than other obligations, goes to the heart of the normative commitments of a political community.

The turn away from formal issues of status towards a concern with function serves to mask the key question of who is the subject of protection – who decides what protection means, when it is needed, how it can be realised and which claimant to authority is able to provide it? Who, in other words, determines the key questions that have been central to the theory and practice of statecraft since the seventeenth century? In the final chapter, I turn to explore the fundamental questions about status and the subject of protection that are raised, but not resolved, by the responsibility to protect concept.

---

[227] Carsten Stahn, *The Law and Practice of International Territorial Administration: Versailles to Iraq and Beyond* (Cambridge: Cambridge University Press, 2008), p. 31.
[228] *Ibid.*, p. 33.   [229] *Ibid.*   [230] *Ibid.*

5

The Question of Status and the Subject of Protection

This book has argued that the responsibility to protect concept offers a normative foundation for the practices of international executive action that have been undertaken in the decolonised world since the late 1950s. Those practices were introduced by Dag Hammarskjöld during his tenure as Secretary-General to fill the 'power vacuums' caused by the liquidation of the colonial system,[1] and have since expanded to create a long-term policing and managerial role for the UN in the decolonised world. The project of implementing the responsibility to protect concept at the UN is an attempt to consolidate the pre-existing but dispersed practices of executive rule into an integrated system. This concluding chapter explores the political implications of the emergence and embrace of the responsibility to protect concept. What might it mean for international officials to describe their authority to rule in the decolonised world as the exercise of a responsibility to protect? What might it mean for the UN to consolidate, integrate and intensify the forms of executive action it has developed to maintain peace in the decolonised world? Does the responsibility to protect concept help to make the practices of international executive rule intelligible in ways that are politically useful?

The crisis of parliamentary democracy in international relations

In one of his very last speeches, Dag Hammarskjöld explained why international executive rule was an important advance over what he termed a 'conference' or parliamentary-based conception of internationalism.

---

[1] UN Secretary-General, 'Introduction to the Annual Report of the Secretary-General on the Work of the Organization', UN GAOR, 16th Sess., Supp. No. 1A, UN Doc. A/4800/Add.1, 1961, p. 7.

> [O]ne of the essential points on which these experiments in international cooperation represent an advance beyond traditional 'conference diplomacy' is the introduction on the international arena of joint permanent organs, employing a neutral civil service, and the use of such organs for executive purposes on behalf of all the members of the organizations. Were it to be considered that the experience shows that this radical innovation in international life rests on a false assumption, because 'no man can be neutral', then we would be thrown back to 1919, and a searching re-appraisal would be necessary.[2]

Throughout his time as Secretary-General, Hammarskjöld argued that it was necessary to abandon the old world of conference diplomacy and the vision of the UN as a static machinery for resolving conflicts, and instead to embrace a new world in which the UN was an instrument of executive action. Hammarskjöld believed that executive rule was the answer to the revolutionary challenges of the modern world, and particularly to the revolution of decolonisation. The time for static conference diplomacy had passed. If peace and protection were to be guaranteed, the UN must be able to take decisions with speed and efficiency. The commitment to public debate was not a value worth defending in the face of Cold War tensions and the threat of nuclear war. As Chapter 2 suggested, Hammarskjöld also failed to treat parliamentary rule as a marker of lawful authority domestically. For example, the fact that Prime Minister Lumumba had the support of both houses of parliament was not considered by UN officials to be a sign of his legitimacy to rule the Congo, but rather an effect of his dangerous and demagogic power to sway his compatriots through appeals to rhetoric. In the post-Cold War era, international administrators have displayed a similar distrust of elected officials and an apparent lack of respect for parliamentary form. Those who advocate increased intervention in the decolonised world are impatient with even the minimal constraints imposed by multilateral diplomacy and negotiation at the UN.

In that sense, justifications for the emergence of executive rule during the era of decolonisation resemble the critique of parliamentary democracy in the name of protection in the inter-war period. Carl Schmitt was one of the inter-war jurists who offered an account of why executive rule should be preferred to parliamentary democracy in revolutionary situations. For Schmitt, like Hammarskjöld in the international arena, it was far from clear that parliamentary democracy, with its commitment to

---

[2] Dag Hammarskjöld, 'The International Civil Servant in Law and in Fact' in Wilder Foote (ed.), *The Servant of Peace: A Selection of the Speeches and Statements of Dag Hammarskjöld* (London: The Bodley Head, 1962), p. 329.

endless conferencing or discussion, was capable of creating unity out of the potential for civil war. In the economic, political and social conditions of the modern world, the institution of parliament had 'lost its moral and intellectual foundation and only remains standing through sheer mechanical perseverance as an empty apparatus'.[3] A new form, perhaps the dictator or the president, was needed to represent the general will of the people. During times of emergency or civil war, the preservation of security depended upon the existence of a strong authority that could command 'a different and higher order of obligation than any of the other associations in which men live'.[4] For Schmitt, 'the totality of this kind of state power always accords with the total responsibility for protecting and securing the safety of citizens'.[5] Schmitt's turn to protection served to explain why executive rule was the answer to the problem of the legitimacy of authority in the revolutionary conditions of the Weimar republic. Direct action and the use of force had everywhere replaced the old bourgeois techniques of peaceful negotiation and public discussion that were the foundation of parliamentarism.

Yet there are other, and perhaps more important, historical and intellectual bases to parliamentary government than 'the bourgeois ideal of peaceful negotiation and agreement'.[6] The political arguments for the creation of an elected representative assembly and the transfer of constitutional power from an aristocratic elite to the people have included not only liberal commitments to openness and discussion, but also absolutist accounts of representation in which one figure or group can speak for the nation as a whole,[7] revolutionary struggles to create parliamentary bodies in which those who have been disenfranchised can gain political power,[8] and anti-fascist attempts to defend a situation in

---

[3] Carl Schmitt, *The Crisis of Parliamentary Democracy*, 2nd edn., Ellen Kennedy trans. (Cambridge: The MIT Press, 1988) (first published 1934), p. 21.

[4] Carl Schmitt, 'Ethic of State and Pluralistic State' in Chantal Mouffe (ed.), *The Challenge of Carl Schmitt* (London: Verso, 1999), p. 196.

[5] *Ibid.*, p. 96.

[6] Richard Thoma, 'Appendix: On the Ideology of Parliamentarism (1925)' in Carl Schmitt, *The Crisis of Parliamentary Democracy*, Ellen Kennedy trans. (Cambridge, Massachusetts: The MIT Press, 1988) (first published 1934), p. 77 at p. 79.

[7] Oliver Arnold, 'Absorption and Representation: Mapping England in the Early Modern House of Commons' in Andrew Gordon and Bernhard Klein (eds.), *Literature, Mapping and the Politics of Space in Early Modern Britain* (Cambridge: Cambridge University Press, 2001), p. 15 at p. 17.

[8] Andrew Sharp, 'The Levellers and the End of Charles I' in Jason Peacey (ed.), *The Regicides and the Execution of Charles I* (Hampshire: Palgrave MacMillan, 2001), p. 181.

which one might reach agreement with an opponent 'under conditions that exclude naked force'.[9] By treating the commitment to conferencing and diplomacy as merely a means to functional ends determined elsewhere, the commitment to parliamentary rule or to negotiation can soon be made to seem an unaffordable luxury.

The impossibility of neutrality

Hammarskjöld declared that international executive rule was premised upon the idea that the Secretary-General in particular, and the international civil service more broadly, were capable of acting 'on a truly international basis' and carrying out their tasks 'without subservience to a particular national or ideological attitude'.[10] If that were shown to be 'a false assumption', then 'a searching reappraisal would be necessary'. While Hammarskjöld consistently defended the claim that the UN could remain neutral as between competing ideologies and impartial as between internal claimants to authority, in practice neutrality did indeed prove impossible. It will also be impossible for the UN to remain neutral as between competing interests, ideologies and claimants to authority as it implements the responsibility to protect concept. This is so for at least three reasons.

First, the implementation of the responsibility to protect concept cannot be a neutral process because the concept grounds authority on the capacity to guarantee protection. Justifying power in terms of the need and capacity to guarantee protection, and privileging de facto over de jure grounds for authority, works to marginalise questions about whether authority was lawfully acquired or whether those exercising power properly represent the people in some strong sense. To make decisions about authority based upon deciding which actor has the will and capacity to guarantee security in a particular territory will inevitability involve privileging certain kinds of claimants to authority over others. The argument that the lawfulness of authority depends upon the fact of protection serves to delegitimise those whose claim to power is based on tradition, on the capacity to realise spiritual ends or on the realisation of self-determination.

<hr>

[9] Ellen Kennedy, 'Introduction' in Carl Schmitt, *The Crisis of Parliamentary Democracy*, Ellen Kennedy trans. (Cambridge, Massachusetts: The MIT Press, 1988) (first published 1934), p. xiii at p. xxvii.
[10] *Ibid.*, p. 346.

Secondly, the implementation of the responsibility to protect concept cannot be neutral because it will require choosing between competing institutional claimants to authority. Hammarskjöld was confident that the UN could remain 'neutral' on the question of who was the lawful authority over a particular decolonised territory. In the Congo, for example, Hammarskjöld claimed that the UN was formally impartial as between the competing claims to authority of the elected Prime Minister, members of Parliament, the President, the commander of the army, Belgian technicians and insurgent secessionists. Yet in the Congo and wherever else it intervenes, the UN cannot be neutral or impartial because those with whom it chooses to deal gain material and political advantages that may even 'exceed the resources that come with *de facto* control over a specific territory'.[11] International recognition, whether in law or in fact, gives a particular claimant to authority advantages such as access to aid, diplomatic ties, military assistance, tax revenues or commercial credibility. International intervention cannot avoid having an effect on the internal politics of states under administration.

Thirdly, deciding which techniques to use in maintaining order and protecting life can never be apolitical, neutral or impartial in the sense used by Hammarskjöld. Administrators whose authority is based on the responsibility to protect will necessarily stand for something – for the preservation of existing entitlements through state neutrality, say, or for redistribution and a commitment to the welfare of the population as a whole. The key techniques of protection utilised by the international community have included security sector reform, administration, control over the movement of peoples, surveillance, punishment, detention, redistribution of property and the use of force. The decision about what protection requires in a particular time and place, and who must make sacrifices in the name of protection, remains inherently political.

As Hammarskjöld recognised, the realisation that neutrality is impossible does indeed throw us back to 1919, when Europe was struggling to come to terms with war and revolution. One of the stakes in the intellectual debates of that period was the nature of the political authority of the state, and the relation of that authority to democracy and to parliamentary rule. In response to the revolutionary situation in which they were

---

[11] William Reno, 'How Sovereignty Matters: International Markets and the Political Economy of Local Politics in Weak States' in Thomas M. Callaghy, Ronald Kassimir and Robert Latham (eds.), *Intervention and Transnationalism in Africa: Global-Local Networks of Power* (Cambridge: Cambridge University Press, 2001), p. 197 at p. 203.

living, European jurists had in large part abandoned questions of the proper subject or author of law as being somehow extra-legal – either too metaphysical or too political. The idea, then being advanced not only in the positivist jurisprudence of lawyers such as Hans Kelsen but also in the sociology of Max Weber and the pluralist political theory of Harold Laski, was that determinations of the validity of a legal order could be made without a normative account of authority. That position was of concern to socialist jurists, such as Hermann Heller.

> Heller regarded the way in which Kelsen makes the state disappear and his consequent emptying of the idea of sovereignty as the most glaring flaw of the Pure Theory. He understood why, in the context of a tendency to create a secular natural law ethic, the doctrine of sovereignty had to be detached from church and theology. But to make the idea entirely subjectless and thus homeless is, he thought, to concede defeat to the likes of Schmitt.[12]

Schmitt was one of the strongest defenders of the idea that the question of whether a law or an administrative decree is valid 'in the formal sense' is an 'essentially political' question.[13] According to Schmitt, the subject did not owe allegiance to the state or its law unless that state can represent the unified people, resolve their competing loyalties and defend their common interest. The state must have a sufficient institutional form 'to establish order' and in addition it must represent something beyond that order if it is to claim 'a unique power and authority'.[14] Schmitt rejected what he described as attempts to 'negate not only the state as the supreme comprehensive unity but also, first and foremost, its ethical demand to create a different and higher order of obligation than any of the other associations in which men live'.[15] For Schmitt, those who dismissed the state as authoritarian or no longer relevant in a world of plural authorities on ethical grounds had in mind 'for purely polemical reasons, the residues of the old "absolutist" states of the seventeenth and eighteenth centuries'.[16] As a result, the '[s]tate then comes to mean apparatus of government, administrative machinery – in short, things which self-evidently can be assessed only for their instrumental value, but cannot attract fidelity or loyalty, and which the different social

---

[12] Dyzenhaus, *Legality and Legitimacy: Carl Schmitt, Hans Kelsen and Hermann Heller in Weimar* (Oxford: Oxford University Press, 1997), p. 172.

[13] Carl Schmitt, *Legality and Legitimacy*, Jeffrey Seitzer trans. (Durham and London: Duke University Press, 2004) (first published 1932), p. 17.

[14] Schmitt, *Roman Catholicism and Political Form*, G.L. Ulmen trans. (Westport: Greenwood Press, 1996) (first published 1923), p. 30.

[15] Schmitt, 'Ethic of State and Pluralistic State', p. 196.   [16] *Ibid.*, p. 202.

groups rightly control, since they share out the residues'.[17] Although it is 'possible to confine the word "state" historically to the absolute state of the seventeenth and eighteenth centuries', that merely serves to make the state into an easier target to attack on ethical grounds. It ignores the historical relation of the word state to the broader 'problem of the political unity of the people'.[18]

As Chapter 4 showed, the functionalist accounts of international jurisdiction that developed to explain the legitimacy of international executive action have also assumed that questions about the lawfulness of authority can be avoided by thinking about the state merely as the 'apparatus of government' or the 'administrative machinery'. Just as positivism left the law homeless in Weimar Germany, so functionalism has left international law 'subjectless and thus homeless' in the situation of decolonisation. Yet while positivism and functionalism may have left the law homeless in theory, they have not done so in practice. In practice, choices must be made about which claimants to authority should be recognised as lawful, and by whom. Schmitt was right to treat the question of whether a law or an administrative decree is valid and must be obeyed as political. Answering that question involves a theory of politics and of authority. Kelsen with his theory of the purity of law, Weber with his preference for empirical sciences of action rather than dogmatic accounts of validity, Hammarskjöld with his theory of neutrality – all tried to treat the normative foundation of authority as a question that could be avoided. But normative questions about authority cannot be avoided, particularly but not only in revolutionary periods – that is, precisely the periods in which protection is invoked. If humanitarian action in the name of protection is to continue – and it will – it needs to be recognised that in practice it involves a theory of the state or of the subject of law. International intervention necessarily recognises some claimants to authority rather than others, and systematically privileges certain institutional forms and practices (such as administration and executive action) over others (such as parliament and conference diplomacy). The effect, as this book has argued, has been the consolidation of a particular form of international executive rule in the decolonised world. In that sense, the practices of protection initiated by Hammarskjöld and consolidated by the responsibility to protect concept have not been, and cannot be, neutral as between worldly interests and ideologies.

[17] *Ibid.*   [18] *Ibid.*

Rethinking functionalism

Contemporary international lawyers assert that formal questions about authority and juridical status have become irrelevant to the exercise of international rule over the decolonised world. Modern international law was self-consciously functionalist in its attitude to international authority for much of the twentieth century. International lawyers do not seek to grasp the juridical form that is created through international executive rule because they understand functionalism to mean abandoning an outdated obsession with form or status and instead attending to the allocation of disaggregated functions of government across a range of different actors.[19] In the self-conscious move from formalism to functionalism, international lawyers were no longer concerned with the 'status' or sovereignty of territories under administration but instead were concerned with 'the welfare of populations'.[20] The state was dismissed as if it were simply one of the many social groups or 'other associations in which men live'.[21] The international order becomes comprehensible as a system in which 'functions' are vested in this or that social group or actor, in the way that a manager might vest a task in this or that organisational department. International intervention is understood as part of a broader development of the 'executive function

---

[19] See, for example, Carsten Stahn, *The Law and Practice of International Territorial Administration: Versailles to Iraq and Beyond* (Cambridge: Cambridge University Press, 2008), pp. 29, 420 (arguing that territorial administration should be understood as a development of the 'executive function of the international community' and that while the 'UN has regularly acted as a functional authority' in the decolonised world, it has not sought to acquire sovereign title to territory through that exercise of authority); Ralph Wilde, *International Territorial Administration: How Trusteeship and the Civilizing Mission Never Went Away* (Oxford: Oxford University Press, 2008), p. 105 (arguing that international territorial administration has no effect upon the 'juridical status' of territories under administration); Gregory H. Fox, *Humanitarian Occupation* (Cambridge: Cambridge University Press, 2008), pp. 32–3 (arguing that the state is just one of many actors that might exercise an authority that has now been 'disaggregated' and dismissing the 'now dated sovereignty question'). For an account of international territorial administration that does explore the formal status of administered territories, see Bernhard Knoll, *The Legal Status of Territories Subject to Administration by International Organisations* (Cambridge: Cambridge University Press, 2008) (arguing that the status of such territories is defined by the fact that the 'international legal order reaches the objects of its concerns directly, through its organ, without the constraining mediation of a sovereign state structure'), p. 412.

[20] Martti Koskenniemi, 'Occupied Zone – "A Zone of Reasonableness"?', *Israel Law Review* 41 (2008), 13 at 31–2.

[21] Schmitt, 'Ethic of State and Pluralistic State', p. 196.

of the international community' and the move towards 'a more central-ised conception of governance' at the 'universal level'.[22] Of course it is much more appealing to speak about the disaggregation of state func-tions than to cling to some outmoded conception of sovereignty or to assert that the principle of sovereign equality really shapes international relations. A functionalist account that emphasises the complexity of global governance 'articulates a project of technological reason that seems, after all, so much more up to date than the Victorian antics of international law'.[23]

Yet earlier functionalists did not question the concept of sovereignty or the form of the state in order to deny the relevance of concepts or forms in general, but rather to deny the *adequacy* of inherited forms to the political situation they faced. Indeed, the political situation to which early functionalists were responding shares many features with the political situation facing international lawyers today. Harold Laski, for example, turned from asking what the state *is* to what the state *does* in an attempt to develop a theory of state responsibility that was adequate to the expansion of state functions. For Laski, writing in 1919, the need to hold the state responsible for the use of public money (held on 'trust') had become evident. This may not have been necessary 'in the days when the functions of government were negative rather than positive in char-acter',[24] but by 1919 this was no longer the case. 'The modern state is . . . nothing so much as a great public-service corporation'.[25] No adequate principle of state responsibility had yet emerged because 'the concepts of our public law have not so far developed that they meet the new facts they encounter'.[26] The linking of government with 'the trappings of medieval monarchy' had led to the centrality of 'the equation "Sovereignty = privilege" which is central to English thought'.[27] Laski recognised that particular officials are always understood to gain their authority from some third term: 'that which gives the official his meaning . . . escapes the categories of law'.[28] In England, that term is 'the Crown; but if we choose to look

---

[22] Stahn, *Law and Practice of International Territorial Administration*, pp. 29–30.

[23] Martti Koskenniemi, 'The Fate of Public International Law: Between Technique and Politics', *Modern Law Review* 70 (2007), 1 at 23.

[24] Harold Laski, 'The Responsibility of the State in England', *Harvard Law Review* 32 (1919), 447 at 451.

[25] *Ibid.*, 452. [26] *Ibid.*

[27] Carol Harlow, 'The Crown: Wrong Once Again?', *Modern Law Review* 40 (1977), 728 at 729–30.

[28] Laski, 'Responsibility of the State', 450.

beneath that noble ornament we shall see vast government offices full of human, and, therefore, fallible men'.[29] The functionalist challenge was then to rethink the 'antiquarian' conception of the state in public law so that 'the real machinery of government' could be 'substituted for the clumsy fiction of the Crown'.[30] In addition, a functionalist approach might reveal that the adherence to stale dogmas had hidden the fact that the state had no greater claim to loyalty than the myriad other groups that existed in the modern world.

> Ours is a time of deep question about the state. Theories of corporate personality have challenged in decisive fashion its proud claim to pre-eminence. Its character of uniqueness seems hardly to have survived the acid test of sceptical inquiry. The groups it has claimed to control seem, often enough, to lead a life no less full and splendid than its own. The loyalty they can command, the fear they may inspire, are near enough to its own to seek comparison with it. Yet dogmas that are none the less fundamental because they are hardly old still haunt our speculations.[31]

Other early functionalists like Felix Cohen also attacked legalism for its attachment to empty forms and metaphysical ideals. Cohen argued that it was necessary to move away from 'legal fictions' that present as 'concepts' and instead look to the '*motions* or *operations*' that they describe.[32] While 'it is useful to invent legal terms to describe the corporate activities of human beings', it is necessary to avoid falling into the trap of believing that those legal terms describe real things.[33] The state or the corporation are just useful fictions to describe collective behaviour, and must be abandoned if they cease to be useful. Cohen wanted 'to substitute a realistic, rational, scientific account of legal happenings for the classical theological jurisprudence of concepts'. The 'functional approach' offered a way to achieve this. Cohen compared functionalism in law to 'functional architecture', which is 'likewise a repudiation of outworn symbols and functionless forms that have no meaning – hollow marble pillars that do not support, fake buttresses, and false fronts'.[34] It is worth noting that the goal of functionalism was to repudiate 'functionless forms' but not to repudiate form altogether – buildings still need pillars and fronts. Cohen called instead for the

---

[29] *Ibid.*, 451.   [30] *Ibid.*

[31] Harold J. Laski, 'The Early History of the Corporation in England', *Harvard Law Review* 30 (1916–17), 561.

[32] Felix Cohen, 'Transcendental Nonsense and the Functional Approach', *Columbia Law Review* 35 (1935), 809 at 825.

[33] *Ibid.*   [34] *Ibid.*, 823.

reinterpretation of legal form: 'the salvaging of whatever significance attaches' to existing concepts 'through the redefinition of these concepts as functions of actual experience'.[35] It was necessary to focus not on the properties of an object but rather on its operations, and to discover what a concept does or the way in which it is recognised in practice.[36] This is functionalism as 'an assault upon all dogmas and devices that cannot be translated into terms of actual experience' – a 'negative' functionalism that is, Felix Cohen says, 'naturally of special prominence in a protestant movement'.[37] Like many protestant movements, legal functionalism aims to abandon empty forms and rituals, and to engage with the real life of the law. The challenge set for legal scholars by functionalism was to try to make legal form meaningful in light of experience and practice.

The form of international rule

How then might the functionalist call to relate legal concepts to 'actual experience' be met in the context of international executive rule? The defining feature of international executive rule is precisely its most visible characteristic – that it is a form of administration. There has been a great deal of recent work in international legal scholarship aimed at 'analyzing global governance as administration' in order to argue that global governance should be 'subject to distinctive administrative law principles'.[38] I do not want to propose that these practices should be understood as administration in order to argue for their subjection to distinctive administrative law principles. Indeed, a focus on administrative law principles of accountability and participation in this situation is part of the problem. Rather, understanding these practices as a specific form of governance (administration) with a particular history can help to make the political stakes of international executive rule intelligible.

International administration has been premised upon the separation of title to and control over territory in the decolonised world.[39] As Chapter 4 showed, that separation of ownership and control has been traced back to the 1950s, when scholars such as Eli Lauterpacht argued that it was necessary to 'distinguish between the two principal meanings

---

[35] Ibid., 827.   [36] Ibid., 809, 827.   [37] Ibid., 822.

[38] Benedict Kingsbury, Nico Krisch and Richard B. Stewart, 'The Emergence of Global Administrative Law', Law and Contemporary Problems 68 (2005), 15 at 19.

[39] Wilde, International Territorial Administration, pp. 99–110.

attributed to the word "sovereignty".[40] Sovereignty could mean both the right of ownership and the control that a state may exercise over territory.[41] The two forms of sovereignty could be split – the important question was who was entitled to exercise jurisdiction and control over a territory and to 'regulate the exploitation of its natural resources'.[42] Lauterpacht's approach can usefully be considered in relation to a legal debate about the distinction between ownership and control over private property that had begun to emerge prior to and during the Second World War in the United States and Europe. In the United States, Adolf Bearle and Gardiner Means argued that the emergence of the public corporation had led to 'a large measure of separation of ownership and control' over property.[43] The corporation had 'destroyed the unity that we commonly call property' by dividing ownership 'into nominal ownership and the power formerly joined to it'.[44] As a result, 'the old atom of ownership' had been dissolved 'into its component parts' and control over industrial property had been 'cut off' from 'beneficial ownership of this property'.[45] Berle and Means argued that this represented a 'radical shift in property tenure'.[46] Similarly, Franz Neumann argued that the rise of the joint stock company in Germany during the same period had meant that 'the capital function' had been 'divorced from the administrative one', and argued that this carried 'the germ for the development of managerial bureaucracy'.[47] Scholars saw the 'division of the functions formerly accorded to ownership' as a development that was revolutionary and potentially destructive in its effects on social relations, its concentration of power in the hands of a centralised management and its overall reorganisation of economic activity.[48]

The separation of ownership and control was related to a shift in the mode of governance. Of particular concern to these scholars was that the separation of ownership and control had led to the creation of a new group or elite class of managers. Where in private corporations and small businesses 'owners managed and managers owned', the separation of the

---

[40] E. Lauterpacht, 'The Contemporary Practice of the United Kingdom in the Field of International Law – Survey and Comment', *International and Comparative Law Quarterly* 5 (1956), 405 at 410.

[41] *Ibid.*   [42] *Ibid.*

[43] Adolf A. Berle Jr. and Gardiner C. Means, *The Modern Corporation and Private Property* (New York: The MacMillan Company, 1933), p. 4.

[44] *Ibid.*, p. 7.   [45] *Ibid.*, pp. 7–8.   [46] *Ibid.*, p. 4.

[47] Franz Neumann, *Behemoth: The Structure and Practice of National Socialism 1933–1944* (New York: Harper and Row, 1944), pp. 284–5.

[48] Berle and Means, *The Modern Corporation and Private Property*, p. 119; *ibid.*, p. 285.

functions of ownership coincided with the rise of a professional class of managers.[49] The authority of this managerial elite was not based upon any particular legal status or formal title to property, but upon the possession and exercise of control over property.[50] As the power of the corporation intensified and control was separated from ownership, it was no longer clear whether the interests of the managers coincided with the interests of the beneficial owners of property, and how if at all the power and privileges of managers could be constrained.[51] This gave rise to legal questions about whether the interests of the managers coincided with the interests of the owners of property, the interests of the employees of the organisation or with the general interest more broadly. Similar concerns were expressed about the growing bureaucratisation of the industrial state. During and after the world wars, control over productive aspects of the state was increasingly vested in an emerging managerial elite. The question of whether those who controlled public money and services were divorced from the interests of the people was of concern both to left and right.[52]

The concept of managerialism was initially discussed critically as a troubling technique of governance that had grown out of the separation between ownership and control. Yet over time, managerialism began to be theorised as a useful technique of control.[53] Managerialism as a philosophy and a practice endorses a division between the managerial or strategic part of an organisation that determines ends, and the operational part of an organisation that performs tasks needed to achieve those ends.[54] Management imparts its thinking to the workforce through

[49] Alfred D. Chandler Jr., *The Visible Hand: The Managerial Revolution in American Business* (Cambridge: Belknap Press, 1977), p. 9.

[50] Jonathan Murphy, 'The Rise of the Global Managers' in Sadhvi Dar and Bill Cooke (eds.), *The New Development Management: Critiquing the Dual Modernization* (London: Zed Books, 2008), p. 18 at pp. 19–21.

[51] Berle and Means, *The Modern Corporation and Private Property*, pp. 121, 353.

[52] See, for example, Vladimir Lenin, *The State and Revolution*, Robert Service trans. (London: Penguin Books, 1992); James Burnham, *The Managerial Revolution* (London: Penguin, 1945).

[53] Anshuman Prasad and Pushkala Prasad, 'The Empire of Organizations and the Organization of Empires: Postcolonial Considerations on Theorizing Workplace Resistance' in Anshuman Prasad (ed.), *Postcolonial Theory and Organizational Analysis: A Critical Engagement* (New York: Palgrave MacMillan, 2003), p. 95 at p. 97.

[54] Ron Kerr, 'International Development and the New Public Management: Projects and Logframes as Discursive Technologies of Governance' in Sadhvi Dar and Bill Cooke (eds.), *The New Development Management: Critiquing the Dual Modernization* (London: Zed Books, 2008), p. 91.

policies, directives or strategies that are linked to funding, while the workforce is accountable to management through reporting on its operations and the extent to which it accomplishes the set tasks.[55] Management techniques such as the requirement that staff performance is audited,[56] the introduction of managed participation as a means of enhancing employee 'ownership' of goals, or the use of the 'project' as a means of increasing efficiency and predictability of outcomes, are used 'to monitor and control the actions of (often distant) others'.[57] Those managerial techniques have now been taken up as a form of rule to control not just employees but whole nations. Managerialism is central to the conduct and scholarly representation of international executive rule. Indeed, managerialism as a technique of control has intensified both within and through the UN since the end of the Cold War.[58] The government of people and places is now conceived of as a series of projects from which lessons can be learned and experience digested.

Managerial techniques of 'local ownership' and disciplinary surveillance themselves grew out of practices of colonial administration and indirect rule that characterised late colonialism in India, Africa and North America.[59] Indirect rule as a form of 'organization and reorganization of the colonial states' was designed 'as a response to a central and overriding dilemma: the native question'.[60] The question facing colonial rulers was 'how can a tiny and foreign minority rule over an indigenous majority?'[61] Indirect rule operated through local laws, customs and leaders as far as possible, with colonial law and the use of force resorted to by colonial powers in the last resort. 'This system did not simply deny sovereignty to its colonies; it redesigned their administrative and political

[55] Ibid., p. 96.
[56] Michael Power, The Audit Society: Rituals of Verification (Oxford: Oxford University Press, 1997); Dean Neu, 'Accounting for the Banal: Financial Techniques as Softwares of Colonialism' in Anshuman Prasad (ed.), Postcolonial Theory and Organizational Analysis: A Critical Engagement (New York: Palgrave MacMillan, 2003), p. 193.
[57] Kerr, 'International Development and the New Public Management', p. 94.
[58] For the related argument that the 'scope and coherence' of managerialism has 'expanded exponentially in recent years', and that the World Bank 'has not only incorporated key postbureaucratic disciplinary strategies into its internal practices, but also externalised them': see Murphy, 'The Rise of the Global Managers', pp. 18–19.
[59] Bill Cooke, 'Participatory Management as Colonial Administration' in Sadhvi Dar and Bill Cooke (eds.), The New Development Management: Critiquing the Dual Modernization (London: Zed Books, 2008), p. 111.
[60] Mahmood Mamdani, Citizen and Subject: Contemporary Africa and the Legacy of Late Colonialism (Princeton: Princeton University Press, 1996), p. 16.
[61] Ibid.

life.'[62] Colonial administrators were given expansive powers to exercise 'control' over the territory, while a 'separate but subordinate structure' was created 'for natives'.[63] The effect was to create two forms of government – 'one defined by sovereignty and citizenship, and the other by trusteeship and wardship'.[64] It is important to note that these two forms of government were 'two parts of a single but bifurcated international system'.[65] What mattered were the relations between the two parts of the system.

These features of indirect rule and techniques of colonial administration have shaped contemporary international executive rule. If we look for example at the way in which international administrators live, in separate 'zones' as in Iraq,[66] or subject to separate regimes of privileges and immunities, we can see the relation to systems of indirect rule which treated governors as spatially and legally distinct from the governed. International executive rule works through local laws where possible, trumping them with administrative regulations and decrees where necessary to achieve the goals determined centrally. Local parliaments and courts are subordinated to international officials. As the institution of territorial administration expands and control is systematically separated from ownership, pressure grows to ensure that those who exercise power (in this case, the administrators) do so for the public benefit. A similar pressure for reform has historically developed in relation to other organisations, such as the Catholic church, the state and the corporation, as their power intensified and they began to be represented as entities whose representatives were separate from their members.[67] In the case of the church, the state and the corporation, reformists demanded that the powers and privileges of those exercising control over the institution be used 'in the common interest'.[68] The question remains how such a demand could be posed to the 'international community', and how it could be made effective in a world of territorially divided states.

The realisation that administration is a specific form of rule with a long history has been met with calls for greater accountability as a means

---

[62] Mahmood Mamdani, *Saviors and Survivors: Darfur, Politics, and the War on Terror* (New York: Pantheon, 2009), p. 277.
[63] Mamdani, *Citizen and Subject*, p. 62.
[64] Mamdani, *Saviors and Survivors*, p. 277.   [65] *Ibid.*
[66] For an account, see Rajiv Chandrasekaran, *Imperial Life in the Emerald City: Inside Baghdad's Green Zone* (London: Bloomsbury, 2007).
[67] Berle and Means, *The Modern Corporation and Private Property*, p. 353.   [68] *Ibid.*

of reforming the practice. Yet it is not enough for lawyers to argue for the development of a global administrative law regime of increased accountability or transparency without also attending to questions of constitutionalism and institutional design. Accountability is a core technique of administrative rule, by which those who are responsible for 'operations' (or means) report on the efficiency of their performance back up a chain of authority to those who formulate 'strategy' (or ends). Similarly, using administrative law to address the turn to administrative rule could be a liberal move, as claimed by the Global Administrative Law project.[69] The history of the turn to administration, however, shows that it could equally be an authoritarian move. For example, in Weimar Germany, a concern with administration took the place of a concern with constitutionalism or state law doctrine. Michael Stolleis has drawn attention to the '"shift towards administrative law" that set in quickly after 1933'.[70] In large part, that shift was connected to the '"settling of the constitutional question" and the functional loss of state law doctrine' that accompanied the rise of Hitler and the 'establishment of the Fuhrer state'.[71] 'Scholars who wished to contribute' and not to appear obstructionist or irrelevant 'had to devote themselves to administration, create the new legal doctrines appropriate to the authoritarian style of leadership, and seek to re-establish the contact with administrative reality that had been lost under the liberal law of the *Rechsstaat*, with its focus on the legal form'.[72] Jurists turned to administrative law 'to avoid the dangerous questions about what form the state would take, questions Hitler monopolized'.[73] A focus on administrative law 'offered a respectable way out, by allowing one to constrain the state with the fetters of the *Rechtsstaat* at least at the lower levels'.[74] Stolleis is not describing 'totalitarian despotism' but something short of it – the authoritarian state theory of the 'conservative revolution', which would seek to 'reconcile conservatism and modernity, a commitment to values and efficiency'.[75]

Looking to administrative law rather than constitutional law as a response to the expansion of the 'executive function of the international community' ignores the question of who is the proper subject or agent of

---

[69] Kingsbury, Krisch and Stewart, 'The Emergence of Global Administrative Law', 51–2.

[70] Michael Stolleis, *A History of Public Law in Germany 1914–1945*, Thomas Dunlap trans. (Oxford: Oxford University Press, 2004), p. 373.

[71] *Ibid.*, pp. 373, 375.   [72] *Ibid.*, p. 375.   [73] *Ibid.*, p. 373.   [74] *Ibid.*   [75] *Ibid.*, p. 374.

these systems of administration.[76] Even in a system built upon increased rationalisation and bureaucratisation, it matters who gets to choose the ends of government. Life can be rationalised 'in very different directions' – the 'modes of rationalization' adopted in a given situation will differ according to the values or presuppositions or ends 'that ground and direct the various ways of leading a rationalized style of life'.[77]

The question of status

The disappearance of the question of status from contemporary legal studies of international rule is thus a symptom of a broader loss. Reading functionalist accounts of international governance, it is hard to remember why there might be reasons to care what form of government is imposed upon a people, or whether they can choose their rulers or decide what ends are to be served by those in power. If policy is determined by global managers and the state is merely one executive agent amongst others of a system directed from elsewhere, what does it matter whether the form of the state, its rulers and its ends are also determined by others?

Yet since the seventeenth century, fundamental questions about politics, authority and the subject of law have been discussed using the language of status or its vernacular equivalent, the state. In medieval Europe, the language of status was used to refer both to the standing of kings or princes and to the condition of the realms or territories over which they ruled.[78] Gradually, status began to be identified with 'the supreme authority vested in the government of the prince' rather than with the broader public welfare of the realm.[79] The 'use of the term *status* and its vernacular equivalents' by early republicans did not express 'a

[76] For the argument that this is the question that functionalism avoids, see Peer Zumbansen, 'Law after the Welfare State: Formalism, Functionalism, and the Ironic Turn of Reflexive Law', *American Journal of Comparative Law* LVI (2008), 769 at 783 ('What functionalism does not answer is who the author of regulation should be').
[77] Donald N. Levine, 'The Continuing Challenge of Weber's Theory of Rational Action' in Charles Camic, Philip S. Gorski and David M. Trubek (eds.), *Max Weber's 'Economy and Society'*: A Critical Companion (Stanford: Stanford University Press, 2005), p. 101 at p. 116.
[78] Quentin Skinner, 'From the State of Princes to the Person of the State' in *Visions of Politics: Renaissance Virtues* (Cambridge: Cambridge University Press, 2002), vol. 2, p. 368 at pp. 369–73.
[79] Gaines Post, 'Status, Id Est, Magistratus: L'Etat, C'est Moi' in *Studies in Medieval Legal Thought: Public Law and the State, 1100–1322* (Princeton: Princeton University Press, 1964), p. 333 at pp. 364–5.

modern understanding of the state as an authority distinct from rulers and ruled'.[80] Nonetheless, English republicans did embrace 'one half of this doubly abstract notion of political power', that is, the distinction between state and government, and expressed this 'as a claim about the independent structures of *stati, états* and states'.[81] Later writers, such as Bodin and Hobbes, sought to counter the revolutionary potential of the idea that the people might also be conceived of as separate from the ruling institutions of the state, by arguing that the people existed as a unity only through their acceptance of common submission to the sovereign.[82] According to Hobbes, without a sovereign the people are nothing, for the 'multitude ... are made *one* person, when they are by one man, or one person, represented'.[83] It is through the creation of the sovereign that the people are unified 'and *unity,* cannot otherwise be understood in multitude'.[84] In such absolutist accounts of sovereignty, the 'status' or state is reduced to the impersonal institutions of government or the administrative machinery of rule.

In time, despite the best endeavours of Bodin and Hobbes, the modern state came to be understood in terms of a three-way abstraction of ruler, ruled and the institutions of government. The relation between the state, the ruler and the people became a core concern – perhaps the core concern – of modern politics. It is that core question that has been dismissed as anachronistic by lawyers who argue that the techniques of control developed to manage decolonisation have rendered the question of juridical status anachronistic. It is now axiomatic that international executive rule has no effect upon the status of territories under administration. The guardian of this new administrative order is the UN. It is thus no longer relevant to ask who is the 'state' – that is, the legal subject with the status to represent the welfare of the people and to lay down the law. As Schmitt prefigured, the abandonment of a concern with the formal question of status renders the subject of protection, and of law, homeless. International administrative regimes, like the authoritarian regimes of twentieth-century Europe, govern according to the principle that '[n]either parties nor associations, neither parliament nor public opinion should be allowed to impair the goal of an objective,

---

[80] Skinner, 'From the State of Princes', p. 386. [81] *Ibid.* [82] *Ibid.*, p. 399.
[83] Thomas Hobbes, *Leviathan,* J. C. A. Gaskin (ed.) (Oxford: Oxford University Press, 2006) (first published 1651), p. 109.
[84] *Ibid.*

task-oriented administration'.[85] The old questions raised by the concept of status have disappeared in such a system.

The responsibility to protect concept is thus of normative significance because it puts the question of authority and its relation to status back on the table. It offers an account of the normative foundation of the form of authority that has been created through the practices of policing and administration conducted in the decolonised world since the 1960s. The responsibility to protect concept asserts that the lawfulness of authority – whether of the state or of the international community – flows from the factual capacity and willingness to guarantee protection to the inhabitants of a territory. The state has the primary responsibility to exercise that authority, but if it fails to do so, the responsibility will shift to the international community acting through the UN. The responsibility to protect concept also seeks to show why that protective function does not vest in just any claimant. Official texts formulating the responsibility to protect concept make clear that the state retains the primary responsibility to protect the people of its territory. Similarly, those texts make clear that the UN rather than, say, the North Atlantic Treaty Organization (NATO) or the US, is the proper representative of the international community and the only legitimate guarantor of international peace. In that sense, the responsibility to protect concept represents an attempt to recover the idea that authority, to be meaningful, must both create order and represent something beyond that order. In the face of a managerial revolution and a functionalist account of government that make questions about the foundations of legal order seem obsolete,[86] the responsibility to protect concept insists upon the centrality of questions about the grounds of authority to the contemporary international situation.

Revolution, counter-revolution and the future of international law

How, on what grounds and by whom legal authority is to be recognised become questions for international law at moments of revolution – the

[85] Michael Stolleis, *A History of Public Law in Germany 1914–1945*, Thomas Dunlap trans. (Oxford: Oxford University Press, 2004), p. 374.
[86] Peter Goodrich (ed.), *Law and the Unconscious: A Legendre Reader* (Basingstoke: Macmillan, 1997), pp. 98–9.

protestant revolutions of the sixteenth and seventeenth centuries, the bourgeois revolutions of the eighteenth century, the communist revolutions of the twentieth century and the revolution that is decolonisation. The linkage of authority and protection has also often emerged at times of civil war or revolution, in order to explain why those who exercise de facto authority should be recognised in preference to other, perhaps more idealistic, claimants to power.

The turn to protection in the state theory of the *Leviathan* was 'the product of the earliest major counter-revolutionary movement in modern European history, the movement of reaction against the ideologies of popular sovereignty initially developed in the Dutch and French religious wars and subsequently restated in the course of the English constitutional upheavals of the mid-seventeenth century'.[87] This book has suggested that the responsibility to protect concept is part of a counter-revolutionary movement in that sense. The practices of rule initiated by Hammarskjöld have privileged executive action over parliamentary debate, and private diplomacy over public contestation. The techniques of surveillance, police action and administration now being consolidated and integrated through the implementation of the responsibility to protect concept have limited the capacity of decolonised states to realise self-determination, to redistribute property, to restructure authority and to exercise power over life and death.

Yet the emergence of the responsibility to protect concept is at the same time part of a revolutionary movement. Hammarskjöld's account of executive action rejected the old forms of imperial rule, and understood the choice facing the European world in stark terms. Faced with 'the breakdown of the European circle of culture, spiritually, politically and geographically', Hammarskjöld's answer was not to 'reach back for the imagined calm of the closed world'.[88] Instead, the challenge was to 'reach ahead towards the glimpse of the synthesis, inspired by the dream of a new culture in which there is achieved, on a level encompassing the whole world, what once seemed to have become a regional reality in Europe'.[89] The UN was the vehicle through which 'the world community might, step by step, grow into organized international co-operation

---

[87] Skinner, 'From the State of Princes', p. 405.
[88] Dag Hammarskjöld, 'Asia, Africa, and the West' in Wilder Foote (ed.), *The Servant of Peace: A Selection of the Speeches and Statements of Dag Hammarskjöld* (London: The Bodley Head, 1962), p. 212 at p. 214.
[89] *Ibid.*

within the Charter'.[90] The creation of a world order would require abandoning the conception of the UN as a static conference machinery – a conception that referred 'to history and to the traditions ... of the past'.[91] The situation of decolonisation required a new conception of the UN as an instrument of executive action that could meet 'the needs of the present and of the future'.[92]

Hammarskjöld's vision was revolutionary, not only for international relations, but also for the occupied states that were to be remade by international administrators. The international forms of rule initiated by Hammarskjöld and authorised by the responsibility to protect concept are revolutionary regimes, designed to eliminate any existing laws, property relations and political cultures deemed illegitimate. Accounts of the law and practice of international executive action offer instruction in how to conduct a revolution and to make certain its effects are real and lasting. In that sense, as a UN official commented in the aftermath of the Congo operation, Hammarskjöld really was 'a Machiavelli of peace'.[93] Yet in a significant departure from the revolutionary manifestos of a Machiavelli or a Marx, the manuals of international rule contain one further significant lesson whose effects are yet to be fully grasped. They teach us that in the twenty-first century, only the 'international community' – rather than the people, or the state, or the proletariat, or the party – may legitimately stage a revolution in the decolonised world. This has had significant implications for the unfinished project of decolonisation.

The project of implementing the responsibility to protect concept aims to consolidate and integrate the practices of executive rule initiated by Hammarskjöld. The tendency from 1960 onwards to treat the largely unconstrained practices of international executive rule in the decolonised world as legitimate exemplifies a trend away from liberalism as the dominant mode of international legal thought. International law, like much modern secular law, has traditionally oscillated between emphasising the consent of states and the collective good as the foundations of its authority.[94] The international legal solution to the tension between individual freedom and worldly authority has classically been liberal – it

---

[90] UN Secretary-General, 'Introduction to the 1961 Annual Report', p. 5.
[91] *Ibid.* [92] *Ibid.*
[93] Conor Cruise O'Brien, *To Katanga and Back: A UN Case History* (New York: Simon and Schuster, 1962), p. 47.
[94] Martti Koskenniemi, *From Apology to Utopia*, 2nd edn. (Cambridge: Cambridge University Press, 2005).

depends upon preservation of a space within which autonomous subjects can freely choose to subject themselves to authority and bind themselves to the order that they bring into being.[95] For Hammarskjöld and many UN officials since, the international community really does represent genuine universality, and individual states (and indeed individuals) obtain their freedom through their association as members of this international community. That is particularly so for newly independent states. As Hammarskjöld stated in the context of the Congo:

> A government without financial means is dependent on those who help it to meet its needs. It may depend financially on another state, or group of states, and thereby tie its fate to that of the donors. Or it may depend on the international community in its entirety, represented by the United Nations, and so remain free. There is no third alternative this side of a complete breakdown of the state through inflation or a speedy disintegration of all social and economic services.
>
> ... These are the hard facts which should be remembered when the relations of the United Nations with the central government are discussed.[96]

Throughout his time as Secretary-General, Hammarskjöld moved towards subsuming the interests of the individual state into the collective interest. His was a revolutionary response to the relation between freedom and authority. In the words of Engels: 'A revolution is certainly the most authoritarian thing there is.'[97]

Institutionalising protection: the work of law and politics

A pessimistic response to the responsibility to protect concept might see it as signalling a regressive return to the authoritarian view of states and their proxies as protectors of individuals living in fear of war and death. This book has (largely) taken the more optimistic view that the attempt to offer a normative account of international executive rule makes visible the importance of the work that is involved in translating concepts such as responsibility and protection into particular political communities and positive laws. The responsibility to protect concept alters the ways

---

[95] Ibid., p. 21.

[96] Andrew W. Cordier and Wilder Foote, Public Papers of the Secretaries-General of the United Nations, Volume V: Dag Hammarskjöld 1960–1961 (New York: Columbia University Press, 1975), p. 163.

[97] Friedrich Engels, 'On Authority' in Robert C. Tucker (ed.), The Marx-Engels reader, 2nd edn. (New York: WW Norton and Co, 1978), p. 730 at p. 733.

in which the presence of international humanitarians and their authority to rule is represented, to themselves and to those they govern. The claim to be intervening on behalf of the universal values of a common humanity was so deeply embedded within a Christian metaphysics of action, that it was difficult for those who believed that the Third World needed saving to experience humanitarian action as political.[98] That vision depended upon projecting the 'inevitable political predicaments of sovereignty and representation' onto the state,[99] and away from the international community. The international community and international law were represented as if they were apolitical and unified,[100] and as if acts of intervention did not themselves set up new relations of domination and exploitation, clashes of interest and unresolved grievances.

Yet such effects are as much part of the constitution of the international community as they are of any state (or indeed any other body politic). There has been inadequate attention paid in the cosmopolitan theory and practice of international executive rule to the ongoing work involved in legitimating (or delegitimating) the 'transformation of power into authority of different kinds'.[101] Instead, the focus has been on the need to transcend the imperfections of the present order, as illustrated by the response of Jürgen Habermas to NATO's intervention in Kosovo. Habermas endorsed NATO's action on the basis that it was understood by Continental European states 'as an "anticipation" of an effective law of world citizenship – as a step along the path from classical international law to what Kant envisioned as the "status of world citizen" which would afford legal protection to citizens against their own criminal regimes'.[102] The proper measurement of humanitarian action was not in terms of what it meant now, in this world, but the extent to which it represented a further step along the path to that coming cosmopolitan order.

---

[98] For a wide-ranging exploration of the Christian metaphysics of international law, see Jennifer L. Beard, *The Political Economy of Desire: International Law, Development and the Nation State* (Oxon: Routledge-Cavendish, 2006).

[99] Gillian Rose, *Mourning Becomes the Law: Philosophy and Representation* (Cambridge: Cambridge University Press, 1996), p. 19 (discussing the general tendency to idealise the concept of community in this way).

[100] Outi Korhonen, 'The Problem of Representation and the Iraqi Elections', *Finnish Yearbook of International Law* 14 (2003), 35.

[101] Rose, *Mourning Becomes the Law*, p. 16.

[102] Jürgen Habermas, 'America and the World (Interview)', *Logos Journal* 3(3) (2004), www.logosjournal.com/issue_3.3/habermas_interview.htm.

In contrast, the shift to justifying the lawfulness of authority on the basis of a responsibility to protect forces its advocates to defend the utility of their actions in concrete situations. Here the question raised by the responsibility to protect – how might subjects be guaranteed security and protection – has the potential to offer a sharper focus for analysis than the much more metaphysical question – how can we bring into being a global civil society to ensure that universal rights and freedoms are guaranteed to all of humanity? Protection cannot be invoked as the grounds of authority today without also invoking the long history of other attempts to legitimise authority through appeals to protection – the violent excesses of Cromwell's Puritan armies, the creation of protectorates as a colonial technique of rule, the return to protection by the counter-revolutionary state theorists of fascist Europe. The writings of Hobbes and Schmitt make visible that the capacity to inspire shock and awe, and to wield the sword or let loose the police, have been part of what is necessary for the security state to last. The prioritising of protection, when accompanied by the empowerment of the executive, the privileging of the interests of private economic actors and the expansion of policing in the name of security, can threaten the well-being of both individuals and populations. As this book has suggested, that history haunts any appeal to protection as a basis for the legitimacy of authority and of law, and politicises the movement between the ideal of protection and its implementation. Perhaps in the end this is what the turn to protection offers – a reminder that judgments about the form and ends of lawful authority are not technical or universally agreed upon, but contested. The responsibility to protect concept might serve to focus attention on the work – of law and of politics – that takes place in the attempt to move *between* metaphysics and physics, universal and particular, ideal and real, or then and now.

BIBLIOGRAPHY

2005 World Summit Outcome, GA Res. 60/1, UN GAOR, 60th sess., 8th Plen. Mtg., UN Doc. A/RES/60/1, 24 October 2005.

Abi-Saab, Georges, *The United Nations Operation in the Congo 1960–1964* (Oxford: Oxford University Press, 1978).

African Commission on Human and Peoples' Rights, Resolution on Strengthening the Responsibility to Protect in Africa, 42nd Ordinary Sess., ACHPR/Res. 117 (XXXXII), 28 November 2007.

Alexander VI, *The Bull Inter Caetera* (1493), as reprinted in Frances Gardiner Davenport (ed.), *European Treaties Bearing on the History of the United States and Its Dependencies to 1648* (Washington DC: Carnegie Institution of Washington, 1917), p. 71.

Alexandrowicz, C. H., 'Doctrinal Aspects of the Universality of the Law of Nations', *British Year Book of International Law* 37 (1961), 506.

'The Theory of Recognition *in Fieri*', *British Year Book of International Law* 34 (1958), 176.

Al-Sayyid-Marsot, Afaf Lutfi, 'The British Occupation of Egypt from 1882' in Andrew Porter (ed.), *The Oxford History of the British Empire: Volume III, The Nineteenth Century* (Oxford: Oxford University Press, 1999), p. 651.

Alvarez, José, 'The Schizophrenias of R2P', *American Society of International Law Newsletter* 23(3) (2007), 1, www.asil.org/newsletter/president/pres070927. html.

Anand, R. P., *New States and International Law* (Delhi: Vikas Publishing House, 1972).

Anghie, Antony, *Imperialism, Sovereignty and the Making of International Law* (Cambridge: Cambridge University Press, 2004).

Appelqvist, Örjan, 'A Hidden Duel: Gunnar Myrdal and Dag Hammarskjöld in Economics and International Politics 1935–1955', *Stockholm Papers in Economic History No 2* (Department of Economic History, Stockholm University, 2008).

'Civil Servant or Politician? Dag Hammarskjöld's Role in Swedish Government Policy in the Forties', *Economic Review* 3 (2005), 33.

Arbour, Louise, 'The Responsibility to Protect as a Duty of Care of International Law and Practice', *Review of International Studies* 34 (2008), 445.

Armitage, David, *The Ideological Origins of the British Empire* (Cambridge: Cambridge University Press, 2000).

Arnold, Oliver, 'Absorption and Representation: Mapping England in the Early Modern House of Commons' in Andrew Gordon and Bernhard Klein (eds.), *Literature, Mapping and the Politics of Space in Early Modern Britain* (Cambridge: Cambridge University Press, 2001), p. 15.

Australian Government Department of Defence, 'Defending Australia in the Asia Pacific Century: Force 2030: Defence White Paper' (Canberra: Australian Government Department of Defence, 2009), www.defence.gov.au/whitepaper/docs/defence_white_paper_2009.pdf.

Balderston, Theo, *Economics and Politics in the Weimar Republic* (Cambridge: Cambridge University Press, 2002).

Barnett, Michael, *Eyewitness to a Genocide: The United Nations and Rwanda* (Ithaea: Cornell University Press, 2003).

Bartelson, Jens, *A Genealogy of Sovereignty* (Cambridge: Cambridge University Press, 1995).

Beard, Jennifer L., *The Political Economy of Desire: International Law, Development and the Nation State* (Oxon: Routledge-Cavendish, 2006).

Bellamy, Alex J., *Responsibility to Protect: The Global Effort to End Mass Atrocities* (Cambridge: Polity Press, 2009).
  'Conflict Prevention and the Responsibility to Protect', *Global Governance* 14 (2008), 135.

Berle, Adolf A. Jr. and Means, Gardiner C., *The Modern Corporation and Private Property* (New York: The MacMillan Company, 1933).

Berman, Harold J., *Law and Revolution II: The Impact of the Protestant Reformations on the Western Legal Tradition* (Cambridge and London: The Belknap Press, 2003).

Black, Christine, McVeigh, Shaun and Johnstone, Richard, 'Of the South', *Griffith Law Review* 16 (2007), 299.

Bolton, John R., 'Letter to UN Member States', 30 August 2005,www.reformtheun.org/index.php/government_statements/c74?theme=alt2.

Brewer, John, *War, Money and the English State 1688–1783* (Cambridge: Harvard University Press, 1988).

Broué, Pierre, *The German Revolution 1917–1923*, John Archer trans. (Chicago: Haymarket Books, 2006) (first published 1971).

Brown, Gordon, 'Lord Mayor's Banquet Speech', 12 November 2007, www.pm.gov.uk/output/Page13736.asp.

Burgess, Glenn, 'Usurpation, Obligation and Obedience in the Thought of the Engagement Controversy', *The Historical Journal* 29 (1986), 515.

Burnham, James, *The Managerial Revolution* (London: Penguin, 1945).

Carlsson, Gunilla, 'The Challenge of Protecting Civilians in Darfur: Sweden's Response', speech given to the ICRC Seminar on the humanitarian challenges in Darfur, 2 July 2007, www.sweden.gov.se/sb/d/8812/a/85206.

Cassese, Antonio, 'Ex iniuria ius oritur: Are We Moving towards International Legitimation of Forcible Humanitarian Countermeasures in the World Community?', European Journal of International Law 10 (1999), 23.

Chandler, Alfred D. Jr., The Visible Hand: The Managerial Revolution in American Business (Cambridge: Belknap Press, 1977).

Chandler, David, 'Unravelling the Paradox of "The Responsibility to Protect"', Irish Studies in International Affairs 20 (2009), 27.

'The Road to Military Humanitarianism: How the Human Rights NGOs Shaped A New Humanitarian Agenda', Human Rights Quarterly 23 (2001), 678.

Chandrasekaran, Rajiv, Imperial Life in the Emerald City: Inside Baghdad's Green Zone (London: Bloomsbury, 2007).

Chomsky, Noam, 'Statement to the United Nations General Assembly Thematic Dialogue on the Responsibility to Protect', United Nations, New York, 23 July 2009, www.un.org/ga/president/63/interactive/protect/noam.pdf.

Cohen, Felix, 'Transcendental Nonsense and the Functional Approach', Columbia Law Review 35 (1935), 809.

Collins, Carole J. L., 'The Cold War Comes to Africa: Cordier and the 1960 Congo Crisis', Journal of International Affairs 47 (1993), 243.

Collins, Jeffrey R., The Allegiance of Thomas Hobbes (Oxford: Oxford University Press, 2005).

Convention Respecting the Free Navigation of the Suez Maritime Canal, 29 October 1888, Supplement to the American Journal of International Law 3 (1909), 123.

Cooke, Bill, 'Participatory Management as Colonial Administration' in Sadhvi Dar and Bill Cooke (eds.), The New Development Management: Critiquing the Dual Modernization (London: Zed Books, 2008), p. 111.

Cordier, Andrew W. and Foote, Wilder, Public Papers of the Secretaries-General of the United Nations, Volume V: Dag Hammarskjöld 1960–1961 (New York: Columbia University Press, 1975).

Cormack, Bradin, A Power to Do Justice: Jurisdiction, English Literature, and the Rise of Common Law, 1509–1625 (Chicago: University of Chicago Press, 2007).

Crawford, James, The Creation of States in International Law, 2nd edn. (Oxford: Oxford University Press, 2006).

Crook, John R. (ed.), 'US Officials Endorse "Responsibility to Protect" through Security Council Action', American Journal of International Law 100 (2006), 463.

Dar, Sadhvi and Cooke, Bill (eds.), The New Development Management: Critiquing the Dual Modernization (London: Zed Books, 2008).

Darwin, John, The Empire Project: The Rise and Fall of the British World System 1830–1970 (Cambridge: Cambridge University Press, 2009).

Deng, Francis M., Kimaro, Sadikiel, Lyons, Terrence, Rothchild, Donald and Zartman, William, *Sovereignty as Responsibility: Conflict Management in Africa* (Washington DC: Brookings Institution Press, 1996).

Development Initiatives, Global Humanitarian Assistance Report 2009 (Wells: Development Initiatives, 2009).

Global Humanitarian Assistance 2000 (Geneva: The Inter-Agency Standing Committee, 2000).

de Vitoria, Francisco, *Political Writings*, Anthony Pagden and Jeremy Lawrance (eds.) (Cambridge: Cambridge University Press, 1991).

de Waal, Alex, 'An Emancipatory Imperium? Power and Principle in the Humanitarian International' in Didier Fassin and Mariella Pandolfi (eds.), *Contemporary States of Emergency: The Politics of Military and Humanitarian Interventions* (New York: Zone Books, 2010), p. 295.

'Darfur and the Failure of the Responsibility to Protect', *International Affairs* 83 (2007), 1039.

Famine Crimes: Politics and the Disaster Relief Industry in Africa (International African Institute, Bloomington: Oxford and Indiana University Press, 1997).

'No Such Thing as Humanitarian Intervention: Why We Need to Rethink How to Realize the "Responsibility to Protect" in Wartime', Harvard International Review (21 March 2007), http://hir.harvard.edu/index.php?page=article&id=1482&p=1.

De Witte, Ludo, *The Assassination of Lumumba*, Ann Wright and Renée Fenby trans. (London: Verso, 2001).

Dixon, Sir Pierson, 'The Secretary General of the United Nations: Mr Dag Hammarskjold', Confidential memorandum to Mr Selwyn Lloyd, 16 January 1958, FO371/137002/UN2303/1 (The National Archives, Kew).

Donini, Antonio, 'The Far Side: The Meta Functions of Humanitarianism in a Globalised World', *Disasters* 34 (2010), S220.

Dorsett, Shaunnagh, 'Mapping Territories' in Shaun McVeigh (ed.), *Jurisprudence of Jurisdiction* (Oxon: Routledge-Cavendish, 2007), p. 137.

and McVeigh, Shaun, 'Questions of Jurisdiction' in Shaun McVeigh (ed.), *Jurisprudence of Jurisdiction* (Oxon: Routledge-Cavendish, 2007), p. 3.

Douglas, Mary, *How Institutions Think* (Syracuse: Syracuse University Press, 1996).

Duncanson, Ian W., 'Reading for Law and the State: Theaters of Problematization and Authority', *International Journal of the Semiotics of Law* 22 (2009), 321.

Dyzenhaus, David, 'Hobbes' Constitutional Theory' in Ian Shapiro (ed.), *Leviathan* (New Haven: Yale University Press, 2010), p. 453.

Legality and Legitimacy: Carl Schmitt, Hans Kelsen and Hermann Heller in Weimar (Oxford: Oxford University Press, 1997).

Elaraby, Nabil, 'United Nations Peacekeeping by Consent: A Case Study of the Withdrawal of the United Nations Emergency Force', *New York University Journal of International Law and Politics* 1 (1968), 149.

Engels, Friedrich, 'On Authority' in Robert C. Tucker (ed.), *The Marx-Engels Reader*, 2nd edn. (New York: WW Norton and Co, 1978), p. 730.

Evans, Gareth, 'From Humanitarian Intervention to the Responsibility to Protect', *Wisconsin International Law Journal* 24 (2006), 703.

   The Responsibility to Protect: Ending Mass Atrocity Crimes Once and For All (Washington DC: Brookings Institution Press, 2008).

Executive Council, African Union, 'The Common African Position on the Proposed Reform of the United Nations: "The Ezulwini Consensus"', 7th Extraordinary Sess., Ext/EX.CL/2 (VII), 7–8 March 2005.

Fasolt, Constantin, *The Limits of History* (Chicago: University of Chicago Press, 2004).

Ferguson, James, *Global Shadows: Africa in the Neoliberal World* (Durham: Duke University Press, 2006).

Focarelli, Carlo, 'The Responsibility to Protect Doctrine and Humanitarian Intervention: Too Many Ambiguities for a Working Doctrine', *Journal of Conflict and Security Law* 13 (2008), 191.

Ford, Richard T., 'Law's Territory (A History of Jurisdiction)', *Michigan Law Review* 97 (1999), 843.

Foucault, Michel, *The Birth of Biopolitics: Lectures at the Collège de France 1978– 1979*, Michel Senellart (ed.) and Graham Burchell trans. (New York: Palgrave Macmillan, 2008).

   Society Must Be Defended: Lectures at the Collège de France, 1975–76, David Macey trans. (London: Penguin Books, 2004) (first published 1997).

Fox, Fiona, 'New Humanitarianism: Does It Provide a Moral Banner for the 21st Century?', *Disasters* 25 (2001), 275.

Fox, Gregory H., *Humanitarian Occupation* (Cambridge: Cambridge University Press, 2008).

Franck, Thomas M., *Recourse to Force: State Action against Threats and Armed Attacks* (Cambridge: Cambridge University Press, 2002).

Fröhlich, Manuel, *Political Ethics and the United Nations: Dag Hammarskjöld as Secretary-General* (London and New York: Routledge, 2008).

Fuller, Lon L., 'Positivism and Fidelity to Law – A Reply to Professor Hart', *Harvard Law Review* 71 (1958), 630.

Gardiner, S. R., *The Constitutional Documents of the Puritan Revolution, 1625– 1660*, 3rd edn. (Oxford: Clarendon Press, 1906).

Garnett, George, *Conquered England: Kingship, Succession, and Tenure 1066–1166* (Oxford: Oxford University Press, 2007).

Global Centre for the Responsibility to Protect, 'Implementing the Responsibility to Protect – The 2009 General Assembly Debate: An Assessment', GCR2P Report, August 2009.

Goodrich, Peter (ed.), *Law and the Unconscious: A Legendre Reader* (Basingstoke: Macmillan, 1997).

Gorski, Philip S., *The Disciplinary Revolution: Calvinism and the Rise of the State in Early Modern Europe* (Chicago and London: University of Chicago Press, 2003).

Gray, Christine, *International Law and the Use of Force*. 2nd edn. (Oxford: Oxford University Press, 2004).

Grotius, Hugo, *The Rights of War and Peace*, Book 2 (Indianapolis: Liberty Fund, 2005) (first published 1625).

Habermas, Jürgen, 'America and the World', *Logos Journal* 3(3) (2004), www. logosjournal.com/issue_3.3/habermas_interview.htm.

Hakluyt, Richard, *A Discourse concerning Western Planting, Written in the Year 1584*, Charles Deane (ed.) (Cambridge: Cambridge University Press, 1877).

Hammarskjöld, Dag, 'Statement in the Security Council Introducing Report: New York, July 20, 1960' in Andrew W. Cordier and Wilder Foote (eds.), *Public Papers of the Secretaries-General of the United Nations, Volume V: Dag Hammarskjöld 1960–1961* (New York: Columbia University Press, 1975), p. 43.

'Interpretation of Paragraph 4 of the Security Council's Third Resolution on the Congo: Leopoldville, The Congo, August 12, 1960' in Andrew W. Cordier and Wilder Foote (eds.), *Public Papers of the Secretaries-General of the United Nations, Volume V: Dag Hammarskjöld 1960–1961* (New York: Columbia University Press, 1975), p. 85.

'Opening Statement in the Security Council: New York, September 9, 1960' in Andrew W. Cordier and Wilder Foote (eds.), *Public Papers of the Secretaries-General of the United Nations, Volume V: Dag Hammarskjöld 1960–1961* (New York: Columbia University Press, 1975), p. 162.

'The New "Santa Maria"' in Wilder Foote (ed.), *The Servant of Peace: A Selection of the Speeches and Statements of Dag Hammarskjöld* (London: The Bodley Head, 1962), p. 40.

'International Service' in Wilder Foote (ed.), *The Servant of Peace: A Selection of the Speeches and Statements of Dag Hammarskjöld* (London: The Bodley Head, 1962), p. 80.

'The Uses of Private Diplomacy' in Wilder Foote (ed.), *The Servant of Peace: A Selection of the Speeches and Statements of Dag Hammarskjöld* (London: The Bodley Head, 1962), p. 170.

'Do We Need the United Nations?' in Wilder Foote (ed.), *The Servant of Peace: A Selection of the Speeches and Statements of Dag Hammarskjöld* (London: The Bodley Head, 1962), p. 200.

'Asia, Africa, and the West' in Wilder Foote (ed.), *The Servant of Peace: A Selection of the Speeches and Statements of Dag Hammarskjöld* (London: The Bodley Head, 1962), p. 212.

'The Development of a Constitutional Framework' in Wilder Foote (ed.), *The Servant of Peace: A Selection of the Speeches and Statements of Dag Hammarskjöld* (London: The Bodley Head, 1962), p. 255.

'The International Civil Servant in Law and in Fact' in Wilder Foote (ed.), *The Servant of Peace: A Selection of the Speeches and Statements of Dag Hammarskjöld* (London: The Bodley Head, 1962), p. 329.

'Last Words to the Staff' in Wilder Foote (ed.), *The Servant of Peace: A Selection of the Speeches and Statements of Dag Hammarskjöld* (London: The Bodley Head, 1962), p. 376.

Hansen, Peo, 'European Integration, European Identity and the Colonial Connection', *European Journal of Social Theory* 5 (2002), 483.

Harff, Barbara, 'How to Use Risk Assessment and Early Warning in the Prevention and De-Escalation of Genocide and Other Mass Atrocities', *Global Responsibility to Protect* 1 (2009), 506.

Harlow, Carol, 'The Crown: Wrong Once Again?', *Modern Law Review* 40 (1977), 728.

Hart, H. L. A., *The Concept of Law* (Oxford: Clarendon Press, 1961).

Haverkamp, Anselm, 'Richard II, Bracton, and the End of Political Theology', *Law & Literature* 16 (2004), 31.

Hayek, F. A., *The Road to Serfdom* (New York: Routledge, 2001) (first published 1944).

Heartfield, James, 'Contextualising the Anti-capitalism Movement in Global Civil Society' in Gideon Baker and David Chandler (eds.), *Global Civil Society: Contested Futures* (London: Routledge, 2005), p. 85.

Hill, Christopher, *Puritanism and Revolution: Studies in Interpretation of the English Revolution of the 17th Century* (New York: St Martin's Press, 1997).

The World Turned Upside Down: Radical Ideas during the English Revolution (London: Penguin Books, 1984).

Hobbes, Thomas, *Leviathan*, J. C. A. Gaskin (ed.) (Oxford: Oxford University Press, 2006) (first published 1651).

On the Citizen (Cambridge: Cambridge University Press, 1998) (first published 1642).

Behemoth or the Long Parliament (Chicago: University of Chicago Press, 1990) (first published 1682).

Hochschild, Adam, *King Leopold's Ghost* (Boston: Mariner Books, 1999).

Holt, Victoria and Taylor, Glyn with Kelly, Max, *Protecting Civilians in the Context of UN Peacekeeping Operations: Successes, Setbacks and Remaining Challenges* (New York: United Nations, 2009).

Hont, Istvan, *Jealousy of Trade: International Competition and the Nation-State in Historical Perspective* (Cambridge, Massachusetts and London: The Belknap Press, 2005).

Hull, Isabel V., *Absolute Destruction: Military Culture and the Practices of War in Imperial Germany* (Cornell: Cornell University Press, 2005).

International Commission on Intervention and State Sovereignty (ICISS), *The Responsibility to Protect* (Ottawa: International Development Research Centre, 2001), www.iciss.ca/pdf/Commission-Report.pdf.

Johnson, Edward, '"The Umpire on Whom the Sun Never Sets": Dag Hammarskjöld's Political Role and the British at Suez', *Diplomacy & Statecraft* 8 (1997), 249.

Kahn, Victoria, *Wayward Contracts: The Crisis of Political Obligation in England, 1640–1674* (Princeton: Princeton University Press, 2004).

'Hamlet or Hecuba: Carl Schmitt's Decision', *Representations* 83 (2003), 67.

Kalb, Madeleine G., *The Congo Cables: The Cold War in Africa – From Eisenhower to Kennedy* (New York: Macmillan, 1982).

Kantorowicz, Ernst H., *The King's Two Bodies: A Study in Medieval Political Theology* (Princeton: Princeton University Press, 1957).

Kapur, Amrita, '"Humanity as the A and Ω of Sovereignty": Four Replies to Anne Peters', *European Journal of International Law* 20 (2009), 560.

Kelsen, Hans, *Collective Security under International Law* (Newport: Naval War College, International Law Studies Series No. 49, 1954).

'Legal Formalism and the Pure Theory of Law' in Arthur J. Jacobson and Bernhard Schlink (eds.), *Weimar: A Jurisprudence of Crisis* (Berkeley and London: University of California Press, 2000) (first published 1929), p. 78.

Kennedy, David, *The Dark Sides of Virtue: Reassessing International Humanitarianism* (Princeton: Princeton University Press, 2004).

Kennedy, Ellen, 'Introduction to Herman Heller', *Economy and Society* 16 (1987), 120.

'Introduction' in Carl Schmitt, *The Crisis of Parliamentary Democracy*, Ellen Kennedy trans. (Cambridge, Massachusetts: The MIT Press, 1988) (first published 1934), p. xiii.

Kennedy, Paul, *The Parliament of Man: The Past, Present and Future of the United Nations* (New York: Vintage, 2007).

Kerr, Ron, 'International Development and the New Public Management: Projects and Logframes as Discursive Technologies of Governance' in Sadhvi Dar and Bill Cooke (eds.), *The New Development Management: Critiquing the Dual Modernization* (London: Zed Books, 2008), p. 91.

Khrushchev, Nikita, 'Statement to the UN General Assembly', UN GAOR, 15th Sess., 882nd Plen. Mtg., Agenda Item 9, UN Doc. A/PV.882, 3 October 1960.

King James VI and I, '*Triplici Nodo, Triplex Cuneus*: or an Apologie for the Oath of Allegiance' in *Political Writings*, Johann P. Sommerville (ed.) (Cambridge: Cambridge University Press, 1994), p. 99.

'A Speech in the Parliament House, as Neere the Very Words as Could be Gathered at the Instant' in *Political Writings*, Johann P. Sommerville (ed.) (Cambridge: Cambridge University Press, 1994), p. 147.

King, Jeff and Hobbins, A. J., 'Hammarskjöld and Human Rights: The Deflation of the UN Human Rights Programme 1953–1961', *Journal of the History of International Law* 5 (2003), 337.

Kingsbury, Benedict, Krisch, Nico and Stewart, Richard B., 'The Emergence of Global Administrative Law', *Law and Contemporary Problems* 68 (2005), 15.

Knoll, Bernhard, *The Legal Status of Territories Subject to Administration by International Organisations* (Cambridge: Cambridge University Press, 2008).

Korhonen, Outi, 'The Problem of Representation and the Iraqi Elections', *Finnish Yearbook of International Law* 14 (2003), 35.

Koselleck, Reinhart, *Critique and Crisis: Enlightenment and the Pathogenesis of Modern Society* (Cambridge: The MIT Press, 1988).

Koskenniemi, Martti, 'Occupied Zone – "A Zone of Reasonableness"?', *Israel Law Review* 41 (2008), 13.

'The Fate of Public International Law: Between Technique and Politics', *Modern Law Review* 70 (2007), 1.

From Apology to Utopia, 2nd edn. (Cambridge: Cambridge University Press, 2005).

'International Law as Political Theology: How to Read *Nomos der Erde*', *Constellations* 11 (2004), 492.

'The Police in the Temple: Order, Justice and the UN: A Dialectical View', *European Journal of International Law* 6 (1995), 325.

Kyle, Keith, *Suez: Britain's End of Empire in the Middle East* (London: I. B. Tauris, 2001).

Laski, Harold, 'The Responsibility of the State in England', *Harvard Law Review* 32 (1919), 447.

'The Early History of the Corporation in England', *Harvard Law Review* 30 (1916–17), 561.

Lauterpacht, E., 'The Contemporary Practice of the United Kingdom in the Field of International Law – Survey and Comment', *International and Comparative Law Quarterly* 5 (1956), 405.

Leader, Nicholas, 'Proliferating Principles; or How to Sup with the Devil without Getting Eaten', *Disasters* 22 (1998), 288.

Lenin, Vladimir, *The State and Revolution*, Robert Service trans. (London: Penguin Books, 1992) (First published 1918).

Levine, Donald N., 'The Continuing Challenge of Weber's Theory of Rational Action' in Charles Camic, Philip S. Gorski and David M. Trubek (eds.), *Max Weber's 'Economy and Society': A Critical Companion* (Stanford: Stanford University Press, 2005), p. 101.

Lidén, Anders, 'Statement on behalf of the European Union at the Security Council Debate on Protection of Civilians in Armed Conflict', UN SCOR, 64th Sess., 6216th Mtg., UN Doc. S/PV.6216, 11 November 2009.

'Statement on behalf of the European Union to the General Assembly Debate on the Responsibility to Protect', UN GAOR, 63rd Sess., 97th Plen. Mtg., UN Doc. A/63/PV.97, 23 July 2009.

Louis, Wm. Roger, 'The Suez Crisis and the British Dilemma at the United Nations' in Vaughan Lowe, Adam Roberts, Jennifer Welsh and

Dominik Zaum (eds.), *The United Nations Security Council and War: The Evolution of Thought and Practice since 1945* (Oxford: Oxford University Press, 2008), p. 280.

Ends of British Imperialism: The Scramble for Empire, Suez and Decolonization (London: I. B. Tauris, 2006).

Luck, Edward C., 'Sovereignty, Choice, and the Responsibility to Protect', *Global Responsibility to Protect* 1 (2009), 10.

'Statement to the UNSC Working Group on Conflict Resolution and Prevention in Africa', 1 December 2008, www.responsibilitytoprotect.org/index.php/eupdate/1965.

The United Nations and the Responsibility to Protect (Muscatine: Stanley Foundation Policy Analysis Brief, August 2008).

MacMillan, Ken, *Sovereignty and Possession in the English New World: The Legal Foundations of Empire, 1576–1640* (Cambridge: Cambridge University Press, 2006).

'Introduction: Discourse on History, Geography, and Law' in John Dee, *The Limits of the British Empire*, Ken MacMillan with Jennifer Abeles (eds.) (London: Praeger, 2004), p. 1.

with Abeles, Jennifer (eds.), *John Dee: The Limits of the British Empire* (London: Praeger, 2004).

Malcolm, Noel, *Aspects of Hobbes* (Oxford: Oxford University Press, 2002).

Mamdani, Mahmood, *Saviors and Survivors: Darfur, Politics, and the War on Terror* (New York: Pantheon, 2009).

Citizen and Subject: Contemporary Africa and the Legacy of Late Colonialism (Princeton: Princeton University Press, 1996).

Marcuse, Herbert, *A Study on Authority*, Joris De Bres trans. (London: Verso, 2008) (first published 1936).

Marsilius of Padua, *The Defender of the Peace*, Annabel Brett (ed.) trans. (Cambridge: Cambridge University Press, 2005) (first published 1324).

Mattingly, Garrett, *Renaissance Diplomacy* (New York: Dover Publications, 1988).

Mazower, Mark, *No Enchanted Palace: The End of Empire and the Ideological Origins of the United Nations* (Princeton and Oxford: Princeton University Press, 2009).

McVeigh, Shaun, 'Subjects of Jurisdiction: The Dying, Northern Territory, Australia, 1995–1997' in Shaun McVeigh (ed.), *Jurisprudence of Jurisdiction* (Oxon: Routledge-Cavendish, 2007), p. 202.

Molier, Gelijen, 'Humanitarian Intervention and the Responsibility to Protect after 9/11', *Netherlands International Law Review* 53 (2006), 37.

Mulaj, Kledja, 'Humanitarian Protection: Prevention, Reaction, and Reconstruction', *Journal of Intervention and Statebuilding* 3(1) (2009), 122.

Muldoon, James, *Empire and Order: The Concept of Empire, 800–1800* (Basingstoke: Palgrave Macmillan, 1999).

Murphy, Jonathan, 'The Rise of the Global Managers' in Sadhvi Dar and
    Bill Cooke (eds.), *The New Development Management: Critiquing the Dual
    Modernization* (London: Zed Books, 2008), p. 18.
'National Security Strategy of the United States (Washington, May 2010), www.
    whitehouse.gov/sites/default/files/rss_viewer/national_security_strategy.pdf.
Nederman, Cary J., *Lineages of European Political Thought: Explorations Along the
    Medieval/Modern Divide from John of Salisbury to Hegel* (Washington DC:
    Catholic University of America Press, 2009).
    'Property and Protest: Political Theory and Subjective Rights in Fourteenth-
    Century England', *Review of Politics* 58 (1996), 323.
Nesiah, Vasuki, 'From Berlin to Bonn to Baghdad: A Space for Infinite Justice',
    Harvard Human Rights Journal 17 (2004), 75.
Neu, Dean, 'Accounting for the Banal: Financial Techniques as Softwares of
    Colonialism' in Anshuman Prasad (ed.), *Postcolonial Theory and
    Organizational Analysis: A Critical Engagement* (New York: Palgrave
    MacMillan, 2003), p. 193.
Neumann, Franz, *Behemoth: The Structure and Practice of National Socialism
    1933–1944* (New York: Harper and Row, 1944).
Nollkaemper, André, 'Constitutionalization and the Unity of the Law of
    International Responsibility', *Indiana Journal of Global Legal Studies* 16
    (2009), 535.
    'Note: Nationalization of the Suez Canal Company', *Harvard Law Review* 70
    (1957), 480.
Nzongola-Ntalaja, Georges, *The Congo from Leopold to Kabila: A People's History*
    (London: Zed Books, 2002).
O'Brien, Conor Cruise, *To Katanga and Back: A UN Case History* (New York:
    Simon and Schuster, 1962).
Orford, Anne, 'The Passions of Protection: Sovereign Authority and Humanitarian
    War' in Didier Fassin and Mariella Pandolfi (eds.), *Contemporary States of
    Emergency: The Politics of Military and Humanitarian Interventions* (New
    York: Zone Books, 2010), p. 335.
    'International Territorial Administration and the Management of Decolonisation',
    International and Comparative Law Quarterly 59 (2010), 227.
    'Jurisdiction without Territory: From the Holy Roman Empire to the Responsibility
    to Protect', *Michigan Journal of International Law* 30 (2009), 981.
    'What Can We Do to Stop People Harming Others? Humanitarian
    Intervention in Timor-Leste (East Timor)' in Jenny Edkins and
    Maja Zehfuss (eds.), *Global Politics: A New Introduction* (London and
    New York: Routledge, 2009), p. 427.
    'Ritual, Mediation and the International Laws of the South', *Griffith Law
    Review* 16 (2007), 353.
    'The Gift of Formalism', *European Journal of International Law* 15 (2004), 179.

Reading Humanitarian Intervention: Human Rights and the Use of Force in International Law (Cambridge: Cambridge University Press, 2003).

Orr, D. Alan, 'The Juristic Foundation of Regicide' in Jason Peacey (ed.), *The Regicides and the Execution of Charles I* (Hampshire: Palgrave MacMillan, 2001), p. 117.

Overton, Richard with William Walwyn's collaboration, 'A Remonstrance of Many Thousand Citizens, 7 July 1646' in Andrew Sharp (ed.), *The English Levellers* (Cambridge: Cambridge University Press, 1998), p. 33.

Pagden, Anthony, *Lords of All the World: Ideologies of Empire in Spain, Britain and France c.1500 – c.1800* (New Haven: Yale University Press, 1995).

and Lawrance, Jeremy (eds.), *Francisco de Vitoria, Political Writings* (Cambridge: Cambridge University Press, 1991).

Panel on United Nations Peace Operations, *Report to the Secretary-General*, UN GAOR, 55th Sess., Provisional Agenda Item 87, UN Doc. A/55/305-S/2000/809, 21 August 2000.

Patterson, W. B., *King James VI and I and the Reunion of Christendom* (Cambridge: Cambridge University Press, 1997).

Peemans, Jean-Philippe, 'Capital Accumulation in the Congo under Colonialism: The Role of the State' in Peter Duignan and L. H. Gann (eds.), *Colonialism in Africa 1870–1960* (volume 4): *The Economics of Colonialism* (London and New York: Cambridge University Press, 1975), p. 165.

Ping, Jean, Chairperson, African Union Commission, Keynote Address at the Round-Table High-Level Meeting of Experts on 'The Responsibility to Protect in Africa', 23 October 2008, www.responsibilitytoprotect.org/index.php/civil_society_statements/1910.

Pitts, Jennifer, 'Boundaries of Victorian International Law' in Duncan Bell (ed.), *Victorian Visions of Global Order: Empire and International Relations in Nineteenth-Century Political Thought* (Cambridge: Cambridge University Press, 2007).

Pocock, J G. A., 'Introduction' in James Harrington, *The Commonwealth of Oceana and A System of Politics* (Cambridge: Cambridge University Press, 1992).

Pope Benedict XVI, 'Address to the General Assembly', 18 April 2008, www.vatican.va/holy_father/benedict_xvi/speeches/2008/april/documents/hf_ben-xvi_spe_20080418_un-visit_en.html.

Post, Gaines, 'Status, Id Est, Magistratus: L'Etat, C'est Moi' in *Studies in Medieval Legal Thought: Public Law and the State, 1100–1322* (Princeton: Princeton University Press, 1964).

Pottage, Alain, 'The Lost Temporality of Law: An Interview with Pierre Legendre', *Law and Critique* 1 (1999), 3.

Power, Michael, *The Audit Society: Rituals of Verification* (Oxford: Oxford University Press, 1997).

Power, Samantha, *Chasing the Flame: Sergio Vieira de Mello and the Fight to Save the World* (New York: Penguin Books, 2008).

Prasad, Anshuman and Prasad, Pushkala, 'The Empire of Organizations and the Organization of Empires: Postcolonial Considerations on Theorizing Workplace Resistance' in Anshuman Prasad (ed.), *Postcolonial Theory and Organizational Analysis: A Critical Engagement* (New York: Palgrave MacMillan, 2003), p. 95.

President of the Security Council, 'Note by the President of the Security Council', UN SCOR, 47th Sess., UN Doc. S/23500, 31 January 1992.

Ratner, Steven R., *The New UN Peacekeeping: Building Peace in Lands of Conflict after the Cold War* (New York: St Martin's Press, 1995).

Reisman, Michael W., 'Through or Despite Governments: Differentiated Responsibilities in Human Rights Programs', *Iowa Law Review* 72 (1987), 391.

Reno, William, 'How Sovereignty Matters: International Markets and the Political Economy of Local Politics in Weak States' in Thomas M. Callaghy, Ronald Kassimir and Robert Latham (eds.), *Intervention and Transnationalism in Africa: Global-Local Networks of Power* (Cambridge: Cambridge University Press, 2001), p. 197.

'Report of the Independent Inquiry into the Actions of the United Nations during the 1994 Genocide in Rwanda', UN Doc. S/1999/1257, 16 December 1999.

Reydams, Luc, *Universal Jurisdiction: International and Municipal Legal Perspectives* (Oxford: Oxford University Press, 2003).

Rieff, David, *A Bed for the Night: Humanitarianism in Crisis* (New York: Simon and Schuster, 2003).

Rose, Gillian, *Mourning Becomes the Law: Philosophy and Representation* (Cambridge: Cambridge University Press, 1996).

Rugema, Bugingo, 'Statement by Rwanda at the Security Council Debate on Protection of Civilians in Armed Conflict', UN SCOR, 64th Sess., 6216th Mtg., UN Doc. S/PV.6216 (Resumption 1), 11 November 2009.

Schachter, Oscar, 'Dag Hammarskjöld and the Relation of Law to Politics', *American Journal of International Law* 56 (1962), 1.

Schechter, Michael G., 'Possibilities for Preventive Diplomacy, Early Warning and Global Monitoring in the Post-Cold War Era; or, the Limits to Global Structural Change' in W. Andy Knight (ed.), *Adapting the United Nations to a Postmodern Era: Lessons Learned* (Hampshire: Palgrave, 2001), p. 52.

Schmitt, Carl, *Political Theology II: The Myth of the Closure of Any Political Theology*, Michael Hoelzl and Graham Ward trans. (Cambridge: Polity Press, 2008) (first published 1970).

Political Theology: Four Chapters on the Concept of Sovereignty, George Schwab trans. (Chicago and London: University of Chicago Press, 2005) (first published 1922).

Legality and Legitimacy, Jeffrey Seitzer trans. (Durham and London: Duke University Press, 2004) (first published 1932).

The Nomos *of the Earth in the International Law of the* Jus Publicum Europaeum, G. L. Ulmen trans. (New York: Telos Press, 2003) (first published 1950).

'Ethic of State and Pluralistic State' in Chantal Mouffe (ed.), *The Challenge of Carl Schmitt* (London: Verso, 1999) (first published 1933).

Roman Catholicism and Political Form, G. L. Ulmen trans. (Westport: Greenwood Press, 1996) (first published 1923).

The Concept of the Political, George Schwab trans. (Chicago and London: University of Chicago Press, 1996) (first published 1932).

The Leviathan in the State Theory of Thomas Hobbes: Meaning and Failure of a Political Symbol, George Schwab and Erna Hilfstein trans. (Westport: Greenwood Press, 1996) (first published 1938).

The Crisis of Parliamentary Democracy, Ellen Kennedy trans. (Cambridge, Massachusetts: The MIT Press, 1988) (first published 1934).

Schwebel, S. M., 'The Origins and Development of Article 99 of the Charter', *British Year Book of International Law* 28 (1951), 371.

Sharp, Andrew, 'The Levellers and the End of Charles I' in Jason Peacey (ed.), *The Regicides and the Execution of Charles I* (Hampshire: Palgrave MacMillan, 2001).

Shlaim, Avi, 'The Protocol of Sèvres, 1956: Anatomy of a War Plot', *International Affairs* 73 (1997), 509.

Simma, Bruno (ed.), *The Charter of the United Nations: A Commentary*, 2nd edn. (Oxford: Oxford University Press, 2002).

'NATO, the UN and the Use of Force: Legal Aspects', *European Journal of International Law* 10 (1999), 1.

Skinner, Quentin, 'From the State of Princes to the Person of the State' in *Visions of Politics: Renaissance Virtues* (Cambridge: Cambridge University Press, 2002) vol. 2, p. 368.

'The Study of Rhetoric as an Approach to Cultural History: The Case of Hobbes' in Willem Melching and Wyger Velema (eds.), *Main Trends in Cultural History: Ten Essays* (Amsterdam: Rodopi, 1994), p. 17.

Smith, Adam, *The Wealth of Nations, Books IV–V* (London: Penguin Books, 1999) (first published 1776).

Smith, Stephen, 'A New Era of Engagement with the World', speech given to the Sydney Institute, 9 August 2008, www.foreignminister.gov.au/speeches/2008/080819_si.html.

Somek, Alexander, 'Austrian Constitutional Doctrine 1933 to 1938' in Christian Joerges and Navraj Singh Ghaleigh (eds.), *Darker Legacies of Law in Europe* (Oxford and Portland: Hart Publishing, 2003), p. 361.

Springborg, Patricia, 'Thomas Hobbes and Cardinal Bellarmine: Leviathan and "The Ghost of the Roman Empire"', *History of Political Thought* XVI (1995), 503.

Stahn, Carsten, *The Law and Practice of International Territorial Administration: Versailles to Iraq and Beyond* (Cambridge: Cambridge University Press, 2008).

'Responsibility to Protect: Political Rhetoric or Emerging Legal Norm?', *American Journal of International Law* 101 (2007), 99.

Stein, Peter, *Roman Law in European History* (Cambridge: Cambridge University Press, 1999).

Stolleis, Michael, *A History of Public Law in Germany 1914–1945*, Thomas Dunlap trans. (Oxford: Oxford University Press, 2004).

Strauss, Leo, 'Notes on Carl Schmitt, The Concept of the Political' in Carl Schmitt, *The Concept of the Political*, George Schwab trans. (Chicago and London: University of Chicago Press, 1996) (first published 1932), p. 90.

Strong, Tracy B., 'How to Write Scripture: Words, Authority and Politics in Thomas Hobbes', *Critical Inquiry* 20 (1993), 128.

Stueck, William, 'The United Nations, the Security Council, and the Korean War' in Vaughan Lowe *et al.* (eds.), *The United Nations Security Council and War: The Evolution of Thought and Practice since 1945* (Oxford: Oxford University Press, 2008), p. 265.

Supiot, Alain, *Homo Juridicus: On the Anthropological Function of the Law* Saskia Brown trans. (London: Verso, 2007).

Szasz, Paul C., 'The Role of the UN Secretary-General: Some Legal Aspects', *New York University Journal of International Law and Politics* 24 (1991), 161.

Terry, Fiona, *Condemned to Repeat?: The Paradox of Humanitarian Action* (New York: Cornell University Press, 2002).

Thoma, Richard, 'Appendix: On the Ideology of Parliamentarism (1925)' in Carl Schmitt, *The Crisis of Parliamentary Democracy*, Ellen Kennedy trans. (Cambridge, MA: The MIT Press, 1988) (first published 1934). p. 77.

Tribe, Keith, *Strategies of Economic Order: German Economic Discourse 1750–1950* (Cambridge: Cambridge University Press, 1995).

Tsagourias, Nicholas, 'Consent, Neutrality/Impartiality and the Use of Force in Peacekeeping: Their Constitutional Dimension', *Journal of Conflict and Security Law* 11 (2009), 465.

Tuck, Richard, *Hobbes* (Oxford: Oxford University Press, 1989).

'The "Modern" Theory of Natural Law' in Anthony Pagden (ed.), *The Languages of Political Theory in Early-Modern Europe* (Cambridge: Cambridge University Press, 1987), p. 99.

Natural Rights Theories: Their Origin and Development (Cambridge: Cambridge University Press, 1979).

UN High-Level Panel on Threats, Challenges and Change, 'A More Secure World: Our Shared Responsibility' (2004).

UN, 'Secretary-General Defends, Clarifies "Responsibility to Protect" at Berlin Event on "Responsibility to Protect: International Cooperation for a Changed World', UN Press Release SG/SM/11701, 15 July 2008, www.un.org/News/Press/docs/2008/sgsm11701.doc.htm.

United Nations Peace Operations 2009: Year in Review (New York: United Nations, 2010).

United Nations Peacekeeping Operations: Principles and Guidelines (New York: United Nations, 2008).

UNHCR, '2008 Global Trends: Refugees, Asylum-seekers, Returnees, Internally Displaced and Stateless Persons', 16 June 2009, www.unhcr.org/4a375c426.html.

UN Secretary-General, 'Remarks at a Stanley Foundation Conference on "Implementing the Responsibility to Protect"', Tarrytown, 15 January 2010, www.stanleyfoundation.org/publications/policy_memo/SGresptoprotect15jan2010.pdf.

'Implementing the Responsibility to Protect: Report of the Secretary-General', UN GAOR, 63rd Sess., Agenda Items 44 and 107, UN Doc. A/63/677, 12 January 2009.

'Address to the Summit of the Africa Union', Addis Ababa, Ethiopia, 31 January 2008, www.un.org/apps/news/infocus/sgspeeches/search_full.asp?statID=180#.

'In Larger Freedom: Towards Development, Security and Human Rights for All', UN GAOR, 59th Sess., Agenda Items 45 and 55, UN Doc. A/59/2005, 21 March 2005.

'We the Peoples: The Role of the United Nations in the 21st Century', UN GAOR, 54th Sess., Agenda Item 49(b), UN Doc. A/54/2000, 27 March 2000.

'Report of the Secretary-General pursuant to General Assembly Resolution 53/35: The Fall of Srebrenica', UN GAOR, 54th Sess., Agenda Item 42, UN Doc. A/54/549, 15 November 1999.

'An Agenda for Peace: Preventive Diplomacy, Peacemaking and Peacekeeping, Report of the Secretary-General Pursuant to the Statement Adopted by the Summit Meeting of the Security Council on 31 January 1992', A/47/277-S/24111, 17 June 1992.

'Introduction to the Annual Report of the Secretary-General on the Work of the Organization', UN GAOR, 16th Sess., Supp. No. 1A, UN Doc. A/4800/Add.1, 1961.

'Introduction to the Annual Report of the Secretary-General on the Work of the Organization', UN GAOR, 15th Sess., Supp. No. 1A, UN Doc. A/4390/Add.1, 1960.

'Second Report by the Secretary-General on the Implementation of Security Council Resolution S/4387 of 14 July 1960 and S/4405 of 22 July 1960', UN SCOR, 15th Sess., UN Doc. S/4417, 6 August 1960.

'First Report of the Secretary-General on the Implementation of Security Council Resolution S/4387 of 14 July 1960', UN SCOR, 15th Sess., UN Doc. S/4389, 18 July 1960.

'Summary Study of the Experience Derived from the Establishment and Operation of the Force: Report of the Secretary-General', UN GAOR, 13th Sess., Agenda Item 65, UN Doc. A/3943, 9 October 1958, annex.

'Second and Final Report of the Secretary-General on the Plan for an Emergency International United Nations Force Requested in the Resolution Adopted by the General Assembly on 4 November 1956 (A/3276)', UN GAOR, 1st Emergency Special Sess., UN Doc. A/3302, 6 November 1956.

UNSGselection.org, 'Ban Ki-moon's Positions on Human Rights, the Responsibility to Protect, International Criminal Court', Issue 34, 19 October 2006, www.unsgselection.org/content/latest-developments/issue-34–19-october-2006-ban-ki-moon's-positions-on-human-rights-the-responsibility-to-protect-international-criminal-court/173.

Urquhart, Brian, 'The Secretary-General – Why Dag Hammarskjöld?' in Sten Ask and Anna Mark-Jungkvist (eds.), *The Adventure of Peace: Dag Hammarskjöld and the Future of the UN* (New York: Palgrave Macmillan, 2005), p. 14.

  Hammarskjöld (New York: W. W. Norton, 1972).

Uvin, Peter, *Aiding Violence: The Development Enterprise in Rwanda* (Connecticut: Kumarian Press, 1998).

Vallance, Edward, 'Oaths, Casuistry, and Equivocation: Anglican Responses to the Engagement Controversy', *The Historical Journal* 44 (2001), 59.

Vander Linden, H., 'Alexander VI and the Demarcation of the Maritime and Colonial Domains of Spain and Portugal, 1493–1494', *American Historical Review* 22 (1916), 1.

Walker, R. B. J., *Inside/Outside: International Relations as Political Theory* (Cambridge: Cambridge University Press, 1993).

Watt, J. A., 'Spiritual and Temporal Powers' in J. H. Burns (ed.), *The Cambridge History of Medieval Political Thought c.350–c.1450* (Cambridge: Cambridge University Press, 1988), p. 367.

Weissman, Fabrice (ed.), *In the Shadow of 'Just Wars': Violence, Politics and Humanitarian Action* (Ithaca: Cornell University Press, 2004).

Weithman, Paul J., 'Religion and Political Philosophy' in Edward Craig (ed.), *Routledge Encyclopedia of Philosophy* (London and New York: Routledge, 1998), vol. 8, p. 224.

Weitz, Eric D., 'Foreword to the English Edition' in Pierre Broué, *The German Revolution 1917–1923*, John Archer trans. (Chicago: Haymarket Books, 2006) (first published 1971), p. i.

West, Robert L., 'The United Nations and the Congo Financial Crisis: Lessons of the First Year', *International Organization* 15 (1961), 603.

Wheeler, Nicholas J. and Egerton, Frazer, 'The Responsibility to Protect: "Precious Commitment" or a Promise Unfulfilled?', *Global Responsibility to Protect* 1 (2009), 114.

Wilde, Ralph, *International Territorial Administration: How Trusteeship and the Civilizing Mission Never Went Away* (Oxford: Oxford University Press, 2008).

Wilson, Peter H., *The Holy Roman Empire 1495–1806* (New York: St Martin's Press, 1999).

Young, Crawford, *Politics in the Congo: Decolonization and Independence* (Princeton: Princeton University Press, 1965).

Zacklin, Ralph, *The United Nations Secretariat and the Use of Force in a Unipolar World: Power v Principle* (Cambridge: Cambridge University Press, 2010).

Zaum, Dominik, 'The Security Council, the General Assembly, and War: The Uniting for Peace Resolution' in Vaughan Lowe, Adam Roberts, Jennifer Welsh and Dominik Zaum (eds.), *The United Nations Security Council and War: The Evolution of Thought and Practice since 1945* (Oxford: Oxford University Press, 2008), p. 154.

Zumbansen, Peer, 'Law after the Welfare State: Formalism, Functionalism, and the Ironic Turn of Reflexive Law', *American Journal of Comparative Law* LVI (2008), 769.

INDEX

administration 4, 5, 7, 11, 13, 39, 42, 50, 56, 70–1, 88, 92–6, 99, 103, 136, 170–2, 184, 187–8, 190, 193, 195, 199–207
Africa 5, 15, 19, 30–2, 43, 45–6, 69, 71, 74, 133
   Congo *see* Congo
   Dafur *see* Sudan (Dafur conflict)
   Egypt *see* Egypt
   Rwanda *see* Rwanda
African Commission on Human and Peoples' Rights 19
Alexander VI (Pope) 145, 148
Allen, William 152
Annan, Kofi 1, 33, 102, 178
Australia, responsibility to protect 18–19

Ban Ki-Moon 2, 17, 105, 180
Bearle, Adolf 200
Belgium, Congo crisis 29–32, 69, 70–7, 79
Bellarmine, Robert 151–5
Blackwell, George 153
Bodin, Jean 206
Bolton, John 24
Bosnia-Herzegovina, international administration 98–9
Boutros-Ghali, Boutros 91
Brown, Gordon 18
Bulls of Donation 145–8
Bunche, Ralph 70

Canada 1, 64
Charles I (King of England) 118, 119
China, Korean War prisoners 50–2
Chomsky, Noam 27
Chou En-Lai 51

civil war 8, 10, 14, 35–7, 81, 92, 97, 109–12, 116, 118, 120–1, 125–30, 133, 136–7, 140, 156, 159, 162, 169–70, 178, 186, 191, 208
Cohen, Felix 198–9
Cold War 5, 7, 30, 35, 90–1, 174, 190
Congo
   de facto authority 78, 80, 83
   executive rule 79–84
   Force Publique 29, 69, 72, 73
   Hammarskjöld's policy 30–2, 74–5, 76–9, 80, 82–3, 84–7
   history of crisis 69–73
   impartiality/neutrality 7
   Katanga 29, 72–3, 75–9
   Port of Matadi 29, 72
   recognition of authority 84–7
   UN Operation in the Congo (ONUC) (1960) 3, 29–30, 69–87
   UN Security Council 73–7
conscience 32, 33, 101–2, 122, 163, 179
Convention of Constantinople (1888) 58–9, 61
Cordier, Andrew 80–4, 98
Cortés, Juan Donoso 126
covenant 37, 113, 114, 115, 119, 121–3, 125
Cromwell, Oliver 118, 212

de facto authority 16, 37, 78, 80, 83, 97, 120
decolonisation 5, 10, 42, 44–6, 56, 58, 63, 67, 69, 71, 87, 90, 108, 163, 169, 190, 195, 206, 208–9
Dee, John 147–8
democracy 129–30, 189–92
Deng, Francis 13–15, 17, 97

Dixon, Pierson 28–9, 61–2
dominium 143–9
Drake, Francis 146
Dulles, John Foster 57, 63–4

early warning 92, 103–4, 136, 182–3
East Timor 7, 93, 94, 100
economics 52–6, 86, 130
Egypt
    Aswan Dam project 57, 63
    British occupation 58–9
    United Nations Emergency Force
        (UNEF) 28–9, 31, 57–68
    see also Suez crisis
Elizabeth I (Queen of England) 146,
    147–8, 152
emergency 61–2, 64–6, 80, 82–3,
    87, 89–90, 95, 128–9, 135, 137,
    169, 191
empire 32, 56–8, 63, 66–7, 162, 166,
    208; see also Holy Roman
    Empire
England
    civil war 36
    Levellers 116, 118
    Norman conquest 116, 117
    see also Hobbes (Thomas)
equality
    sovereignty 66
    UN Charter 47
Erastus, Thomas 152
European Union (EU), responsibility
    to protect 21
executive powers
    authority 97–103
    dynamic executive action 3, 5,
        42, 44
    expansion 5–6, 90–103
    form of international rule 199–205
    international practices 42–108
    managerialism 94–7
    politics 133–8
    responsibility to protect 106–8, 133–8
    systematisation 6–10, 87–90
    UN Secretary-General 3–5, 26, 47

Ferdinand and Isabella 145–8
Ford, Richard 144

France
    Congo 29, 73
    Suez 28–9, 31–2, 59–63, 65–6
Freiburg school 54
Friends of the Responsibility
    to Protect 20
Fuller, Lon 14
functionalism 5, 15, 40, 170–1, 175–7,
    187–8, 192, 195, 197–9, 205

genocide 7–9, 21–2, 101, 104, 136,
    179–82, 184–5
Genocide Convention 23
Germany
    Communist Party 126
    Freiburg school 54
    Weimar Republic 125–6, 129,
        191, 195
    World War I 37, 110

Hakluyt, Richard 147
Hammarskjöld, Dag
    African policy 30–2, 45–6
    Congo crisis 30–2, 74–5, 76–9, 80,
        82–3, 84–7
    discretionary powers 11
    economic thinking 52–6
    executive powers 3–5, 6–7, 12–13,
        28, 42–3, 47, 87–90
    impartiality/neutrality 7, 30–2, 43,
        47–56, 141–2
    independence 48–50
    international rule 42–108
    Korean War prisoners 50–2
    peace in decolonised world 44–5
    preventive diplomacy 45
    role of state 52–6
    Suez crisis 3, 5, 28–32, 35, 43, 57–68,
        87, 89–90
    Swedish civil service 52–4
    system building 47
Hart, H. L. A. 14, 25
Hayek, Friedrich 54, 55
Heller, Herman 194
Henry VIII (King of England) 152
Hitler, Adolf 126, 204
Hobbes, Thomas
    authority 124–5

counter-revolutionary theorist 116–20
covenant 37, 113, 114, 115, 119,
   121–3, 125
divided obligations 155–61
lawful authority 35–7, 120–4, 139–40
liberal/revolutionary state forms 38
natural law 112–25
preservation of life 112–25
protection/representation/state 112–16
religious wars 109–10
sovereignty 118–19, 120–1, 122–5
Holy Roman Empire 37, 120, 140, 143,
   145, 148–50, 157
human rights 32–3, 102, 104, 119, 164,
   166, 168, 176–7 186
humanitarian intervention 15–16,
   28–9, 32–4, 72–4, 137, 211

ICISS see International Commission on
   Intervention and State
   Sovereignty
impartiality 5–8, 10, 32, 47, 64–5, 80,
   83, 85–7, 90, 96–8, 101–3, 106,
   179, 187, 192–3
international civil servant 5–6, 11, 28,
   43, 47–50, 65, 187, 192
International Commission on
   Intervention and State
   Sovereignty (ICISS),
   Responsibility to Protect (2001) 1,
   13, 15–16, 33–4, 103, 104, 137
ICISS see International Commission on
   Intervention and State
   Sovereignty
international relations
   conference diplomacy 5, 44–7
   parliamentary democracy 189–92
Iraq 33, 36
Israel 59–64

James I (King of England) 116, 153,
   154–5
jurisdiction
   control 143–50
   decolonised world 164–78
   form/function 164–78
   international 164–78
   limits 27, 151–5

proliferation of claims 175–8
recognition 39–40, 139–88
responsibility to protect 178–86
states 143–50
UN Charter 164–7
UN/functionalism 167–72
universal see universal jurisdiction

Kasavubu, Joseph 30, 69, 73, 80–1
Kelson, Hans 194, 195
Keynes, John Maynard 53
Khrushchev, Nikita 141
Korean War, American prisoners 50–2
Kosovo
   international administrators 7, 93, 94–5
   NATO action (1999) 32–3, 40, 176–8

Laski, Harold 197–8
Lauterpacht, Eli 171, 199–200
Leopold II (King of Belgium) 70
Levellers 116, 118
Lie, Trygve 48
Loutfi, Omar 61
loyalty 48–50, 65, 122, 128, 153, 156,
   174, 187, 194, 198
Luck, Edward 17, 20, 105
Lumumba, Patrice 30, 31, 69, 73, 78,
   80–3, 84, 190

Maistre, Joseph de 126
managerialism 94–7, 189, 200–2
Marsilius of Padua 151–2
Means, Gardiner 200
Mobutu, Joseph Désiré (Sese Seko) 83–4
Mounir, Akram 180

Nasser, Gamal Abdel 57
natural law 113–14, 121, 124–5, 134–5,
   162, 194
Neumann, Franz 200
neutrality 6–8, 31–2, 42–3, 47–8, 50,
   52–3, 55–6, 66, 78, 81, 85–6, 90,
   96–8, 101–2, 106, 187, 190, 192–3,
   195
Non-Aligned Movement,
   responsibility to protect 20, 24
non-governmental organisations
   (NGOs), managerial structure 96

North Atlantic Treaty Organisation
(NATO), Kosovo action (1999)
32–3, 40, 176–8

order 14

Papacy 38, 115, 139–40, 143, 145–9,
159, 186
parliament 10, 12, 46, 68, 79, 81–5, 94,
96, 99–100, 117–18, 121, 129–30,
134, 137, 153, 167, 169, 183,
189–95, 203, 206, 208
Paul V (Pope) 153
peacekeeping 42–3, 57, 64–6, 68, 87, 92,
94, 96–7
Pearson, Lester Bowles 64
Petritsch, Wolfgang 98–9
Pius V (Pope) 152
police action 27–34, 59, 62, 63, 133–4,
165, 169, 189, 208
power vacuum
decolonised world 43, 45, 109
preventive diplomacy 45
prevention 42–3, 87, 91, 103, 105–6,
136, 174, 183–5
Protocol of Sèvres (1956) 59

Ramos-Horta, José 101
recognition 14–15, 36, 38–9, 41, 80,
83–6, 97–8, 102, 106, 112, 120–1,
124, 128, 132, 162–3, 165, 187,
193, 195, 207
Reformation 115, 150, 152, 160
representation 1, 12, 26–7, 31, 33, 36–8,
40, 46, 52, 85–6, 98, 112, 115,
118–19, 123–5, 129–32, 141, 156,
186, 191–2, 194, 206
revolution 35, 37–8, 109, 111, 113–14,
116–18, 126, 133, 135, 140, 162,
164, 190–1, 193, 195, 200, 204,
206–7, 209
Roman law 144–5
Rwanda 7–8, 98

safe havens 8, 9, 101
Schacter, Oscar 12–13
Schmitt, Carl
civil war 125–30

European order 125–30
friends/enemies 130–3
lawful authority 37, 110–11
neutrality 194–5
parliamentary democracy 190–1
responsibility to protect 125–30
Schwebel, Stephen M. 12
self-determination 16, 41, 46, 67, 85,
115, 119–20, 134, 136, 164–6, 169,
178, 192, 208
Smith, Adam 54, 117
Smith, Stephen 18–19
Solemn League and Covenant 122
sovereignty
acquisition 114
equality 66
Hobbes (Thomas) 118–19, 120–1
ICISS see International Commission
on Intervention and State
Sovereignty
jurisdictional limits 27
responsibility 13–15
Spain 145–8
Srebrenica
impartiality/neutrality 7, 8
safe havens 9, 101
status 38–41, 79, 87, 117, 131, 140,
171–2, 187–8, 196, 201, 205–7
Stolleis, Michael 204
Sudan, Dafur conflict 18
Suez crisis
Anglo-French action 59–60
canal nationalisation 57–60
future of UN 66–8
UN Emergency Force (UNEF) 28–9,
31, 57–68
UN General Assembly 60–4
Sweden
Dafur conflict 18
Hammarskjöld's career 52–4

Treaty of Tordesillas 146
Treaty of Versailles 126
Tshombé, Moise 77, 78
Tunisia 74

UN Charter
equality 47

international executive powers
    10–13
jurisdiction 164–7
peace 44
Secretary-General 4, 6, 10–13, 26,
    49, 50
UN Convention on Privileges and
    Immunities (1946) 95
UN Emergency Force (UNEF)
    creation 3, 57, 61–6
    Hammarskjöld's role 64–6
UN General Assembly
    responsibility to protect 20–1
    Suez crisis 60–4
    voting power 46–7
    World Summit Outcome (2005) 2,
        17, 23, 24, 25, 104, 180–4
UN High Commission for Refugees
    (UNHCR) 93, 98
UN Interim Administration Mission in
    Kosovo (UNMIK) 94–5
UN Operation in the Congo (ONUC)
    (1960) 3, 29–30, 69–87
    Egypt (Suez crisis) 28–9, 31, 57–68
UN Operation in Somalia
    (UNOSOM) 95
UN peacekeeping
    Department of Peacekeeping
        Operations (DPO) 93
    emergence 57
    immunities 95
    impartiality/neutrality 7–8
    mandates 92–3
    UNEF see UN Emergency Force
UN Secretary-General
    Agenda for Peace 91
    Annan (Kofi) 1, 33, 102, 178
    Ban Ki-Moon 2, 17, 105, 180
    Boutros-Ghali (Boutros) 91
    executive powers 3–5, 26, 47
    Hammarskjöld see Hammarskjöld
        (Dag)
    impartiality/neutrality 6
    Lie (Trygve) 48
    political role 10–13, 50–2
    quiet diplomacy 50–2
    UN Charter 4, 6, 10–13, 26,
        49, 50

UN Security Council
    Congo 73–7
    responsibility to protect 24
    threats to peace 91
UN Transitional Administration in
    East Timor (UNTAET) 94, 100
Union of Soviet Socialist Republics 74,
    79
United Kingdom
    Congo 73
    East Timor 100
    responsibility to protect 18
    Suez 28–9, 31–2, 58–66
United Nations (UN)
    civilian operations 93
    decolonised world 3–6, 56
    humanitarian intervention 93–4
    international jurisdiction 164–78
    post-Cold War 90–4
    secular church 172–5
United States
    Congo 74, 80
    decolonised world 56–7, 63, 67–8
    FBI investigations 48–50
    Fifth Amendment 48, 49
    Korean War prisoners 50–2
    responsibility to protect 21–2
    Suez crisis 57, 60, 63, 67–8
universal jurisdiction
    civil peace 151–5
    Holy Roman Empire 27, 140, 143,
        145–50
    Papacy 27, 139, 140, 143, 145–50
    reformation 150–61
    see also jurisdiction
universality 31–2, 46, 67, 110, 132, 160,
    177, 179, 210
Urquhart, Brian 4

Vitoria, Francisco de 147
von Mises, Ludwig 54

Weber, Max 194, 195
Wigforss, Ernst 53
World Summit Outcome (2005) 2, 17,
    23, 24, 25, 104, 180–4, 187

Youlou, Fulbert 82